STUDIES IN POLITICAL TRANSITION

Edited by Klaus Bachmann

VOLUME 10

PETER LANG

International Criminal Tribunals as Actors of Domestic Change

Klaus Bachmann/Gerhard Kemp/Irena Ristić (eds.)

International Criminal Tribunals as Actors of Domestic Change

The Impact on Institutional Reform

VOL 2

PETER LANG

Bibliographic Information published by the Deutsche Nationalbibliothek
The Deutsche Nationalbibliothek lists this publication in the Deutsche
Nationalbibliografie; detailed bibliographic data is available in the internet
at http://dnb.d-nb.de.

Library of Congress Cataloging-in-Publication Data
A CIP catalog record for this book has been applied for at the Library of Congress.

This publication was financially supported by the Polish National Research Center
(Narodowe Centrum Nauki) through the grant nr. 2012/06/A/HS5/00249 and a
grant awarded by the Polish Ministry of Science and Higher Education based on
decision nr 215443/E-560/S/2013-1. Klaus Bachmann and Gerhard Kemp also
extend their gratitude to the Robert Bosch Foundation, where they were able to work
on the final version of both volumes during their fellowship at the Robert Bosch
Academy in Berlin in 2017 and to STIAS, the Stellenbosch Institute for Advanced
Study, Wallenberg Research Center at Stellenbosch University, Stellenbosch 7600,
South Africa. The views expressed in this book are those of the authors and should
not be attributed to the staff, officers or trustees of the Robert Bosch Foundation.

ISSN 2191-3307
ISBN 978-3-631-77089-4 (Print)
E-ISBN 978-3-631-77090-0 (E-PDF)
E-ISBN 978-3-631-77091-7 (EPUB)
E-ISBN 978-3-631-77092-4 (MOBI)
DOI 10.3726/b14787

© Peter Lang GmbH
Internationaler Verlag der Wissenschaften
Berlin 2018
All rights reserved.

Peter Lang – Berlin · Bern · Bruxelles · New York ·
Oxford · Warszawa · Wien

This publication has been peer reviewed.

www.peterlang.com

Foreword to the 2. Volume

This is the second volume of the publication "International Criminal Tribunals as Actors of Domestic Change. The impact on institutional reform", which is one of the results of a five-years research project carried out by Klaus Bachmann, Irena Ristić and Gerhard Kemp and which was financed by the Polish National Science Centre (Narodowe Centrum Nauki).[1] We, the authors, have decided to split the publication into two volumes and to do without a replication of the theoretical and methodological introduction as well as the acknowledgements, which the interested reader will find at the beginning of volume 1, where we explain the background of the project and the methods, through which we tried to find out, whether and eventually how International Criminal Tribunals (ICTs) trigger internal reforms in countries affected by their jurisdiction.

We decided to split the publication into two volumes in accordance with the results of the field research. The latter clearly identified cases in which ICT decisions had an impact on institutional reform on the ground, but it also revealed the sometimes cunning strategies of governments in dealing with unwanted ICT interference in their domestic politics. The latter cases are gathered in this second volume. Here, we have to do with cases of open defiance towards ICT decisions and their mission, with the building up of facade institutions, whose sole aim was to claim inadmissibility of the respective case before the ICC and with cases, where a government openly confronts an international tribunal with hostility. The reader may nevertheless be surprised about some of the details of these cases. Sometimes, such facade institutions start to live their own life, partly against the will and the intents of those, who created them, sometimes, certain norms find their way into the legislation even of an ICT-hostile country,

1   This publication was financially supported by the Polish National Research Center (Narodowe Centrum Nauki) through the grant nr. 2012/06/A/HS5/00249 and a grant awarded by the Polish Ministry of Science and Higher Education based on decision *nr 215443/E-560/S/2013-1*. Klaus Bachmann and Gerhard Kemp also extend their gratitude to the Robert Bosch Foundation, where they were able to work on the final version of both volumes during their fellowship at the Robert Bosch Academy in Berlin in 2017 and to STIAS, the Stellenbosch Institute for Advanced Study, Wallenberg Research Center at Stellenbosch University, Stellenbosch 7600, South Africa, where they were able to discuss the results of the project with Dire Tladi from the University of Pretoria and other STIAS fellows.

sometimes, ICC cases in one country have collateral, unexpected and unintended consequences in other countries.

This second volume ends with an a conclusion, a bibliography and an index of names which include the sources and names from both volumes.

Klaus Bachmann, Irena Ristić, Gerhard Kemp

Contents

IV) Special Cases: South Sudan, Ukraine and Russia

Amani M. Ejami

Igor Lyubashenko

Klaus Bachmann, Irena Ristić, Gerhard Kemp

II) Domestic Change in Cases of Adaptation Toward ICT Decisions

Amani M. Ejami

The Impact of the International Criminal Court on the Reform of the Judiciary in Sudan

1. Criminal Accountability and the Sudanese Judiciary

Since the referral of the Darfur case to the International Criminal Court (ICC) by the United Nations Security Council (UNSC) in 2005, a series of events in Sudan has influenced the Sudanese justice system. Such impact is evident by the establishment of new institutions, the Special Criminal Court on the Events in Darfur (SCCED), the Special Prosecutor for Crimes against Humanity, the Justice and Reconciliation Commission, and the Gender Violence Unit. War crimes and crimes against humanity for the first time are added to Sudanese law. The ICC referral had coincided with the signing and implementation of the Comprehensive Peace Agreement (CPA) in 2005 between the Government of Sudan and the Sudan People's Liberation Movement (SPLM), which ended up a two decade long civil war between the North and South of Sudan, which eventually led to the secession of South Sudan as an independent country in 2011.[1] The issue of justice and accountability has not been part of neither the CPA nor its predecessor, the Addis Ababa Accord 1972, despite the atrocities and serious violations of Human Rights and humanitarian law committed during the six-decade long civil war. The perpetrators of these crimes were shielded by blanket amnesties, leaving the impunity door wide open for further atrocities. Experiences of Human Rights Watch show that the "lack of justice for violent crimes too often fosters further abuses."[2] The recent ongoing ethnic conflict in South Sudan is practical proof of the accuracy of this experience. The Darfur conflict has not been resolved within the CPA and the Sudanese government insisted that the negotiations be understood solely as a North-South affair.[3] As such the international and regional mediators pressed the government and the

---

1   The Comprehensive Peace Agreement is available at: http://unmis.unmissions.org/Portals/UNMIS/Documents/General/cpa-en.pdf

2   Human Rights Watch, *Ending the Era of Injustice; Advancing Prosecutions for Serious Crimes Committed in South Sudan*, December 2014, available at: https://www.hrw.org/report/2014/12/10/ending-era-injustice/advancing-prosecutions-serious-crimes-committed-south-sudans

3   P. Adwok Nyaba, *South Sudan: The State We Aspire To*, Cape Town 2013, 113.

Darfur rebels to conclude a separate peace agreement for the Darfur conflict. Consequently, the Darfur Peace Agreement (DPA) was signed in 2006 between the Sudan Government and a faction of the Sudan Liberation Movement/Army (SLMA) led by Minni Minawi, whereas the other faction, under the name Sudan Liberation Movement (SLM) led by Abd Elwahid M. Nour, and the Justice and Equality Movement (JEM) led by Khalil Ibrahim boycotted the accord. Accountability was taken out of the agenda by the government, which argued that this issue had been referred to the ICC.

The DPA 2006 failed and fighting intensified not only between the government and the rebels, but also between the rebels themselves. In 2007 the ICC Prosecutor issued two summonses followed by arrest warrants against two government officials. The government refused to co-operate with the ICC, risking a confrontation not only with the ICC but also with the international community in general.[4] This confrontation ended with the issuance of an arrest warrant against the President, Omer Al Bashir, for committing war crimes and Crimes against Humanity in addition to genocide. It was the first such arrest warrant against a sitting president.[5] The Sudanese government, which is under the enormous pressure of economic and commercial sanctions imposed unilaterally by the USA since 1997, which were further renewed in 2007, has maintained very antagonistic and hostile relations with the USA since the imposition of the Sharia laws in 1983. Consequently, the Sudanese government has perceived the court as an attempt of the Western UNSC members to change the Sudanese government by issuing an arrest warrant.[6] The government of Sudan launched a campaign against the ICC and has so far gained the solidarity of many African and Arab governments. In 2009, the African Union Peace and Security Council (PSC)

In Sudan, the notion "North-South affair" refers to the relations between South Sudan and Sudan. When referrence is made to "the West" this means, in the Sudanese context, usually the relations between Darfur (whose three provinces are situated in the Western part of the country) and the central government in Khartoum.

4   K. El-Gizouli, "The Erroneous Confrontation: The Dialectics of Law, Politics and the Prosecution of War Crimes in Darfur" in: S. M. Hassan and C. E.Ray (eds), *Darfur and the Crises of Governance in Sudan; A critical Reader*, Ithaka: Cornell University Press 2009, 261.

5   The next one would be the ICC arrest warrant (for Crimes against Humanity) against Uhuru Kenyatta in Kenya (see Gerhard Kemp's chapter later in this volume).

6   S. M. H. Nouwen and W. G. Werner, "Doing Justice to the Political: The International Criminal Court in Uganda and Sudan", *The European Journal of International Law* Vol. 21 (2010) available at: http://www.ejil.org/pdfs/21/4/2120.pdf

formed an investigation committee on Darfur headed by former South African President Thabo Mbeki. The African Union High Panel on Darfur (AUHPD) was created to investigate violations of Human Rights and humanitarian law and to make recommendations for accountability, peace, justice and reconciliation in Darfur.[7] The AU PSC also mediated another peace accord in Doha (Qatar), which led to the adoption of the Doha Peace Document on Darfur (DDPD) between the government of Sudan and a faction of JEM. The mediators and the parties to the accord agreed to put the issue of accountability on the agenda of the negotiations. A chapter on transitional justice was included in the agreement. Therefore, one can argue that the inclusion of accountability in the DDPD was directly impacted by the intervention of the ICC, because accountability had not been part of the DPA.

Against this background, this chapter covers two sections. Its first section concentrates on Sudan, and gives an overview of the Sudan conflict in general as well as a chronology of the relations between Sudan with the ICC. It outlines the Sudanese government's responses to atrocity-related accountability before the ICC. Then it identifies the legal and institutional developments subsequent to the ICC's judicial intervention in Sudan. All these changes within the justice system shall be described in the context of the general political environment and the international pressure on Sudan, which inclined the Sudanese government to regard the ICC as a tool of Western countries to subdue the Sudanese government.[8]

---

7 At the AU inaugural meeting in Durban, the African leaders signed the "Protocol Relating to the Establishment of the Peace and Security Council of the AU" which came into force on 26 December 2003. The Protocol defines the PSC as "a standing decision-making organ for the prevention, management and resolution of conflicts. The PSC shall be a collective security and early-warning arrangement to facilitate timely and efficient response to conflict and crisis situations in Africa". The Protocol also stipulates that "The Peace and Security Council shall be supported by the Commission, a Panel of the Wise (POW), a Continental Early Warning System (CEWS), an African Standby Force (ASF) and a Special Fund." See more at: http://www.peaceau.org/en/page/38-peace-and-security-council#sthash.ZLIbVhXR.dpuf.

8 The United Nations Security Council issued sixteen resolutions concerning Sudan in the period June 2004–May 2006. This was seen by the Sudan Government as an obvious example of the politicization of the UNSC Resolutions, taking into consideration the failure of UNSC to adopt similar resolutions with regard to other Human Rights violations in the world, especially the Israel-Palestinian conflict. (Sudan News Agency).

2. The Historical Background of the Conflicts in Sudan

Sudan has long history of civil wars. Armed conflict has been present in one form or another for the last six decades. The War between North and South was rampant across Sudan even before its independence in 1956. Both parts where formally ruled by the Anglo-Egyptian Condominium between 1899 and 1956, but the territory and the administration were largely controlled by the British, who entrenched and deepened the divide between the two halves of Africa's largest country. Until today, the North is predominately Muslim, while the Southern regions are mostly Christian and animist. Owing to the geographical, political, historical, and cultural differences between the South and the North, the British devised a system of a separate administration for each of the parts.[9]

In August 1955, already before the British withdrawal, the announcement that the British officers were to be replaced with Arabs provoked the Equatoria Corps, a unit of Southern Sudanese Soldiers, to start a mutiny that launched Sudan's first civil war.[10] It ended with the 1972 Addis Ababa Agreement between the Southern Insurgents, called the *Anya Nya,* and the government of Sudan, which granted significant regional autonomy to southern Sudan.[11] The discovery of oil in 1979 in the South and the construction in 1980 of a huge canal designed to divert water from the Nile for Egypt's benefit prompted President Jaafar Muhammad Numeiri (1969–1985) to repudiate the Addis Ababa accord unilaterally.[12]

The situation deteriorated when President Jaafar Nimeiri introduced Sharia Law in 1983, leading to the second civil war under the leadership of Dr. John Garange, the founder of the Sudan People Liberation Movement (SPLM). However, on 30 June 1989, a military coup led by Omar Al Bashir overthrew the Sudanese government, introduced Islamic policies and enrooted the perception in the North that the conflict was a "jihad" of the North against the (non-islamic) South. As a result this has led to the most tragic cycle of suffering. Those who died in the south on the regime's side were convinced that they would go straight

---

9   In line with this policy, the British passed the Closed Districts Ordinance of 1920 and The Passports and Permits Ordinance 1922. These laws required the use of passports and permits for travellers shuttling between the two parts of the country.

10 G. Prunier, 'A wealthy North, A Worn-Out South and Dispute over Oil; Sudan peace Accord won't end war', Le Monde diplomatique 14 February 2005.

11 Addis Ababa Peace Accord 1972, available at; http://peacemaker.un.org/sites/peace-maker.un.org/files/SD_720312_Addis%20Ababa%20Agreement%20on%20the%20Problem%20of%20South%20Sudan.pdf

12 Ibid, page 2.

to paradise. The Sudanese government started serious negotiations with SPLM in 2002 after the 9/11 attacks. In 2002, SPLM and the Sudanese Government signed the Machakos Protocol as a roadmap to a broader peace agreement. This protocol provided for a ceasefire and for the South the right to seek self-determination.[13]

In February 2003, the Western province of Darfur rose against the central government when the Sudan Liberation Movement/Army (SLM/A) and JEM began fighting against the government in Khartoum. Darfur is an entirely Muslim region populated by black Africans and Arabs with a total population of 7,516,000 divided into more than 30 ethnic groups.[14] There are different explanations for the causes of the conflict. Some of these reasons are relating to the land, water access, monopoly on power by the Arabs and to the socio-economic and political marginalization of the Darfur region. There is another copycat factor, which stems from the conflict solution between the Sudanese government and the South. When Darfur's inhabitants saw that the SPLM would probably profit from 20 years of war by obtaining 50% of the oil revenues and a seat in the central government, they rebelled in the belief that only violence would secure them a seat at the negotiating table. During 2003–2004, the attacks against civilians forced an estimated 2.7 million people into displacement, including around 250,000 refugees who went to Chad. Tens of thousands were killed or wounded and women and girls were raped, creating an immense longing for justice, accountability, and reconciliation.[15]

In September 2004, the American Secretary of State, Colin Powell declared the events in Darfur "genocide."[16] Powell's statement was followed by the calls of the United States for the establishment of a UN Commission of Inquiry to determine whether the Sudanese government and its militias are guilty of genocide.[17]

---

13 Machakos Protocol 2002 available at: http://www.smallarmssurveysudan.org/fileadmin/docs/documents/HSBA-Docs-CPA-2.pdf
14 Central Bureau of Statistics – The Ministry of Cabinet, *Sudan in Figures 2009–2013*; http://www.cbs.gov.sd/files.php?id=15#&panel1-5
15 Report of the African Union High-Level Panel on Darfur (AUHPD), page 46, dated 29.10.2009. Available at: http://southsudaninfo.net/wp-content/uploads/reference_library/reports/quest_peace_darfur%20au2009.pdf
16 Gl. Kessler and C. Lynch, 'US calls Killings in Sudan Genocide, Washington Post 10.9.2004, available at: www.washingtonpost.com/wp-dyn/articles/A8364-2004Sep9.html
17 The position of the USA was criticized by some Sudanese journalists, like Mahjoub Mohammed Salih, the Editor in Chief of Al Ayaam Daily News Paper, who accused the USA of double standards with regard to the ICC, because the US did not ratify the Rome Statute and tried to keep their soldiers out of the ICC's reach.

That same month, in September 2004, the UNSC requested the UN Secretary General (UNSG) to establish an international commission of inquiry, to investigate reports of violations of international humanitarian law and Human Rights law in Darfur and to determine whether or not acts of genocide had occurred, and if so, to identify the perpetrators of such crimes.[18]

As the conflict in Darfur was escalating, the Comprehensive Peace Agreement (CPA) was signed in 9 January 2005 ending 21 years of civil war between North Sudan and the South, leaving two million people dead and four million people displaced. The CPA granted South Sudan autonomy for six years, after which a referendum on the question of independence would be held. The referendum was held on 8 January 2011, and the people of South Sudan voted almost unanimously for independence. Consequently, South Sudan became an independent State on the 9 July 2011. The Darfurians were hoping that the Darfur conflict would be solved within the CPA framework, and as the African Union High Panel on Darfur had stated in its report: "Many were hopeful that the Darfur conflict could be settled within the CPA framework. However, the Sudan Government was unwilling to make additional concessions to Darfur. The SPLM was eager to proceed with completing the CPA negotiations. However, rather than seeing the CPA and its democratisation provisions as an opening through which they could gain their political rights by democratic means, many Darfurian leaders instead saw the CPA as an exclusive agreement that privileged southern Sudan at their expense."[19]

As a result of international pressure, the Sudanese Government signed the Darfur Peace Agreement (DPA) 2006 with a faction of Sudan Liberation Army led by Minnei Minawi in 2006.[20] The non-inclusion of other rebel factions weakened the agreement and as such did not manage to end the hostilities.

In 2010, new peace talks between rebels and the government in Doha under the auspices of the AU organ, the African Peace and Security Council, led to a framework agreement in July 2011, known as the Doha Document for Peace in Darfur (DDPD). This agreement, like its predecessor, failed to end the hostilities in Darfur since it was signed with only one faction of JEM. As a result, violence escalated again.[21]

---

18 UNSC Resolution 1564 (2004). Adopted on 18 September 2004. S/RES/1564 (2004), available at: www.responsibilitytoprotect.org/files/SC_Res1564_18Sep2004.pdf
19 Report of the African Union High-Level Panel on Darfur (AUHPD), 37.
20 Darfur Peace Agreement 2006, available at; http://www.un.org/zh/focus/southernsudan/pdf/dpa.pdf
21 Human Rights Watch, World Report 2011, www.hrw.org

3. The National and International Legal Framework

The Sudanese legal system is grounded in British common law and Islamic law, which was introduced in 1983. Sources of law are Sharia law, judicial precedents and customs. The judiciary consists of regular, special and customary courts. Sudan adopts a dualist approach to international law whereby international law provisions apply only when implemented through domestic legislation. Sudan adopted The Interim National Constitution of 5 July 2005 (INC), as part of the CPA framework.[22] However, article 27(3) of the INC 2005 provided that "all rights and freedoms enshrined in international Human Rights treaties, covenants and instruments ratified by the Republic of the Sudan shall be an integral part of this Bill."

The Sudanese government is bound by a number of international Human Rights treaties: the International Covenant on Civil and Political Rights (ICCPR),[23] the International Covenant of Economic, Social and Cultural Rights (ICESCR),[24] the Convention on the Rights of the Child (CRC),[25] the Convention on the Elimination of all forms of Racial Discrimination (CERD),[26] the Convention on the Prevention and Punishment of the Crime of Genocide,[27] and an African Charter on Human and People's Rights.[28] The Sudanese government is also bound by International Humanitarian Law, including the four Geneva Conventions of 1949,[29] the Optional Protocol to the Convention on the Rights of the Child on the involvement of Children in armed conflict,[30] the Protocol Additional to the Geneva Conventions of 12 August 1949 and relating to the protection of Victims of Non-International Armed Conflicts Protocol (II),[31] and the Convention for the Protection of Cultural Property in the Event of Armed Conflicts.[32] However, the country neither incorporated crimes against humanity, nor war crimes nor genocide in its penal law up to 2008, although the country

---

22 Article 106- 107 of the Interim Constitution 2005.
23 Joined as a party on 18 June 1986.
24 Sudan joined as a party on 18 June 1986.
25 Joined as a party on 24 July 1990.
26 Joined on 20 April 1977.
27 Joined as a party 13 October 2003.
28 Ratification on 18 February 1986.
29 Ratification on 23 September 1957.
30 Ratification on 26 August 2005.
31 Joined as a party 13 July 2006.
32 Ratification on 23 July 1970.

was engaged in a series of civil wars in the South since independence and was involved in the current crisis in Darfur.

4. The Response to War Crimes Before the ICC Referral

During the first civil war in Sudan, which began in 1955, both the government forces and *Anya-Nya* committed various Human Rights violations. Massacres were carried out in South Sudan during 1964–1965. In 1972, the Addis Ababa Peace Agreement was signed, which contained a general amnesty covering the years of war.[33] Following this peace accord, two laws were adopted; the first one was The Southern Provinces Regional Government Act of 1972, under which "the southern provinces of the Sudan shall constitute a Self-Government Region within the Democratic Republic of The Sudan" with legislative and executive organs and the English language as the official language in the South.[34]

The second law was The Amnesty Act of 1972. According to it, amnesty was granted to "any person who has on or after the 18th day of August, 1955, committed inside or outside Sudan an illegal act or omission in connection with mutiny, rebellion or sedition in the Southern Region in the Sudan." Accordingly, "no action against such person civil or criminal shall be taken and that any person undergoing sentence or in custody pending investigation or trial shall be released."[35] According to this law, more than two thousand detainees and prisoners for crimes connected with the rebellion were released. The victims were pressing the government to take action against the perpetrators of violations, which did not bear any fruit. Among the victims was a man from west Equatoria in the South, who had his ears and lips cut-off by men of *Anya-Nya* movement, after having been charged with spying. His claim for compensation was denied by the Law of General Amnesty.[36]

In Sudan, the experience of using the law to prosecute Human Rights violations has been the limited experience of the 1985–86 transitional limited period. Immediately after the fall of President Nimeiri in 1985, Sudanese Human

---

33 The signing of the Addis Ababa Agreement signed in March 27, 1972, to end 16 years of civil war between the northern Khartoum forces and southern Anya-nya rebels. Part of the agreement includes the creation of the autonomous region of South Sudan, with Juba as its capital.

34 Laws of the Sudan, Volume 6 (1971–1973) 5th edition, articles 3, 4 and 5.

35 The Laws of the Sudan, Volume 6 (1971–1973), articles 3, 4 of the Amnesty Law 1972.

36 A. Mekki Medani, *Crimes Against International Humanitarian Law in Sudan (1989–2000),* Dar El Mostaqbal El Arabi, 2001, 27.

Rights activists pressed for the prosecution of persons who had committed Human Rights abuses during the Nimeriri regime, which assumed power in May 1969 by a military coup against a democratic government (1964–1969). The government successfully prosecuted the leaders of the original 1969 coup for overthrowing a democratically elected government, and six members of the May coup were convicted and imprisoned. Despite this, the government failed to set up a special prosecutor's office or a special court to assist the victims to litigate.

Although the Darfur atrocities were more publicized abroad, the conflict in the South was much more entrenched than of the one in Darfur, with deeper ethnic, political and religious roots; countless villages were destroyed, girls and women were raped, whole families were brutally killed, children abducted into forced labour or even sold as slaves.[37] An estimated 2 million civilians were killed, more than six times the number thought to have been killed in Darfur.[38] Despite that, no one was held accountable for the atrocities in the South and no changes were made to the existing justice institutions and laws in order to prosecute war crimes and crimes against humanity. The consequences are a deepening of the cleavages among the involved groups and an entrenchment of tensions between them. In this respect, the escalating cycles of revenge killings that characterize inter-communal and politically motivated conflicts in South Sudan can be seen as a direct consequence of the pervasive culture of impunity in the country. People do not have confidence in the state to provide justice, so they take matters into their own hands to seek retribution. Since impunity is the norm, individuals that engage in revenge killings can be confident that they will not be punished for their crimes as long as they have the upper hand in the conflict.[39]

5. The International Criminal Court and Sudan

Sudan signed the Rome Statute of the ICC on 8 September 2000, but has not ratified it. However, the ICC could assume jurisdiction over cases referred to it by the UNSC acting under chapter VII of the UN Charter under the complementarity principle.[40] Before it did, in May 2004, President Al Bashir established the

---

37 H. F. Johnson, *Waging Peace in Sudan; the Inside Story of the Negotiations that ended Africa's Longest Civil War*, Sussex 2011, 3, 4.

38 J. Mclure, 'Sudan's Civil War is even worse that Darfur', Newsweek, 1.8.2009.

39 A Working Paper by D K. Deng, 'Special Court for Serious Crimes (SCSC): A Proposal for Justice and Accountability in South Sudan' (May 2014), working paper of the South Sudan News Agency, available at: http://www.southsudannewsagency.com/news/press-releases/special-court-for-serious-crimes-in-south-sudan.

40 Article 17 of the Rome Statute.

National Commission of Inquiry to investigate crimes committed in Darfur.[41] The National Commission confirmed that both the government and the rebels in Darfur had committed war crimes. It also found that rape had occurred, although had not been widespread and systematic. The National Commission was later described by the ICID as devoid of impartiality and as being under great pressure to approve the government's claims.[42]

Between July 2004 and November 2004, the UNSC issued several resolutions calling upon the Sudanese government to take steps to end the violence and Human Rights violations in Darfur and bring to justice *Janjaweed* militia leaders and their associates who were accused of Human Rights and international humanitarian law violations as well as other atrocities.[43] In January, The International Commission of Inquiry on Darfur (ICID) submitted its report to the UNSG.[44] The report did not consider the atrocities in Darfur to amount to genocide,[45] but it confirmed that serious violations of Human Rights law and humanitarian law had been committed. A sealed list of 51 individuals against whom evidence existed for such violations was submitted to the UNSG. The list included Sudanese army officers, militia commanders, and foreign military officers. The ICID recommended to the UNSC to refer the Darfur case to the ICC according to article 13 (b) of the Rome Statute. The ICID stated that, "The Sudanese justice system is unable and unwilling to address the situation in Darfur. This system has been significantly weakened during the last decade."[46] Two months later the UNSC, acting under chapter VII of the UN Charter, decided to refer the situation in Darfur since 1 July 2002 to the Prosecutor of the ICC by adopting UNSC resolution 1593.[47] This is considered as the first ever such referral that gave jurisdiction to the ICC.[48] At the beginning of June, the

---

41 Presidential Order number 97/2004 dated 8/5/2004.

42 ICID report, page 118.

43 Resolution 1556 (2004), SC RES 1556, UN DOC S/RES/1556(2004) 30th July,2004; Resolution 1564 (2004), SC Res 1564, UN Doc S/RES/1564(2004) Sep 18th 2004; Resolution 1574 (2004) SC RES 1574, UN Doc S/RES/1574(2004)November 19th 2004.

44 ICID report dated 25th January 2005, http://www.un.org/news/dh/sudan/com_inq_darfur.pdf

45 Note 6, page 4.

46 Note 6, page.

47 Resolution 1593 (2005) adopted by the UNSC at its 5158th meeting on 31 March 2005. (S/RES/1593 (2005). http://www.icc-cpi.int/nr/rdonlyres/85febd1a-29f8-4ec4-9566-48edf55cc587/283244/n0529273.pdf

48 A. de Waal, Darfur, 'The court and Khartoum; The politics of State Non-Co-Operation', in: N. Waddell and P. Clark (eds), *Courting Conflict? Justice, Peace and the ICC in*

ICC prosecutor opened an investigation.[49] It lasted until February 2007, when the prosecution requested an arrest warrant against Ahmed Harun, a former State Minister in the Humanitarian Affairs Ministry and currently Governor of the Southern Kordofan State and Ali Kushayb, a militia (Janjaweed) commander. The prosecution claimed that Harun had recruited, funded and armed the Militia/Janjaweed to supplement the Sudanese Armed Forces (SAF), and that both suspects had committed massive crimes against the civilian population. According to the prosecuton, Kushayb was a key part of that system, personally delivering arms and leading attacks against villages.[50] On that basis pre-trial chamber 1 of the ICC issued an arrest warrant for 51 counts of crimes against humanity and war crimes against Haroun and Kushayb. In November 2008, three rebel commanders, Bahar abu Garda, Abdallah Banda and Salah Jerbo were accused of responsibility for deadly attacks against peacekeepers in Haskanita in 2007 and were also summoned by the ICC prosecutor.[51] Abu Garda appeared voluntarily before the ICC. His case was heard from 19 to 29 October 2009. On 8 February 2010, the pre-trial chamber decided not to confirm the charges against him. His case never went to trial. This was different with another case, which aroused much more public attention in the world and soured the relations between the ICC and the Sudanese government much more. On 14 July 2008, the Prosecution presented its evidence to Pre-Trial Chamber 1, requesting an arrest warrant against President Omer Al Bashir for 10 charges of genocide, crimes against humanity and war crimes. The Prosecution alleged that President

---

Africa, London: The Royal African Society 2008, 29, available at: http://www.lse.ac.uk/internationalDevelopment/research/crisisStates/download/others/ICC%20in%20Africa.pdf

49 Press report of the ICC prosecutor, available at: http://www.icc cpi.int/en_menus/icc/press%20and%20media/press%20releases/2005/Pages/the%20prosecutor%20of%20the%20icc%20opens%20investigation%20in%20darfur.aspx

50 The Prosecutor v. Ahmad Muhammad Harun ("Ahmad Harun") and Ali Muhammad Ali Abd-Al-Rahman ("Ali Kushayb") ICC-02/05-01/07, http://www.icc cpi.int/en_menus/icc/situations%20and%20cases/situations/situation%20icc%200205/related%20cases/icc%200205%200107/Pages/darfur_%20sudan.aspx.

51 The Prosecutor v. Ahmad Muhammad Harun and Ali Muhammad al Abd-al-Rahman, Case No.
ICC-02/05-01/07 (hereinafter Harun and Kushayb case)
The Prosecutor v. Bahar Idriss Abu Garda, http://www.icc-cpi.int/en_menus/icc/situations%20and%20cases/situations/situation%20icc%200205/related%20cases/icc02050209/Pages/icc02050209.aspx

Al Bashir had used the state apparatus to commit massive crimes in Darfur.[52] At that stage, the ICC pre-trial chamber did not yet endorse the genocide charges, but in March 2009 issued an arrest warrant against President Omer Hassan Al Bashir, accepting seven counts of crimes against humanity and war crimes, while rejecting three counts of genocide.

On 3 February 2010, the Appeals Chamber found that the Pre-Trial Chamber applied an erroneous standard of proof and directed the pre-Trial Chamber to decide on the basis of the correct standard of proof whether a warrant of arrest for genocide should be issued. On 8 February 2010, pre-trial chamber 1 decided to confirm the charges of genocide against President Al Bashir. At the beginning of the following month, the ICC issued another arrest warrant against a member of the Sudanese government, this time against Abdel Raheem Muhammad Hussein, the defence minister, for seven counts of crimes against humanity and six counts of war crimes committed in Darfur.[53]

The response of the Sudanese government to these charges took place against the backdrop of its general relations with the West, especially its tempestuous relations with the US. The Sudan and the US had maintained unstable relations since the 1960s. Sudan broke diplomatic relations with the US in June 1967, following the outbreak of the Arab-Israeli War. Relations improved after July 1971, when the Sudanese Communist Party attempted to overthrow President Nimeiri, and Nimeiri suspected Soviet involvement. US assistance for resettlement of refugees following the 1972 peace settlement with the South improved bilateral relations. US relations with Sudan were strained again during the 1990s. Sudan backed Iraq in its invasion of Kuwait and provided sanctuary and assistance to Islamic terrorist groups in the early and mid-1990s.[54] In October 1997, the US imposed comprehensive economic, trade, and financial sanctions against the Sudan in connection with the civil war with the South.[55]

Once US Secretary of State Colin Powell had labelled the conflict in Darfur "genocide" in 2004, the international media and US newspapers picked up

---

52 The Prosecutor v. Omar Hassan Ahmad Al Bashir, http://www.icc-cpi.int/en_menus/icc/situations%20and%20cases/situations/situation%20icc%200205/related%20cases/icc02050109/Pages/icc02050109.aspx

53 The Prosecutor v. Abdel Raheem Muhammad Hussein, http://www.icc-cpi.int/en_menus/icc/situations%20and%20cases/situations/situation%20icc%200205/related%20cases/icc02050112/Pages/icc02050112.aspx

54 Available at: http://www.state.gov/outofdate/bgn/sudan/194934.htm

55 Sudan Sanctions Program, http://www.treasury.gov/resource-center/sanctions/Programs/Documents/sudan.pdf

Powell's statement and started comparing this conflict with the one Rwanda in 1994.[56] This had a strong impact on the tenth commemoration of the genocide in Rwanda, where Darfur was framed as "another Rwanda" and became a test case for the many commitments of "never again" that political leaders readily asserted after the massacres in Rwanda in 1994.[57] As a consequence, the US did not veto Resolution 1593 which referred the crisis in Darfur to the ICC, but abstained instead.

In response to the Government of Sudan's continued complicity in unabated violence occurring in Darfur, President Bush imposed new economic sanctions on Sudan in May 2007. The sanctions blocked assets of Sudanese citizens implicated in Darfur violence, and also additionally sanctioned companies owned or controlled by the Government of Sudan. Sanctions continue to underscore US efforts to end the suffering of the millions of Sudanese affected by the crisis in Darfur. Within that political context, the Sudan government declared that it would not co-operate with the ICC and declared the ICC proceedings a conspiracy to weaken the country and prepare for the government's removal from power, accusing the ICC as a neo-colonial tool of the West.[58] Consequently, the government was non-cooperative with the ICC. As Alex De Waal put it, "Sudanese leaders simply do not believe that the ICC is independent of political pressures and they don't see the court as distinctive from other punitive measures imposed upon them."[59]

First, the Sudanese government expelled thirteen International Non-Governmental Organizations providing humanitarian assistance in Darfur and shut down three local NGOs, claiming they had cooperated with the ICC.[60] The second Vice-President declared in a press conference that, the government would "combat" the ICC decision in coordination with regional and international organizations, including the Arab league and the African Union as well

---

56 For the conflict in Rwanda in 1994, see Christian Garuka's chapter in the first volume of this publication.

57 D. Brunk, 'Dissecting Darfur: Anatomy of a Genocide Debate', *International Relations*, vol 22, No 1, 25–44.

58 Sudan News Agency; Special Report; Sudan and the International Security Council (5.6.2006), 11.

59 De Waal, *Courting Conflict*, 33.

60 Al sahafa News Paper, June 2010, 5980 available at: www.alsahafasd.net/details. php?articleid=2207

as "friends and supporters" such as China and Russia.[61] Since then, many Arab and African countries have expressed concern over the fallout from the ICC investigations.[62]

The Sudanese government gained the support of African Union member states against the ICC claiming that the ICC is targeting African states and African leaders. Accordingly, the AU has expressed its grave concerns about the ICC and its case against President Al Bashir. The AU requested the UNSC to defer the proceedings against Al Bashir, but the UNSC never did so.[63] As a result of the ICC indictments against Al Bashir and the subsequent indictment of Kenyan president Uhuru Kenyatta, the ICC has been perceived as being "anti-African" and the AU has urged its members to "speak with one voice" against criminal proceedings at the ICC against sitting presidents.[64] The AU General Assembly passed a decision on Africa's Relationship with the International Criminal Court, according to which "The Assembly reiterates the AU's concern on the politicization and misuse of indictments against African leaders by ICC as well as at the unprecedented indictments of and proceedings against the sitting President and Deputy President of Kenya in light of the recent developments in the country."[65] On 12 December 2014, the ICC prosecutor decided to shelve the

---

61 Sudantribune, Sudan Plans to undertake Campaign against ICC Decision, 4.3.2009, available at: www.sudantribune.com/spip.php?inframe&page=imprimable&id-article= 30381,

62 Ibid.

63 Decision on the Meeting of African States Parties to the Rome Statute of the International Criminal Court (ICC), Doc. Assembly/AU/13(XIII), adopted by the Thirteen Ordinary Session of the Assembly in Sirte, Libya, 3 July 2009. Available at: http://www.au.int/en/sites/default/files/ASSEMBLY_EN_1_3_JULY_2009_AUC_ THIRTEENTH_ORDINARY_SESSION_DECISIONS_DECLARATIONS_%20 MESSAGE_CONGRATULATIONS_MOTION_0.pdf
The UNSC can defer a ICC prosecution for a year (and eventually prolong the deferral as long as it has the required majority) under art. 16 of the Rome Statute.

64 M. Taddele Maru, 'The Future of the ICC and Africa: the Good, the Bad, and the Ugly', Al Jazeera, available at: www.aljazeera.com/indepth/opinion/2013/10/future -icc-africa-good-bad-ugly-20131

65 Extraordinary Session of the Assembly of the African Union, 12 October 2013, Addis Ababa, Ethiopia, available at: http://webcache.googleusercontent.com/search?q=ca che:OQ8pg8F2PH4J:https://www.iccnow.org/documents/Ext_Assembly_AU_Dec_ Decl_12Oct2013.pdf+&cd=1&hl=en&ct=clnk
For the Kenyan cases and the relations between Kenya and the ICC see also Gerhard Kemp's chapter in this volume.

Darfur investigation for lack of support from the Security Council, complaining the UNSC did not take measures to could compel Al Bashir and his co-defendants to face the court.[66] President Al Bashir claimed victory over the ICC by saying that, "the ICC raised its hands and admitted that it failed," and "the Sudanese people have defeated the ICC and have refused to hand over any Sudanese to the colonialist court."[67]

6. The ICC's Impact on Accountability, Justice, and Peace

Accountability and justice was never part of the CPA 2005. The parties to the CPA agreed only to "initiate a comprehensive process of national reconciliation and healing throughout the country as part of the peace building process."[68] The CPA did not include any provision for amnesty. Nevertheless, no person was held accountable for committing atrocities during the war. Following the signing of the CPA, the Office of the United Nations High Commissioner for Human Rights found that accountability had never been executed in South Sudan;

> "In Southern Sudan and the traditional areas there are signs that a culture of accountability will be difficult to institute. Violence and documented intimidation tactics carried out by members of the SPLM have discouraged victims from filing complains."[69]

However, the CPA provided for the establishment of six independent commissions,[70] namely, the National Electoral Commission, the National Human Rights Commission, the National Judicial Service Commission,[71] the National Civil Service Commission, an *ad hoc* Commission to monitor and ensure

---

66 K. Abdelaziz, 'Sudans President Omar Al Bashir claimsvictory over ICC after it drops Darfur war crimes investigation', The Independent 14.12.2014, available at: http://www.independent.co.uk/news/world/africa/sudans-president-omar-albashir-claims-victory-over-icc-after-it-drops-darfur-war-crimes-investigation-9924471.html

67 Ibid.

68 CPA, Chapter II, I.7.

69 Second Periodic Report of the United Nations High Commissioner for Human Rights on the Human Rights Situation in Sudan, (27 January 2006), 32.

70 CPA 2005, art.2.10 part two; Power Sharing.

71 Established by the National Judicial Service Commission Act 2005. The Commission is responsible for the general administration of the national Judiciary with regards to the approval of the budget and general policy of the Judiciary; making recommendations to the President of the Republic with respect to the appointment of the Chief Justice and his deputies, justices of the National Supreme Court and other judges within the Judicial System, as well as recommendations for judges dismissal to the Chief Justice and any other function prescribed by the law. According to article 131 of the Interim

accuracy and transparency of the referendum of self determination for the people of the South Sudan, and the Fiscal and Financial Allocation and Monitoring Commission.[72] The CPA was followed by the incorporation of these provisions into the National Interim Constitution, which was adopted in 2005. In October 2005, the Minister of Justice established a Law Reform Committee (LRC) to ensure compatibility with the CPA and the Interim National Constitution 2005, in particular the Bill of Rights. This was an important recognition by the government that the law was in need of reform.

During the Peace talks between the government and the Darfur armed movements mediated by the African Union (AU) and conducted in Abuja in 2006, the issue of accountability for Human Rights abuses was taken off the table as the mediation team argued that the UN had already referred Darfur to the ICC.[73] These negotiations were also impacted by the ICC indictments. Thus, when the leaders of the armed movements demanded that the government apologize for crimes committed in Darfur and asked for compensations to the victims of these crimes, the government refused, arguing that doing so would amount to an admission of culpability in the context of the ICC investigations.[74] The Al Bashir's arrest warrant was also put on the negotiation table during the Doha peace talks.[75] The AU argued "that the search for justice should be pursued in a way that does not impede or jeopardize efforts aimed at promoting lasting peace."[76] The African Union High-Level Panel on Darfur, which was formed following the ICC arrest warrant against Al Bashir, issued its report in October 2009 with recommendations that "encouraged the Sudanese parties, with the Support of the Joint Chief Mediator, to ensure that issues of impunity, accountability and reconciliation and healing were appropriately addressed during the negotiations aimed at reaching a comprehensive peace agreement." Following this recommendation, PSC reinstated accountability and justice into the Doha

---

Constitution 2005, the Commission is answerable to the President of the Republic, despite other articles, (art.128) guarantee the independence of the judiciary.

72 CPA 2005, art. 2.10.1
73 Note 10, page 33.
74 De Waal, *Darfur, the Court and Khartoum*, 33.
75 S. Nouwen, 'International Justice and the prevention of Atrocities; Case Study': Darfur (ECFR background paper), November 2013, 8.
76 AU Decisions on the Abuse of the principles of Universal Jurisdiction adopted in Sharm El Sheikh in July 2008 as well as the activities of the ICC in Africa adopted in January and July 2010, 2011, 2012 and May 2013.

talks. The PSC observed in its report that dropping accountability from the Abuja talks had been "an error".[77]

In the context of the AU's antagonistic relation with the ICC, which was directly affected by the issuance of arrest warrants against Al Bashir, the DDPD set out transitional justice mechanisms. It demanded justice and reconciliation to be based on certain principles, including "ensuring that all perpetrators of violations of Human Rights and international humanitarian law are held accountable" [78] and "justice, accountability, recognition of wrongdoing, forgiveness and commitment to non-repetition." [79] The DDPD also acknowledged the victims' right to compensation.[80] In addition, the parties to the DDPD further agreed on a process for reconciliation and to establish an independent Truth, Justice and Reconciliation Commission.[81] The DDPD also called upon the Sudanese judiciary to establish a Special Court for Darfur with jurisdiction over gross violations of Human Rights and humanitarian law committed in Darfur since February 2003 and it urged this court to apply Sudanese criminal law, international criminal law and international humanitarian and Human Rights law.[82] A prosecutor for the special court was to be appointed in order to bring perpetrators to justice.[83]

It is also worth mentioning that a general amnesty followed the adoption of the DPA 2006 by a Presidential decree.[84] Special Rapporteur Sima Samar found: "The wording of the amnesty is ambiguous and unclear; it does not outline the crimes for which amnesty will be granted, nor does it provide the procedures for applications for amnesty, which makes it unclear whether there are any limitations to the crimes that can be pardoned."[85] Under this decree, an amnesty was given to two low-level officers convicted in Al Fashir for the murder of a thirteen-year-old boy who died from torture while in custody.[86] Unlike the

---

77 Ibid.
78 Article 55 (General Principles for Justice and Reconciliation), section 283 of the Doha Document For Peace In Darfur 2011.
79 Ibid, section 290.
80 Ibid, Article 57, sections (301, 302, 303. 304).
81 Ibid, Article 58, sections 311–321.
82 Ibid, Article 59, section 322 and 324.
83 Ibid, section 323.
84 The General Amnesty, issued by Presidential Decree No. 114 on 11 June 2006, Article 364 of the Darfur Peace Agreement 2006 which provided for (the release of persons detained in connection with the conflict without any restrictions).
85 Report of the Special Rapporteir on the Human Rights situation in Sudan, 20.9.2006.
86 Ibid.

DPA, the general amnesty clause in the DDPD has expressly excluded certain crimes from the application of the amnesty. These crimes are, "war crimes, crimes against the humanity, crimes of genocide, crimes of sexual violence, and gross violations of Human Rights and humanitarian law."[87]

It could be argued that the non-inclusion of accountability and justice within the DPA in 2006 and the subsequent inclusion of the same within the DDPD were directly influenced by the ICC intervention in Sudan in general, and the issuance of the arrest warrant against the President in particular, and that "it was the search for an alternative to the ICC that triggered the negotiation on transitional justice and the accountability to be put back in the agenda because of the debate around the arrest warrant for the Sudanese President."[88] This argument could be seen in light of the AUHPD report, which suggested a hybrid court to try crimes committed in Darfur and also in the subsequent AU decision to expand the jurisdiction of the African Court on Human and People's Rights to try war crimes, crimes against humanity, and genocide. In addition to that, the Sudanese government has declared several times that the SCCED would substitute the ICC.

7. Changes in Sudanese Legislation

7.1. Changes in Criminal Law

Criminal laws in Sudan have either been repressive by their very nature or been used in a repressive way. They have also failed to protect individuals from crimes committed by state officials during peace times as well as during war.[89] This includes the 1983 September laws and Public order laws. Such laws are incompatible with Human Rights obligations and have been characterized by the absence of international crimes and a legacy of impunity. The ICID confirmed the weakness of the state in that respect and concluded:

> "Repressive laws that grant broad powers to the executive have undermined the effectiveness of the judiciary, and many of the laws in Sudan today contravene basic Human Rights standards. Sudanese criminal laws do not adequately proscribe war crimes

---

87   DDPD article 60.
88   Nouwen, *International Justice and the Prevention of Atrocities*, 8.
89   REDRESS & KCHRED, 'Priorities for Criminal Law Reform in Sudan: Substance and process, An options paper prepared by REDRESS and KCHRED' January 2008, available at: http://www.redress.org/downloads/publications/Options_Paper_Law_Reform%20FinalEngl.pdf

and crimes against humanity, such as those carried out in Darfur, and the Criminal Procedures Code contains provisions that prevent the effective prosecution of these acts."[90]

As a result of such weakness within the criminal justice system in Sudan, the ICID recommended to the UNSC that the situation in Darfur be referred to the ICC. After this referral, and in particular after the ICC arrest warrant against the Sudanese President, the Government of Sudan endorsed amendments to the Criminal Act 1991 by adding a new chapter (chapter 18) incorporating the international crimes of genocide, crimes against humanity, and war crimes.[91] A special committee formed in the Ministry of Justice following the ICC intervention in Darfur had drafted these amendments. The incorporation of these crimes as part of the Sudanese criminal justice system is a significant step towards combating impunity and repression of the Human Rights and humanitarian law violations.[92] However, these amendments cannot be applied retroactively and accordingly cannot cover the violations between 2003 until the date of issuance. The Criminal Law of 1991 provides that "the law in force at the time of commission of the offence shall apply."[93]

7.2. Changes in the Criminal Procedures Act

The Criminal Procedure Act 1991 was also amended in 2009. This amendment prohibited investigations or proceedings outside the country against any Sudanese person accused of committing any violation of international humanitarian laws, including crimes against humanity, genocide, and war crimes. They also prohibit anyone in Sudan from assisting in the extradition of any Sudanese for prosecution of the above crimes.[94] This amendment reflects the government's fears with regard to the ICC intervention and to further ensure that no Sudanese individual will be prosecuted by the ICC. One can argue that this amendment directly resulted from the ICC intervention and the arrest warrants which were

---

90 Report of the International Commission of Inquiry on Darfur to the United Nation-Secretary General, page (5), 25 January 2005. Available at: http://www.un.org/news/dh/sudan/com_inq_darfur.pdf
91 Articles 187–192 of the Criminal Law 1991 as amended 2009.
92 M. Abdelsalam Babiker, 'The Prosecution of International Crimes under Sudan's Criminal and Military Laws', in: Lutz Oette (ed): *Criminal law reform and transitional justice: Human Rights perspectives for Sudan*, Burlington 2011, 163.
93 Article 4 of the Criminal Law 1991.
94 Criminal Procedures Act 1991, Article (3).

issued against Sudanese officials. It then would constitute an attempt to adapt to the ICC rather than comply with its decisions.

7.3. Changes in the Armed Forces Act

The Sudan Armed Forces Acts were characterized by the absence of any clause concerning the criminalization and prosecution of war crimes and crimes against humanity. The first military law since the independence of Sudan was The Armed Forces Act of 1957. This law was repealed by the Nimeiri Military Regime (1969–1985) which issued the Armed People's Act 1983, which covered war-related crimes, including the inhumane treatment of prisoners of war, looting and the protection of humanitarian organizations. After the collapse of the Nimeiri regime in 1985, the Civilian Government that took power (1985–1989), repealed the 1983 Act and replaced it with the Armed Forces Act of 1986, which again lacked any humanitarian provisions. The current government replaced the 1986 Act with the People's Armed Forces Act 1999 which also did not include humanitarian provisions.

The 1999 Armed Forces Act was repealed in 2007 and the Armed Forces Act of 2007 was introduced. This new Act has incorporated the international crimes of genocide, crimes against humanity, and war crimes. It introduced war crimes offences committed by combatant personnel against civilians during military operations; articles 154 on offences against persons enjoying special protection; article 155 on attacks against civilians; article 162 on threatening and displacing the populace and offences against prisoners of war.[95] The new law also established for the first time an office of military prosecution.[96] This system is parallel to the public prosecution office in the civilian justice system.

7.4. International Obligations

On 26 July 2005, Sudan became a State Party to the Optional Protocols on the Convention on the Rights of the Child on the Involvement of Children in Armed Conflict and the on the Sale of Children, Child Prostitution, and Child Pornography. On 26 August 2005, Sudan ratified the Additional Protocol (II) to the Geneva Conventions of 12 August 1949 relating to the protection of Victims of Non-International Armed Conflicts.

---

95 Babiker, *The Prosecution*, 171.
96 Art. 60 (Branch II of Military Organs and their Powers) of the MFA 2007.

7.5. The Issue of Sexual Violence in Darfur

Since the outbreak of war in Darfur in 2003 and until this chapter was written, sexual violence occurred and continues to occur throughout the region, both in the context of continuing attacks on civilians, and during periods of relative calm. International reports have confirmed that rape has been systematic and widespread. In many cases women were raped in public, in the open air, in front of their husbands, relatives or the wider community. Rape is first and foremost a violation of the Human Rights of women and girls; in some cases in Darfur, it is also clearly used to humiliate the woman, her family and her community.[97]

The UN ICID in January 2005 concluded that government forces and Janjaweed militias had used rape and sexual violence as a "deliberate strategy with the aim of terrorizing the population, ensuring control of the movement of the IDP population."[98] In the mostly Muslim province of Darfur, sexual violence is an extremely sensitive topic. Women and girls often do not admit to being sexually abused because they fear social stigmatization and do not trust the authorities to take action. The humanitarian organization *Médecins sans Frontières* (MSF) treated almost 500 women and girls between October 2004 and February 2005 in South Darfur, who represented a fraction of the total number of cases given the chronic under-reporting of rape.[99] The government responded that this could not happen among Darfurian Muslims and that therefore all these reports are exaggerated. Thus a criminal case was filed in Sudan against MSF. The Dutch Ambassador interfered and the case was suspended.

7.6. Changes in Legislation Concerning Sexual Violence

When the Sharia Law was introduced in 1983, the Sudanese Penal Code 1974 was repealed because adultery had been permitted under the 1974 Code so long as the two parties had reached the age of consent and agreed to have sexual intercourse. As a result, many laws were repealed to incorporate Sharia principles, these laws are commonly known as the September Laws because they were issued in September 1983. Among these laws was the 1983 Penal Code, which

---

97 Amnesty International, *Darfur. Rape as a Weapon of War*, 2004, available at: http://www.amnestyusa.org/node/55614
98 International Commission of Inquiry Report, para. 353, http://www.icc-cpi.int/library/cases/Report_to_UN_on_Darfur.pdf
99 The Crushing Burden of Rape: Sexual Violence in Darfur A briefing paper by Médecins Sans Frontières, Amsterdam, 8 March 2005 http://www.doctorswithoutborders.org/sites/usa/files/sudan03.pdf

had exempted the South from the application of "Hudud" punishments, that is 40 lashes for drinking alcohol. The new law also made adultery punishable by stoning to death if committed by a married Muslim, or with a penalty of 100 lashes if the perpetrator is not married. The Code also punished rape, and assault on persons or animals. The current Penal Code 1991 preserved the Islamic principles of the 1983 Code.

Section 145 of the Criminal Law 1991 defines adultery as having intercourse without a lawful bond, in which both parties are equally guilty, regardless of consent. If a person is married, the punishment is stoning to death. If not, punishment entails 100 lashes. Since the peoples of South Sudan are Non-Muslims, the Southern states of Sudan were exempted from the application of the harsh "Hudud" Sharia punishments, such as amputation, whipping up to hundred lashes and retribution. Therefore in Southern Sudan, the punishment for adultery was up to one-year imprisonment, or a fine, or both; if married, then up to three years in prison, or a fine, or both. Sodomy was punishable in the North by up to 100 lashes and also liable to up to five years imprisonment, for a second conviction 100 lashes and up to five years imprisonment; for a third time, the punishment was death or life imprisonment.

Rape is defined in Section 149 of the Criminal Law 1991 as "adultery or sodomy" on a person without consent. Consent is not acceptable if the accused has authority over or is entrusted with the care of the victim. The punishment for rape is 100 lashes and imprisonment up to 10 years. This definition has created a situation of confusion between adultery and rape about the applicable rules of evidence. The required proof for adultery is either four male eyewitnesses or confession. As a result of such confusion, if a woman claims to have been raped and fails to present the required proof, she will be under the risk of being accused of adultery because she confessed to having illegal sexual intercourse.

Despite the government of Sudan's denial of systematic rape in Darfur, it has nevertheless taken positive steps to combat sexual violence:

– In November 2005, the government of Sudan launched a National Action Plan on combating sexual violence in Darfur.[100]
– A gender violence unit was established by a decision of the Council of Ministers to follow up the implementation of the action plan of combating violence against women. The unit reports to the Minister of Justice. It formulates

---

100 Ministry of Justice, 'Combating violence against woman and children', Ministry of Justice publications unit, Khartoum 2005 (in the possession of the author).

policies on gender-based violence and organizes studies and research on the scale, causes, and manifestations of the phenomenon in the Sudan.[101]
- A women's investigation bureau was established in the state of South Darfur.
- The Ministry of Justice also issued in August 2007 a forceful declaration affirming the Sudanese government's "zero tolerance" for sexual violence and renewing its commitment to implementing the National Action Plan.[102] The declaration also reaffirmed the implementation of Criminal circular 2 of 2005 allowing women in Darfur to legally seek medical care without filling out Form 8 – the police Form that has to be filled out when violence is reported.[103]
- Several trainings for the police on international humanitarian law were also held and the numbers of female police were increased in the belief that women will feel more comfortable reporting sexual violence to a female officer.[104]
- Within the amended Armed Forces Act 2007, provisions were made prohibiting attacks on civilians during war, including violence against women.

8. Institutional Reform

8.1. The Special Criminal Court and the Events in Darfur

The Sudan Chief Justice has wide powers to set up special courts and determine their jurisdictions.[105] Between 2001 and 2003 he established eight special courts in Darfur to try armed robbery, sale of illegal arms and robbery and other crimes specified in the statutes. These courts were composed of two military judges and one civilian. The special courts were abolished in 2003 and replaced by the Special Criminal Courts in Darfur with some improvement in their composition, which was then headed by civilian judges to try war-related crimes, and legal representations were allowed, which had previously often been denied.[106]

---

101 Ibid.
102 The Declaration for Combating Violence against Women in Darfur (2007).
103 Ibid.
104 L. *Tønnessen*, "From impunity to Prosecution? Sexual Violence in Sudan beyond Darfur", NOREF Report, February 2012, available at: http://www.peacebuilding.no/Regions/Africa/Sudan-and-South-Sudan/Publications/From-impunity-to-prosecution-Sexual-violence-in-Sudan-beyond-Darfur
105 Judiciary Act 1986, art. 10(e), and Criminal Procedures Act 1991, art. 6, 10 and 14.
106 International Commission of Jurists, The Administration of Justice in Sudan: The Case of Darfur, June 2007. pp 13, 15.

On 7 June 2005, one day after the ICC Prosecutor announced that he was initiating investigations on Darfur, the Chief Justice established the Special Criminal Court on the Events in Darfur (SCCED).[107] Part two of the Order establishing the court gives it territorial jurisdiction over Darfur and makes it competent to try the following:

- Acts that constitute crimes under the Sudan Criminal Act 1991 and any other Penal Acts.
- The criminal information submitted to it by the committee formed by the Minister of Justice (by order no: 3/2005 dated 19.1.2005) to investigate the alleged contraventions stated in the report of the fact-finding committee.[108]
- Any other criminal information under any other law in accordance with a decision made by the Chief Justice.

The government declared that the SCCED would substitute for the ICC. Following the establishment of the SCCED, the Minister of Justice announced as well that the court had started investigations concerning the 51 individuals that were identified by the ICID, and he further added that Ali Kosheib was under arrest for three months as a result of the criminal investigations.

According to the Minister of Justice, the investigation had shown there was no criminal case against Haroun.[109]

In 2006 Chief Justice established two additional chambers to the special courts in Darfur, headquartered in Geneina city and Nyala city.[110] The main court was based in El Fashir city.[111] This could have been an opportunity to demonstrate a genuine willingness to deal with the alleged crimes domestically, but that has not occurred. These courts have thus far tried few cases in comparison with the total amount of crimes, all related to theft or individual murders, none involving

---

107 Order of Establishment of Special Criminal Court on the events of Darfur; issued by the Chief Justice in June 2005. The court consists of three Judges, the President of the court, a Supreme Court Judge, and two judges from the court of appeals.

108 According to the recommendations of the National Commission of Inquiry, which was established in 8/5/2004 and submitted its report in January 2005, a Judicial Commission of Inquiry was established by the Minister of Justice to undertake criminal investigations on the events of Darfur. This Commission later submitted the cases to the SCCED.

109 Sudan News Agency (SUNA); Sudan and the International Criminal Court; Special Report March 2007.

110 Chief Justice Order's numbers 1128 and 1129, dated November 2006.

111 Geneina, El Fashir and Nyala City are the largest cities in Darfur.

crimes covered by the Rome Statute. They have failed to prosecute any high-level official within the chain of command, and Sudan's laws have not been amended to allow such a possibility. Broad immunity provisions remain in place, creating obstacles for the prosecution of members of the armed forces (including the Popular Defence Forces and some militias), national security agencies, and the police.[112]

The SCCED has been widely criticized for its lack of independence and impartiality. The court was not established by a law, but by an Order from the Chief Justice who is appointed and accountable to the president of Sudan, under power given to the Chief Justice to set up courts and determine their jurisdictions and procedures. This has also been criticized by the Africa Union High-Level Panel on Darfur, which found the present judicial system to be neither able nor willing to prosecute violations committed in Darfur. It recommended the introduction of hybrid tribunals – mixed courts composed of Sudanese and non-Sudanese judges and prosecutors in order to try violations of humanitarian law in Darfur –, the creation of a truth and reconciliation commission, and the awarding of reparations to victims.[113] Since the issuances of the AUPD report, Sudan has done little to promote accountability.[114] Instead, judicial proceedings were initiated against individuals suspected of assisting the ICC, including journalists, activists, students, policemen, and even Sudanese UNAMID staff members.[115]

8.2. The Special Prosecutor for Crimes against Humanity

Another related institutional development was the appointment of a Special Prosecutor for Crimes against Humanity.[116] The Special Prosecutor was tasked with exercising the prescribed powers in the Criminal Procedure Act 1991. He was to investigate breaches of international humanitarian law, international

---

112 K. El Jizooli, 'Sudan: the Wrong Confrontation between the Government and the ICC; a paper prepared for a regional workshop "For the Peace in Darfur"', (11–12 May 2007), 90 (on record with the author).

113 The African Union established in 2009, the African Union Panel on Darfur (AUPD), to investigate the situation on the ground and to make recommendations to the AU on peace, justice and reconciliation in Darfur. The AUPD presented its report on 29 October 2009.

114 Human Rights Watch; World Report 2013, 175.

115 Human Rights Watch, World Report 2010, 33. UNAMID is the abbreviation for United Nations Mission in Darfur,

116 Minister of Justice Decree: Establishment of a Special Prosecutor for Crimes against Humanity 2005, 18 September 2005.

conventions to which Sudan was a party, and any other relevant law in relation to crimes against humanity, as well as crimes defined in other laws, which would threaten or infringe on human security.

In August 2008, the Sudanese Minister of Justice appointed a Special Prosecutor for Darfur (SPD) to investigate crimes from 2003 onward. This appointment took place one month after the ICC Prosecutor had announced that he would seek an arrest warrant against Al Bashir. On 8 October 2008, Sudanese justice officials announced that the SPD had completed an investigation into allegations against Ali Kosheib. Consequently, Kosheib was arrested.[117] The SPD was eventually removed from his position as Prosecutor. The SPD was succeeded by other three Prosecutors, all of them either resigned or were removed from ther office. Accordingly, the period of 2008–2012 witnessed the appointment of four Prosecutors.[118] The current Prosecutor was appointed following the Signature of Doha Peace Agreement 2011 between the government of Sudan and the Justice and Equality Movement.

8.3. The Justice and Reconciliation Commission

A Justice and Reconciliation Commission was established in March 2013 to, *inter alia,* address issues of impunity and build a culture of confidence, peace, and reconciliation. The Commission has sub-offices in the three Darfur states and most of its 25 appointed members are judges, lawyers, and legal advisers.[119] This Commission was one of the institutions provided for under the DDPD 2011. This Commission has not been able to function owing to the lack of funding. However, the Sudanese government has recently released funds in fulfilment of its obligation under the DDPD, which may help the Commission to start functioning.[120] The Minister of Justice made a declaration concerning the commitment of the Sudanese government to the transitional justice mechanisms provided for under the DDPD, and stating that the continuous fighting in Darfur has delayed the functioning of the Justice and Reconciliation Commission.[121]

---

117 SUNA, Note 41.

118 www.aljazeera.net/home/print/7dcab3c3

119 OHCHR REPORT 2013.

120 Press statement issued by the UN Independent Expert on the situation of Human Rights in the Sudan, Professor Mashood Adebayo Baderin, at the end of his second mission to the Sudan (10 February 2013). Available at: www.sudantodayonline.com/news.php?action=show&id=9092

121 www.moj.gov.sd/detiles.php

9. Changes in Budget Allocations

The government of Sudan is committed under the DDPA to allocating funds from the national budget to support the voluntary return and reintegration of IDPs and refugees.[122] The government has also agreed to establish a compensation fund for damages suffered by the IDPs, refugees, and victims of the conflict. The government has agreed to pay two hundred million USD.[123] Funds also were allocated to social services.[124] The government also is committed to allocating funds to the Darfur Reconstruction and Development Fund for up to two billion USD.[125] The Sudan government has stated to the ICCCR committee that 100 million SDG were allocated to the gender violence unit in the state's general budget.[126] According to the 2015 general budget, 62 million SDG are allocated to the Darfur Compensation Fund, and 33.80 million SDG to Darfur Peace Fund. However, all these transfers were the result of the government's obligations resulting from the DDPA or from commitments to international bodies other than the ICC. Nevertheless, the (unknown) expenses for maintaining the bodies created in order to provide accountability, which are described above, can be counted as triggered by the ICC.

10. The Efficiency in Implementing the Reforms

As will be illustrated in the case of Kenya,[127] the incorporation of International Criminal Law concepts into Sudanese law has no retroactive effect. Therefore, the Sudanese cannot claim the ICC cases against members of the Sudanese government and the armed forces to be inadmissible, because the post factum introduction of international crimes into Sudanese law does not enable the Sudanese judiciary to prosecute these crimes. There are also other legal gaps that Sudan would need to close. Command responsibility is not part of Sudanese criminal law. This kind of criminal liability would enable the prosecution to reach out to the higher echelons in the chain of command. In addition to that, the confusion that exists between article 145 and 149 (rape and adultery) also needed to

---

122 Article 54, section 274 DDPD 2011.
123 Ibid section 273.
124 Ibid article 20.
125 Article 21, section 142 DDPD.
126 Replies to the list of issues (CCPR/C/SDN/Q/3) in connection with the third periodic report of the government of Sudan concerning International Covenant on Civil and Political Rights (CCPR/C?SDN/3) (on record with the author).
127 See Gerhard Kemp's chapter on Kenya in this book.

be addressed. It has also been noted that even after the inclusion of war crimes and crimes against humanity in Sudanese criminal law, no one was prosecuted for committing these crimes. So far the prosecutions before the SCCED were directed against low-ranking officers and some rebels for committing theft, robbery, murder, and weapons trafficking. There has never been any prosecution for serious war crimes.[128]

In 2006, the head of the unit dealing with violence against women within the Ministry of Justice stated the total number of sexual crimes in the three Darfur states to be as low as 64 cases.[129] But until 2007, only one single rape case was prosecuted before the Darfur Special Court, and all the accusations against the suspects were dismissed.[130]The Darfur Human Rights Council noted that "efforts have been made to address the consequences of rape in Darfur through better access to medical and social care; however, less work has been done on prevention and accountability."[131] Victims and their families fear the consequences of reporting cases to the authorities. One reason is Sudan's adultery law. If a victim is unmarried and pregnant and fails to convince the police that she did not consent to sex, the police may charge her with adultery (*zina*). Under *Sharia* (Islamic law), the pregnancy of an unmarried woman is *prima facie* evidence of guilt. According to one set of official statistics, the courts of Darfur tried 10 cases of rape in 2006, among which seven ended with convictions. In October 2007, the Sudanese Ministry of Justice reported that Darfur courts had tried 20 cases of rape in 2007. Only once Darfur courts awarded compensation.[132]

The Minister of Justice has facilitated victims' access to medical care in some places, but this approach has not been applied uniformly. Some police and community leaders who advise victims still believe that they must report the crime to the police before they seek medical care, although a ministerial circular regulation has relieved victims from this obligation. This amendment resulted from the pressure of humanitarian agencies, which repeatedly voiced concerns that the need to go to the police first prevented survivors from seeking healthcare.

The National Intelligence Security Service Act of 1999 (NISSA), the Armed Forces Act 1986 and the Police Forces Act 1999 all include provisions which

---

128 K. El-Gizouli, *The Erroneous Confrontation*, 261.
129 Sudan Human Rights Council, *Articles on Violence Against Women*, (Violence against Women and Children), Atiat Mustafa, 2006, 62.
130 International Commission of Jurists, Sudan Judiciary System; Darfur Case, October 2007, 47. (On record with the author)
131 Ibid.
132 Information is in the possession of the author.

grant extensive immunities to members of the NSSF, the members of Police and Armed Forces, thus making their prosecution for the most serious crimes almost impossible.[133] These provisions ensure that none of the government's officers be compelled to give information about the actions performed in the course of their duty. Civil or criminal actions against such persons for acts committed in connection with their duty can only be brought with an approval from their superiors. Members of the Police, NISSA, and Armed Forces appear before special courts, rather than the regular criminal courts.[134] However, some NISSA officers were tried for Human Rights abuses, although the number of cases brought against them remained much below the number of alleged perpetrators of Human Rights violations.[135]

---

133 Police Forces Act 1999, art. 46, 47; National Security Service Act 1999, art. 33 and art. 41 together with the Armed Forces Act 1986.
134 The Police Court, The Military Court and the NISSA court.
135 Second Periodic Report of the United Nations High Commissioner for Human Rights on the Human Rights Situation in Sudan, 27 January 2006, in the author's possession.

III) Lack of Domestic Change in Consequence of Open Defiance Toward ICT Decisions

Klaus Bachmann, Amani M. Ejami

The ICC and Institutional Reform – The Case of Libya

1. The Libyan Revolution and its Aftermath

According to the narrative in most academic and popular-science accounts of the Libyan contribution to the Arab Spring, Libya's revolution, which toppled Muhammar Al-Gaddafi in 2011, started on 17 February. But the protests against Gaddafi and his regime had started earlier in 2011. They certainly were inspired by the protests in Tunisia and Egypt, but focused on domestic problems like housing and corruption. The protests began in several big towns in January. In February, the they spread to the capital, where they took on a violent character, including the throwing of Molotov cocktails on police buildings and the police responding with rubber bullets, water cannons and beating. For 17 February, the opposition called for a "Day of Rage", which was followed in several towns and took on a scope that inclined the security forces to use live ammunition against the protesters. Protesters torched public buildings. Benghazi was the first town taken over by the opposition.[1] In other towns, especially in the eastern part of the country, soldiers and policemen switched sides and fought with the protesters. The patterns of the protests already revealed regional, tribal and political divisions, which would later cause the breakdown of the opposition movement into rivalling factions. But in early 2011, these divisions were obfuscated by the anti-Gaddafi stance of all opposition forces and the fierce resistance the Gaddafi regime offered against the advance of opposition fighters. As the tribal and regional divisions started to affect the cohesion of the army, more and more soldiers switched sides, providing the opposition with heavy weaponry and even tanks and military aircraft. Almost from the beginning of the uprising, the opposition was supported from outside, since the strong repressions under Gaddafi had forced dissidents to go abroad and the opposition could only meet and coordinate actions in foreign countries.

There are also strong indications of crimes being committed by all conflict parties from the beginning of armed hostilities. At the end of 2011, Amnesty

---

1   D. Vanderwalle, "Libya's uncertain revolution", in: P. Cole, and B. McQuinn (eds), The Libyan Revolution and its aftermath, Oxford, New York (kindle edition) 2015.

International (AI) published a large report listing and categorizing the abuses in legal terms. The report also assessed the policy of the National Transitional Council (NTC) and its followers, recognizing their limited influence on militias and individual fighters on the ground. AI conceded that the sudden escape of Gaddafi's forces had left a power vacuum, which left space for personal revenge actions and spontaneously emerging groups, whose aim was to uphold a minimum of security in their neighbourhood, but which were untrained and unaware of Human Rights obligations and acted under stress and fear. However, the report also details cases of gross abuses on a mass scale, which had gone unpunished and were downplayed by the NTC and its organs. One of these abuses was the execution of more than 50 Gaddafi supporters, 50 foreign fighters and two Libyans, who were massacred in Derna after opposition forces had taken the local garrison. Western media outlets also reported revenge killings of captured or surrendered foreign fighters, called mercenaries[2], which were often justified with racist arguments. These attacks were directed against Africans, even when there was no circumstantial evidence to regard them as combatants.[3] Compared with the 2–3 million foreign immigrants in Libya at the outbreak of the conflict, the number of mercenaries was relatively small and the likelihood of becoming a victim of popular outrage was much higher for innocent people than for actual mercenaries.[4] The AI report found: "[t]he allegations about the

---

2   In legal terms, mercenaries are commercial fighters which do not hold the citizenship of the country on whose behalf they are fighting. The Gaddafi regime's practice of granting Libyan citizenship to armed supporters, recruited from African tribes in neighbouring countries, whose tribal leaders supported Gaddafi, made the assessment whether these people were or were not mercenaries extremely difficult, even for the UN expert panel charged with the supervision of the UN arms embargo against Libya. See: Final report of the Panel of Experts in accordance with paragraph 24 (d) of resolution 1973 (2011), S2012/163 and Final report of the Panel of Experts in accordance with paragraph 10 (d) of resolution 2040 (2012), S/2013/99, both available at: http://www.un.org/sc/committees/1970/experts.shtml

3   Prior to the conflict, Libya had also attracted a number of foreign civilian workers, some of whom were killed by opposition fighters under the premises that they were hidden mercenaries. V. Prashad: *Arab Spring, Libyan Winter*. Okaland, Baltimore, Edinburgh 2012, 226–227.

4   On the links between economic immigration (mostly from Chad) into Libya under Gaddafi, forced returns (often due to increasing racism and supremacist attitudes in Libya) and the treatment of Africans during the revolution see also: K. F. Hansen, 'Political and Economic Effects of Qaddafi's Death on Chad', Note de l'IFRI, December 2013, available at: www.ifri.org/sites/default/files/atoms/files/noteifriocpkfhansen.pdf

use of mercenaries proved to be largely unfounded. Many captured Al-Gaddafi fighters, including those interviewed by Amnesty International in Benghazi and Misratah, were in fact Libyan nationals, including individuals from places such as Sabha in the south-west of Libya and from the Tawergha region east of Misratah."[5]

Tawergha is a crime site which was not covered by the Amnesty Report. The town is situated on the road between Sirt and Misratah, one of the first towns whose population rose against Gaddafi. The latter's troops used it as a stronghold during the two-month long siege of Misratah, committing numerous war crimes against its population. When the balance of power shifted and the oppositional Misratah Brigade seized Tawargha, the population was severely punished for what the oppositional fighters regarded as the inhabitant's collaboration with the regime. Reporters from the Telegraph and the BBC, entering the town later in 2011, found it virtually empty. About 30,000 people had been chased away and deported to other parts of the country. According to Misratah commanders, the purpose of the expulsions had been to erase the town. Inhabitants, they declared to reporters, would never be allowed to come back.[6]

Government forces were more often accused of mass atrocities and international crimes by the media. Some media even wrote about the genocide, which was allegedly underway in Libya.[7] The most frequent accusations pointed to cruelties of the security forces against protesters, the use of heavy weapons and the air force against (opposition held) civilian targets such as residential

---

5   Amnesty International, 13.9.2011, 'Libya: The battle for Libya: Killings, disappearances and torture', available at: https://www.amnesty.org/en/documents/MDE19/025/2011/en/

6   A. Gilligan, 'Gaddafi's ghost town after the loyalists retreat', The Telegraph 11.9.2011, available at: http://www.telegraph.co.uk/news/worldnews/africaandindianocean/libya/8754375/Gaddafis-ghost-town-after-the-loyalists-retreat.html and T. Kafala, "'Cleansed' Libyan town spills its terrible secrets'", BBC 12.12.2011, available at: http://www.bbc.com/news/magazine-16051349. See also: Human Rights Watch, 'Libya: Militias Terrorizing Residents of "Loyalist" Town', October 2011, available at: http://www.hrw.org/news/2011/10/30/libya-militias-terrorizing-residents-loyalist-town

7   BBC: 'Libya's deputy envoy to the UN:'"What's happening is genocide"' BBC 21.2.2011. Initially the genocide claim was levelled by oppositional politicians against government forces, later, after the armed intervention by NATO countries, it was usually directed against the bombing and against the persecution of alleged African mercenaries, which were labelled as "black genocide" and, according to the authors of these claims, supported by NATO. See for example the anonymous website: http://humanrightsinvestigations.org.

areas, and the use of rape as a means of intimidating oppositional civilians.[8] Some of these accusations, which were published by media outlets, were neither confirmed by Human Rights investigators, nor by the ICC prosecution. When ICC Prosecutor Luis Moreno Ocampo, who had made allegations about Viagra-supported mass crimes, allegedly ordered by Gaddafi, applied for an arrest warrant against Gaddafi, Abdullah Al Senussi and Saif al-Islam in May 2011, no charges concerning sexual violence were included. The application only contained the charges of murder and persecution as elements of crimes against humanity.[9] The pre-trial chamber's decision on Ocampo's application for an arrest warrant does not mention rape nor any kind of sexual violence and concentrates on the use of the security sector for carrying out a policy of organized and centrally commanded persecutions against the civilian population and for war crimes.[10]

The three ICC cases related to Libya were the consequence of one of the two United Nations Security Council's very controversial referrals based on art. 13b

---

8   In June 2011, Ocampo had told reporters that hundreds of women had been raped in the Libyan government clampdown on the popular uprising and that Gaddafi had ordered the violations as a form of punishment. The prosecutor said there was even evidence that the government had been handing out doses of Viagra to soldiers to encourage sexual attacks. See: The Guardian, 9.6.2011, available at: http://www. theguardian.com/world/2011/jun/08/gaddafi-forces-libya-britain-nato; See also: P. Cockburn, 'Amnesty questions claim that Gaddafi ordered rape as weapon of war', The Independent 24.6.2011, available at: http://www.independent.co.uk/news/world/africa/ amnesty-questions-claim-that-,gaddafi-ordered-rape-as-weapon-of-war-2302037. html; and V. Prashad, *Arab Spring, Libyan Winter*, 216–217. Cherif Bassiouni, head of an UN-panel inquiring international crimes in Libya at the same time, called the claims about mass rapes "hysteria", suggesting, that Ocampo's allegations had been based on false evidence. See: The Herald Sun, 10.6.2011, available at: http://www. heraldsun.com.au/news/breaking-news/libya-rape-claims-hysteria-investigator/ story-e6frf7jx-1226072781882

9   Prosecutor's Application Pursuant to Article 58 as to Muammar Mohammed Abu Minyar Gaddafi, Saif Al-Islam Gaddafi and Abdullah Al-Senussi.ICC 01/11, 16 May 2011, available at: http://www.icc-cpi.int/iccdocs/doc/doc1073503.pdf. Based on this document, it is impossible to establish the precise scope of the allegations against the three, since the whole part concerning evidence was redacted.

10 Decision on the Prosecutor's Application Pursuant to Article 5 8 as to Muammar Mohammed Abu Minyar Gaddafi, Saif al-Islam Gaddafi, and Abdullah Al-Senussi, ICC-01/11, 27.6.2011, available at: http://www.icc-cpi.int/iccdocs/doc/doc1099314. pdf

of the Rome Statute.[11] The UNSC made this decision on 26 February 2011, at a time when the revolution in Libya was already in full swing.[12] The UNSC referral was approved together with a list of sanctions against Libya, which also included an arms embargo on the country and an assets freeze and travel ban for the family of Muhammar Al-Gaddafi and some government officials. A no-fly zone had been approved in March on the basis of a different UNSC resolution.[13] Beginning from 19 March 2011, NATO started to launch air strikes against military targets in Libya connected to the Gaddafi government.[14] The intervention was based on UNSC resolution 1973, which called to protect the civilian population. This mandate was interpreted in a very broad and flexible way that empowered the intervening forces to attack any military convoy moving toward civilian buildings. During the uprising in Tripoli, NATO aircraft coordinated its actions with the insurgents and with Quatari officers and hit 24 out of 28 command centres of the government forces, enabling the insurgents to take over the Libyan capital.[15] From the beginning, the no-fly zone was directed against the government side alone, since the opposition only managed to take over individual airplanes, but did not have its own air force. The UNSC resolution did not authorize foreign soldiers to enter Libya and NATO claimed not to have "boots on the ground", but individual member states like France and Britain had special forces operating as advisors and forward air controllers in Libya, who helped direct the air strikes to their targets.[16] The mere timing of the UNSC referral, which overlapped with NATO's intervention against the Gaddafi government, was likely to create the impression of ICC bias. This impression was reinforced by the referral's content. Under the resolution's paragraph 6, the UNSC decided "that nationals, current or former officials or personnel from a

---

11 The first was the referral against Sudan's ruling president Omar Al Bashir and several other high-ranking government officials. The Gaddafi and Sensussi case was the second.

12 UNSC res. 1970 (2011), available at: http://www.un.org/press/en/2011/sc10187.doc.htm

13 UNSC res. 1973 (2011) available at: http://www.un.org/press/en/2011/sc10200.doc.htm

14 F. Wehrey, 'NATO's Intervention', in: Peter Cole and Brian McQuinn (eds), *The Libyan Revolution and its Aftermath*. Oxford (kindle edition) 2015.

15 Ibid and P. Cole and B. McQuinn, 'The Fall of Tripoli part 1' and 'the fall of Tripoli part II'; both in: P. Cole and B. McQuinn (eds), *The Libyan Revolution and its Aftermath*. Oxford (kindle edition) 2015.

16 Wehrey, NATO's intervention.

State outside the Libyan Arab Jamahiriya[17] which is not a party to the Rome Statute of the International Criminal Court shall be subject to the exclusive jurisdiction of that State for all alleged acts or omissions arising out of or related to operations in the Libyan Arab Jamahiriya established or authorized by the Council, unless such exclusive jurisdiction has been expressly waived by the State." The paragraph excluded ICC jurisdiction over crimes committed by US citizens during the air strikes. The other intervening countries of the anti-Gaddafi alliance – Great Britain, France and Canada – were all parties to the Rome Statute.[18] In November 2011, ICC prosecutor Luis Moreno Ocampo announced investigations concerning crimes committed by NATO troops and opposition fighters during the air raid on Libya[19], but he left a few months later without having submitted any arrest warrant for confirmation. His successor Fatou Bensouda never came back to this topic, although in May 2012, Human Rights Watch published the results of an extensive investigation into eight incidents of NATO bombing, which had caused the deaths of 72 civilians, one third of whom had been under 18 years old. In two out of the eight cases, HRW did not find any evidence for the existence of a legitimate military target during the time when the place had been bombed. NATO did not reveal any testable information about the targets.[20]

2. Relations Between the ICC and Post-Revolutionary Libya

The above-mentioned background of the conflict is relevant for the context of the ICC referral, because it was likely to create the impression of the ICC as NATO's judicial arm.[21] The perception of the ICC as an ally in regime change in Libya was

---

17 "Libyan Arab Jamahiriya" was the official name of Libya under Gaddafi.

18 The UNSC also burdened the parties to the Rome Statute with the cost of the ICC intervention, "recognizing that none of the expenses incurred in connection with the referral, including expenses related to investigations or prosecutions in connection with that referral, shall be borne by the United Nations and that such costs shall be borne by the parties to the Rome Statute and those States that wish to contribute voluntarily."

19 The Telegraph 2.11.2011, available at: http://www.telegraph.co.uk/news/worldnews/africaandindianocean/libya/8866007/Libya-Nato-to-be-investigated-by-ICC-for-war-crimes.html

20 HRW, 'Unacknowledged Deaths Civilian Casualties in NATO's Air Campaign in Libya', 13.5.2012, available at: https://www.hrw.org/report/2012/05/13/unacknowledged-deaths/civilian-casualties-natos-air-campaign-libya

21 A similar situation occured as the result of the Kosovo conflict in 1999, when NATO intervention against the Federal Republic of Yugoslavia (Serbia and Montenegro) overlapped with the decision of Louise Arbour, the ICTY's chief prosecutor, to issue

further strengthened by the lack of any ICC investigation into crimes committed by the opposition and the fact that the ICC referral was later actually followed by regime change, although the latter was rather the consequence of the air strikes and the shift in the military balance on the ground to the advantage of the opposition forces than of the ICC referral and the subsequent arrest warrants.[22] The impression of the ICC's partiality was reinforced by the ICC's reluctance to investigate the apparent murder of Muammar Al-Gaddafi. Despite Human Rights groups urging the ICC to investigate his murder, the ICC remained passive and instead continued investigations against the remaining suspects, against whom arrest warrants had been issued. Both of them were members of the Libyan *ancien regime* under Gaddafi: Saif Al-Islam Gaddafi, honorary chairman of the Gaddafi International Charity and Development Foundation, who was widely regarded as *de facto* Prime Minister, and Abdullah Al-Senussi, colonel in the Libyan Armed Forces and head of the Military Intelligence. The arrest warrant and the proceedings against Muammar Al-Gaddafi were terminated by the ICC in November 2011.

Relations between the ICC and the Libyan interim authorities quickly became strained despite the fact that the ICC was widely regarded as a factor in the weakening of the Gaddafi regime and had, to some extent, contributed to its fall. No longer than a few days after the UNSC referral, the ICC prosecutor initiated an investigation, and on 16 May 2011, the ICC pre-trial chamber issued the three arrest warrants. On 19 November 2011, Saif al-Islam Gaddafi was arrested and flown to Zintan, where he remained in the hands of local militia. On 17 March 2012, Senussi was arrested in Mauritania when flying in from Morocco on a false Malian passport.[23] Mauritania, which is not a signatory state to the

---

an indictment against the then ruling president of Yugoslavia, Slobodan Milošević. For details, see Jovana Mihajlović Trbovc' chapter on Serbia in the first volume of this publication.

22 Some authors question the assumption about NATO air strikes being responsible for a shift on the ground and argue that at that stage, the opposition already had the upper hand over Gaddafi's (badly commanded and demoralized) army and the airstrikes' purpose was for the intervening countries to get a better hold of Libya's postwar development. H. Campbell, *Global NATO and the Catastrophic Failure in Libya*, New York 2013, 155–161 and K. Engelbrekt, Ch. Wagnsson, M. Mohlin (eds), *The NATO Intervention in Libya*. New York, London 2015.

23 The Telegraph 17.3.2011, available at: http://www.telegraph.co.uk/news/worldnews/africaandindianocean/libya/9150099/Muammar-Gaddafis-spy-chief-Senussi-arrested-in-Mauritania.html

Rome Statute, extradited him to Libya, ignoring the ICC arrest warrant and French requests for extradition.[24] Press reports alleged that the transaction had cost the NTC 200 mln USD.[25] Initially, he was held in the custody of the Libyan government in Tripoli. But in July 2014, the radical *Libya Dawn* movement overran Tripoli and took hold of the government premises, including the justice ministry and the prisons, which made Senussi a prisoner of the new authorities and deprived the pro-Western government, which went to Tobruk, of control over his person.[26]

Under the provisions of the Rome Statute, both defendants could only be tried at the ICC if the latter found the Libyan judiciary unwilling or unable to try them on its own. The UNSC referral did not relieve the ICC from this admissibility test. Until Senussi's arrest in Mauritania, Libya had clearly been unable to put him on trial, but it was well willing to go after him. The ICC was eager to carry out the proceedings against Senussi and Saif al-Islam Gaddafi, but the Interim Transitional National Council wanted them tried in Libya. Already on 1 May 2012, the Libyan government had filed an admissibility challenge to the ICC, arguing that the case against Saif al-Islam should be left to the Libyan judiciary. A court building had been prepared for the trial. However, at that time, Saif al-Islam was held by a militia in Zintan, over which the government in Tripoli had only very limited leverage. When in June, a team from the ICC's Office of Public Counsel for the Defence (OPCD), led by Australian lawyer Melinda Taylor went to Zintan to talk to Saif Al-Islam, they were arrested on allegations of spying and undermining Libya's security. They were released after 26 days, following an apology from the ICC president. The ICC announced an investigation into the Libyan allegations about Taylor having carried a coded letter from a prominent member of the Gaddafi entourage, who at that time was beyond the reach of the Libyan authorities and was suspected of conspiring to help Saif Al-Islam escape from prison. The result of the investigation was never published, and and Taylor criticized the ICC strongly after her release[27] and ceased to work

24 BBC, 'Mauretania deports Libya Spy chief Abdullah Al-Senussi', 5 September 2012, available at: http://www.bbc.com/news/world-africa-19487228.

25 M. Kersten, "Justice after the war: The International Criminal Court and post-Gaddafi Libya", in: K. Fisher and R. Stewart (eds), *Transitional Justice and the Arab Spring*. London, New York: Routledge 2014, pp. 189–190.

26 Klaus Bachmann's interview with former Minister of Justice Salah El-Marghani (in office between November 2012 until August 2014) in Leiden in September 2015.

27 According to information available at the Press Office of the ICC in July 2015, the ICC had never completed the investigation into the four lawyers' conduct in Zintan,

for the tribunal.[28] The incident spoiled relations between the ICC and the Libyan government, but at the same time let rumors about a deal between the ICC and the Libyan government flourish.[29] It also made clear that the ICC staff would face manifold obstacles if it acted against the interest of the Libyan government, including dangers for staff members' personal security.

The admissibility test was more difficult to pass in the case of Saif Al-Islam, who was in custody of militia, who in principle were friendly to the official Libyan government, but refused to hand him over. A willingness of the Libyan government to try Saif al-Islam was out of the question. But the Rome Statute does not provide any guidance on how to assess a state's ability to try an accused under conditions of power diffusion in a post-conflict country. Rather than focusing on this issue, the judges discussed at length whether the charges brought against Saif Al-Islam were exactly the same as the ones for which he was to be tried at the ICC. There, the Libyan government's approach to the case had hardly been convincing. Zintan had charged Saif al-Islam first with minor crimes related to financial fraud, corruption, insulting the Libyan flag and undermining national security. The latter two charges were a repercussion of the Melina Taylor affair.[30] Only later were charges added which mirrored those contained in the ICC arrest warrant and relating to war crimes and crimes against humanity committed during the revolution, including the import of mercenaries from other African

because it had not obtained the necessary information from the Libyan government. Kaus Bachmann's interview with Fadi El Abdallah from the ICC Public Affairs Unit.

28 M. Rout, V. Vasek, 'Australian lawyer Melinda Taylor, freed after being held in Libya, is reunited with her family', The Australian 3.7.2012, available at: http://www.theaustralian.com.au/national-affairs/aussie-lawyer-melinda-taylor-leaves-libya/story-fn59niix-1226415228687; C. Stephen, J. Borger, L. Harding, 'Libya accuses Australian ICC official of passing secret letter to Gaddafi's son', The Guardian 25.6.2012, available at: http://www.theguardian.com/world/2012/jun/25/melinda-taylor-libya-accuse-spying

29 C. Stephen, 'Melinda Taylor lashes out at Libya and ICC', Libya Herald 16.12.2012.

30 The New York Times: 'Libya: Qaddafi's Son Appears in a Tribal Court and Reuter', 19.9.2013, available at: http://www.nytimes.com/2013/09/20/world/africa/libya-qaddafis-son-appears-in-a-tribal-court.html?ref=topics
See also the draft translation of a press conference held by Mohamed Al-Alagi, from the National Council for Public and Human Rights and others on 2.5.2013 in Zintan. The transcript was tendered at the ICC, the video of the conference is available at: http://www.youtube.com/watch?v=vdwDrENFrmg&feature=youtu.be

countries and personally participating in the shooting of unarmed prisoners of war.[31] At the ICC, Libya's representatives argued that the Zintan indictment and the charges prepared by the National Prosecutor were "much broader than the ICC's investigation, both in its temporal and geographical scope."[32] The government also conceded that they did not encompass all the incidents mentioned in the arrest warrant. Another Achilles' heel of the Libyan case at the ICC was the absence of command responsibility in the Libyan investigation. There he was mainly charged with crimes committed personally, whereas the ICC prosecution focused on crimes committed indirectly through Saif al-Islam's use of the military and state machinery.[33]

In the pre-trial chamber's decision about the admissibility of Saif al-Islam's case, the discussion concerning Libya's ability and readiness to judge him comprised only 7 pages as compared to the 24 dedicated to the issue whether his Libyan indictment included the same conduct and events as the ICC arrest warrant.[34] Nevertheless, some observers concluded that the lack of control over Saif's person had been the real reason why the ICC judges had agreed to leave Senussi to the Libyan judiciary and pressed the Libyan government to deliver Saif.[35] There were also speculations that the Zintan trial was not about bringing Saif al-Islam to justice, but about sheltering him. They were based on the assumption, that Zintan had sided with former Gaddafi supporters their conflict with other power centres and used Saif al-Islam as a bargaining chip in the

---

31 Owen Bowcott: 'Saif Gaddafi should go on trial in Libya, war crimes tribunal told', The Guardian 1.5.2012, available at: http://www.theguardian.com/world/2012/may/01/saif-gadaffi-trial-libya-icc

32 Judgment on the appeal of Libya against the decision of pre-trial chamber I of 31 May 2013 entitled "decision on the admissibility of the case against Saif al-Islam Gaddafi" ICC-01/11-01/11-OA4, par 52, available at: http://www.icc-cpi.int/iccdocs/doc/doc1779877.pdf

33 Judgment on the appeal of Libya against the decision of pre-trial chamber I of 31 May 2013 entitled "decision on the admissibility of the case against Saif al-Islam Gaddafi" ICC-01/11-01/11-OA4, par 62, available at: http://www.icc-cpi.int/iccdocs/doc/doc1779877.pdf

34 ICC pretrial chamber I: Decision on the admissibility of the case against Saif al-Islam Gaddafi. ICC-01/11-01/11, 31.5.2013, available at: http://www.icc-cpi.int/iccdocs/doc/doc1599307.pdf. The pre-trial decision was confirmed on appeal almost exactly a year later on 21.5.2014.

35 This was mentioned as the main reason by ICC spokesman Fadi El Abdallah and by Thomas Verfuss, the president of the Association of Journalists at the International Criminal Court in interviews with Klaus Bachmann in The Hague I July 2015.

UN-brokered peace negotiations.[36] Supporters of this interpretation could point to Saif al-Islam's year-long pre-trial arrest.

In May 2014, the appeals chamber rejected the Libyan appeal entirely and confirmed the findings and interpretations of the pre-trial chamber, with two out of five judges dissenting. On 10 December 2014, pre-trial chamber I decided to refer the matter to the Security Council of the United Nations, finding that Libya had failed to to surrender Saif Al-Islam Gaddafi to the Court. Ocampo's concept of positive complementarity echoed in the courtroom when the chamber emphasized that it did not intend "to sanction or criticize Libya but solely to seek the assistance of the Security Council to eliminate the impediments to cooperation."[37]

The situation was different with regard to the Senussi case. When Libya's inadmissibility challenge was discussed before the ICC pre-trial chamber, it was relatively easy to prove that Libya was eager and able to bring him to justice. At that time, the officially recognized government of Libya[38] had taken him into custody and indicted him for crimes committed under domestic law. The most controversial point of the Senussi case was therefore not whether Libya was willing and able to judge him at home, but whether the Libyan judiciary would prosecute him for the same crimes, for which the arrest warrant had been issued and whether the Libyans would be able to deliver a fair trial. The latter point was strongly emphasized by Senussi's lawyers[39],

---

36 L. Hilsum, 'Saif al-Islam Gaddafi: the prophet of his own doom', The Guardian 25.8.2015, available at:
    http://www.theguardian.com/world/2015/aug/05/saif-al-islam-gaddafi-prophet-of-own-doom-libya (it should be noticed, that the article was written after the ICC appeals judgment concerning admissibility).

37 The chamber also criticized the Libyan government's failure to return materials, which had been confiscated from the Melina Taylor team in Zintan. See: The prosecutor v. Saif al-Islam Gaddafi. Here: Decision on the non-compliance by Libya with requests for cooperation by the Court and referring the matter to the United Nations Security Council, 10.12.2014, ICC-01/11-01/11-577, available at: www.icc-cpi.int/iccdocs/doc/doc1879914.pdf

38 On 30.11.2011 a majority of 102 UN member states voted in favor of the recognition of the NTC as the official Libyan government. Already in July, 30 UN member states had recognized it bilaterally. The Guardian: 'Libyan rebels win international recognition as country's leaders', 15.7.2011, available at: http://www.theguardian.com/world/2011/jul/15/libyan-rebels-international-recognition-leaders

39 Since the Zintan militia isolated Senussi, he had been unable to directly hire defence counsel. But under the Rome Statute, the Office of the Public Counsel for the Defence (OPCD) took over.

who claimed that Senussi was deprived of his basic right to an effective defence, because Libya did not allow defence lawyers to meet their client. In its verdict, the pre-trial chamber rejected this allegation, arguing that the procedure in Libya had not yet reached a stage at which the lack of consultation with a defence counsel amounted to a violation of the accused's fair trial rights. But not only Senussi's lawyers were in favour of trying him in The Hague, the interventions of the Office of Public Counsel for the Defence (OPCD) went in the same direction. It even accused the ICC prosecution of double standards and of siding with the Libyan government. The prosecution saw its purpose not in securing Senussi's transfer to The Hague, but in supporting Libyan efforts to try him at home. This was contrary to the stance of the biggest international Human Rights NGOs, which all wanted the accused to stand trial at the ICC. The elephant in the room was of course another issue, which transpired through the verdict of the pre-trial chamber: capital punishment and the question in how far the ICC could act as a norm entrepreneur in Libya and use its limited leverage to incline the Libyan government to take its Human Rights commitment seriously.[40] If tried in Libya, Senussi (and Saif Al-Islam, too) would face a possible death sentence and execution. If tried in The Hague, the most severe punishment would be a life-long prison term. But there is no provision in the Rome Statute that would charge the ICC with the task of fostering the implementation of international Human Rights norms or, more specifically, contributing to the abolition of capital punishment. Many signatory countries to the Rome Statute (but far from all of them) do not apply or carry out the death penalty, but they do so because of their adherence to international conventions other than the Rome Statute. And Libya was not even a signatory state to the Rome Statute.

The second elephant in the room was the issue of whether the ICC should declare a case admissible if the challenging country was able and willing to try a suspect, but would most likely not do so in a fair way. Here, the pre-trial chamber set a very low threshold for an inadmissibility challenge, declaring that a violation of a defendant's rights would in itself not empower the pre-trial chamber to assume the inability of a country to "genuinely carry out an

---

40 I am grateful to Thomas Verfuss, the president of the Association of Journalists at the International Criminal Court (AJICC) for directing my attention to these points during an interview in July 2015 in The Hague.

investigation or prosecution." This would only be possible if an investigation or prosecution would be conducted with a "lack of independence and impartiality" and in a manner that was "inconsistent with the intent to bring the person to justice." In such a case, the court would only be able to establish inadmissibility if one or more or the scenarios in art. 17 par. 2 and 3 of the Rome Statute were met.[41] These scenarios are, however, restricted to a situation, in which a country strives to avoid punishing a defendant. They do not describe situations, in which a government or another state organ intends to hold a defendant accountable in a way that does not require his prosecution, for example in the framework of a truth-seeking or truth-telling procedure which involves conditional amnesty. They also do not describe situations, in which a country seeks to convict and punish a defendant at any rate.[42]

The appeals chamber confirmed the decision of the pre-trial chamber. Already in its first paragraph, which summarizes the verdict, the judges did not regard it as their duty to base their findings about admissibility on an evaluation "whether the due process rights of a suspect have been breached per se. In particular, the concept of proceedings 'being conducted in a manner which, in the circumstances, is inconsistent with an intent to bring the person concerned to justice', should generally be understood as referring to proceedings which will lead to a suspect evading justice in the sense of not appropriately being tried genuinely to establish his or her criminal responsibility, in the equivalent of sham

---

41 Art 17/2 says: "The proceedings were or are being undertaken or the national decision was made for the purpose of shielding the person concerned from criminal responsibility for crimes within the jurisdiction of the Court referred to in article 5;

    (b) There has been an unjustified delay in the proceedings which in the circumstances is inconsistent with an intent to bring the person concerned to justice;

    (c) The proceedings were not or are not being conducted independently or impartially, and they were or are being conducted in a manner which, in the circumstances, is inconsistent with an intent to bring the person concerned to justice."

    Art 17/3 adds: "In order to determine inability in a particular case, the Court shall consider whether, due to a total or substantial collapse or unavailability of its national judicial system, the State is unable to obtain the accused or the necessary evidence and testimony or otherwise unable to carry out its proceedings."

42 (Pre-trial) Decision on the admissibility of the case against Saif al-Islam Gaddafi. 31.5.2013, ICC-01/11-01/11, available at: http://www.icc-cpi.int/iccdocs/doc/doc1599307.pdf

proceedings that are concerned with that person's protection."[43] The judges did not go so far as to regard any possible violation of an accused's rights as irrelevant to an admissibility decision and conceded that violations might be so egregious "that the proceedings can no longer be regarded as being capable of providing any genuine form of justice to the suspect, so that they should be deemed, in those circumstances, to be inconsistent with an intent to bring the person to justice." The appeals chamber did not define such situations, but the emphasis was clear: a government could infringe the rights of an accused and still effectively claim inadmissibility before the ICC, as long as the infringements were not "egregious" and did not amount to a "sham trial" and as long as the trial demonstrated the intent to "bring him to justice."[44] Such a case would only be inadmissible before the ICC if fair trial rights were violated in order to acquit or otherwise exonerate a defendant. Because fair trial rights predominantly serve the interest of the defence and tend to compensate a defendant's disadvantages with regard to the prosecution, the appeals decision in Senussi was likely to create an imbalance in admissibility matters to the detriment of defendants. But the criticism of this decision was not so much inspired by concerns about equality between defence and prosecution in domestic trials, over which the ICC could claim primacy, but by disappointment about the ICC's reluctance to act as a norm entrepreneur in transition countries. The ICC verdicts on admissibility in the Senussi case were regarded as a major backlash for Human Rights by many observers from Human Rights organizations, because the ICC pre-trial chamber (and subsequently the appeals chamber) refused to use admissibility decisions as Human Rights safeguards.

For the purpose of this chapter, the admissibility challenges in the Senussi (and the Saif Al-Islam) case are important for another reason: because they demonstrate the ICC's unwillingness to act as an influencer on domestic legal reform in Libya, contrary to what the ICTY and the ICTR had tried in the framework of their outreach programs and completion strategies. Ocampo's notion of "positive complementarity" came close to the latter's policy, but it was rejected by

---

43 Decision on the admissibility of the case against Mr. Abdullah Al-Senussi", ICC-OI/II-OI/IIOA6, 24.7.2014, available at: http://www.icc-cpi.int/iccdocs/doc/doc1807073.pdf

44 It is worth noticing that the judges' definition of a "sham trial" only included proceedings intended to exonerate a defendant; they did not mention the opposite possibility, that a "sham trial" be carried out in order to scapegoat a defendant without proving his or her guilt.

the judges when they claimed Saif Al-Islam for the ICC.[45] The ICC was regarded by many as an actor that had driven regime change in Libya, side-by-side with NATO and the NTC, but when it came to domestic change during transition, it stopped short of influencing internal politics. Had the ICC pre-trial chamber openly addressed the elephants in the room (Libya's ability to judge the suspects and the death penalty issue), domestic legislative change would have been more likely, and Libya would have been more inclined to do what Rwanda and some of the former Yugoslav successor republics had done – to adopt modern Human Rights standards and universal jurisdiction (and to implement them in practice). Countries under ad hoc tribunals' jurisdiction had done so in order to be allowed to take over cases from the respective international tribunal or in order to prevent it from stepping in. Libya would probably have done it, too, in order to have the cases declared inadmissible. Such a move would have at least been more likely if the judges had claimed both defendants because of the low quality of the justice that was meted out to them. But with the pre-trial chamber restricting the scope of its arguments to issues explicitly mentioned in the Rome Statute, there was no chance for the ICC to trigger domestic change and support reform toward the rule of law in Libya.

3. Legal Change

One of the first crucial decisions about the future of Libya was made by the Interim Transitional National Council, which gathered the opposition against the Gaddafi regime and, in August 2011, issued what it called a "Draft Constitutional Charter for the transitional stage".[46] The Charter stated, among others, the "principal source of legislation" to be "Islamic Jurisprudence (Sharia)". Article 4 of the Charter obliged the state to "seek to establish a political democratic regime to be based upon the political multitude and multi-party system in a view of achieving peaceful and democratic circulation." Article 6 promulgated equal rights for all citizens and forbade discrimination, and art. 7 declared that "Human Rights and his basic freedoms shall be respected by the State. The state shall commit itself to join the international and regional declarations and charters which protect such rights and freedoms." Thus, the obligation to ratify international Human Rights

---

45 Kersten, *Justice after the war*, 192.
46 Draft Constitutional Charter for the transitional stage, available at (in an English translation): http://portal.clinecenter.illinois.edu/REPOSITORYCACHE/114/w1R3bTIKE lG95H3MH5nvrSxchm9QLb8T6EK87RZQ9pfnC4py47DaBn9jLA742IFN3d70VnOY ueW7t67gWXEs3XiVJJxM8n18U9Wi8vAoO7_24166.pdf

treaties was already enshrined in the basic law of post-revolutionary Libya. Moreover, the obligation to ratify international conventions and build democracy was not only with the future state, but, according to art. 17, with the Interim Transitional National Council itself, which was "to ratify the international agreements and to establish the bases of the civil constitutional democratic state." The Council declared itself to be the highest legislative body at the same time and forbade Council members to seek any position in the executive. The Charter also provided for the *nulla poene sine lege* principle, the presumption of innocence – a fair trial requirement –, the independence of the judiciary, and the prohibition to establish exceptional courts. Nevertheless, this was always directed towards the future. When the revolution ended, international crimes[47] formed no part of the Libyan Criminal Code, although the Code predated Gaddafi's rule and had been adopted under the monarchy.[48] The Libyan judiciary could only prosecute crimes committed during the revolution as far as they were defined in the Penal Code as "Felonies and Misdemeanors against the Public Interest", the "Person of the State", "the State" or individuals.

3.1. The Constitutional Charter and the Libyan Judiciary

Originally, the Charter was only meant to serve as an interim solution in a situation where the country had abolished the old order, but did not yet have any available sources of legitimacy that could be derived from existing institutions. The Interim Transitional National Council was aware that it also lacked this kind of legitimacy. According to the Charter, the legitimacy of the new order was to be derived from new elections and a constitutional referendum. The Council envisaged a road map from revolution to a new political order, which included a declaration of liberation, after which the Council would create an interim government, the promulgation of a law regulating the elections of a "National Public Conference", the appointment (by the Council) of a National Supreme Commission for elections, and finally the election of the "National Public Conference". During the first meeting of the latter, the NTC would dissolve, making way for the new institutions. According to the Charter, the National Public Conference would elect a government and a "Constitutional Power",

---

47 International crimes here refer to genocide, crimes against humanity and war crimes as they are defined in the Rome Statute, the Geneva Conventions and Additional Protocols, and the Convention for the Prevention and Punishment of Genocide.

48 Libyan Arab Jamahiriya Penal Code, available in English at: https://www.unodc.org/tldb/showDocument.do?documentUid=8542

whose aim would be the elaboration of a draft constitution. The latter was to be submitted to a plebiscite requiring a 2/3 majority for approval.

At the beginning, this road map was implemented relatively smoothly. In July 2012, elections were held, the General National Congress (with 200 members) was created and it appointed the members of the constituent assembly, leading to the dissolution of the Interim National Transitional Council. The GNC became the main legislative authority in Libya with an interim mandate scheduled to end on 8 February 2014, when it was to be succeeded by a permanent elected parliament. In November 2012, Ali Zaidan became prime minister and formed a government. But in December 2013, a majority in the General National Congress adopted a law imposing Sharia and extended its own term for a year beyond the 1.5 year period for which the General National Congress had been elected. General Khalifa Haftar, commander of the Libyan Army, called for the appointment of a technical government and early elections, and then mobilized the Army against the General National Congress and the government.

Then the whole constitutional road map became obsolete, because the country split apart in a civil war. So did the parliament, and across the country rival militias started to control parts of the country's territory, shifting their loyalties between the two governments and parliaments in Tobruk and Tripoli and the former hot spots of anti-Gaddafi resistance in Benghazi and other big cities. Nevertheless, in the absence of a new constitution (and the impossibility of applying the constitution from the Gaddafi regime to the current situation), the NTC's constitutional declaration remained the main point of reference for the courts in the country, which had been vested with autonomy by article 32 of the declaration. Due to the relative autonomy judges had enjoyed under Gaddafi, the judiciary remained almost untouched by the revolution and was also sheltered from later vetting efforts. Even after the split of the country into competing power centers, the law used to be applied relatively coherently across the spheres of influence.[49] The most prominent proof thereof is the fate of law no. 37, which was passed by the NTC in 2011 and forbade, in a cursory and vague way, propaganda for the Gaddafi regime, criticism of Islam and the Libyan revolution. In May 2012, Prime Minister Abdurrahim El-Kib declared at a conference in London that "Law 37 and other such laws" would soon disappear. "I guarantee that once we get to elections and have a National Congress formed, such laws will disappear from the scene."[50] "Lawyers for Justice in Libya" challenged Law 37 before the Libyan Supreme

---

49 Klaus Bachmann's interview with Libyan Ambassador Breik A. Swessi in the Netherlands in September 2015.
50 Libya Herald, 25.5.2012.

Court. The hearing began in early June and ended after less than two weeks. On 14 June 2012, the Libyan Supreme Court struck down Law 37, finding it incompatible with the NTC's Constitutional Declaration.[51] The Supreme Court's verdict was the first judicial review over NTC legislation by the court and it confirmed the Constitutional Declaration's status as the highest law in Libya. The verdict also strengthened the Declaration's Human Rights commitments, which were partly contradicted by some of the NTC's laws and by the practice of the authorities.

The judiciary remained intact and the recognition of the Constitutional Declaration as the basic law overarching revolutionary lawmaking also prevailed when the country itself split apart. When the *Libya Dawn* authorities in Tripoli put Saif Al-Islam on trial in May 2015, Zintan recognized the jurisdiction of the court in Tripoli de facto by enabling him to participate in the proceedings via videolink.[52]

Before the Libyan authorities managed to get hold of Saif Al-Islam and Senussi, the NTC prepared a draft decree, which never came into force but which foresaw the incorporation of the Rome Statute's definition of genocide, crimes against humanity and, war crimes into the Libyan Criminal Code.[53] If the decree had become law, the mere fact that the Libyan judiciary could prosecute the same crimes as the ICC would have been an argument in Libya's admissibility challenge. But back in 2011, such a move was unnecessary, because until the apprehension of Saif Al-Islam and Senussi, the NTC regarded the ICC as an ally in dealing with the Gaddafi past, not as a rival. However, the bill never became a law and until this chapter was written, Libya had not taken over the Rome Statute's international crimes' concepts.[54]

---

51 Libya Herald, 14.6.2012.
52 According to Salah El-Marghani, the Tobruk government declined to recognise the judgment in Tripoli. Klaus Bachmann's interview with Salah El-Marghani, former Minister of Justice, in Leiden in September 2015.
53 The document was tendered during the inadmissibility procedures at the ICC as document ICC-01/11-01/11-144-ANXJ, dated from 15.5.2012, available at: http://www.icc-cpi.int/iccdocs/doc/doc1398585.pdf
54 This was established in an amici curiae report in the case of *the prosecutor v. Saif al-Islam Gaddafi and Abullah Al-Senussi*. Lawyers for Justice in Libya and Redress Trust's observations persuant to rule 103 of the rules of procedure and evidence, ICC-01/11-01/11, 8 June 2012, available at: http://www.icc-cpi.int/en_menus/icc/situations%20and%20cases/situations/icc0111/related%20cases/icc01110111/court%20records/filing%20of%20the%20participants/amicus%20curiae/Pages/172.aspx,

3.2. Command Responsibility

In 2013, the House of Representatives (at that time still based in Tripoli and with a pluralistic composition) passed law no. 10/2013, which introduced the concept of command responsibility for international crimes into the Criminal Code. Until then, Libya's traditional Criminal Code had only criminalized different aspects of complicity.[55] Since the ICC pre-trial chamber had admonished the Libyan government in the Saif Al-Islam case about the lack of such a concept in Libyan law and had argued that prosecuting an accused for the same conduct as a direct perpetrator was not the same as prosecuting him for command responsibility for this very conduct, law no. 10/2013 can be seen as triggered by the ICC's refusal to declare the Senussi case inadmissible. It was actually passed in April – one month before the appeals decision about the inadmissibility challenge was made public.[56]

3.3. Amnesties and the ICC

ICC influence is less obvious when it comes to amnesties. Under the conditions of reconstruction and an ongoing power struggle in Libya, an amnesty which could have helped to win over former rank-and-file fighters for Gaddafi would have been feasible for two main reasons: after the split of the country, it would have strengthened the support for the Tobruk government (and accordingly the Tripoli government, if it had done the same), and it would have emptied Libya's overcrowded detention sites, which were often beyond both governments' control. According to Amnesty International and Human Rights Watch reports, thousands of detainees have been vegetating and rotting in Libyan prisons, apprehended during the revolution by anti-Gaddafi forces and held by rivalling militias without trial or even without being formally indicted. In April 2013, Amnesty International estimated their number only in Tripoli at 2500. Many of them had apparently been tortured during their confinement.[57]

---

55 Law no. 10/2013 is available (in Arabic only) on: www.startimes.com/f.aspx?t=32716988
56 Art. 5 of Law no. 10 (2013) on the Criminalization of Torture, Forced Disappearances and Discrimination contains the concept of command responsibility and was passed by the General National Congress on 14.4.2013. The law is available in English at: http://www.security-legislation.ly/sites/default/files/files/lois/306-Law%20No.%2010%20of%202013_EN.pdf
57 Amnesty International, "Libya: new report shows that abductions by armed groups is rampant", available at: http://www.amnesty.org.uk/press-releases/libya-new-report-shows-abductions-armed-groups-rampant and

There were several occasions when amnesties were declared (in the form of political decisions or as laws). Back in 2011, and before the NTC made way for the GNC, the NTC passed a number of highly controversial transitional justice decisions, among them was Law no. 35, "On an Amnesty for Some Crimes", and Law no. 38 regarding "Some Procedures Relating to the Transitional Period." Law no. 35 excluded torture and rape from the amnesty and did not say anything about the treatment of international crimes. Critics argued that both laws taken together amounted to a blanket amnesty for war crimes and crimes against humanity which the NTC granted itself and its supporters, and that this amnesty would undermine the rule of law in Libya.[58] The law did not raise much attention abroad, and only specialized Human Rights organizations and lawyers discussed its implications. Law no. 38 foresaw an amnesty for fighters against the Gaddafi regime, if their crimes had been committed as part of the opposition during the revolution. The same law excluded the Gaddafi family and the Revolutionary Committees from any future amnesty and reconciliation effort.[59]

Law no. 38's article 4 provided for a blanket amnesty for "acts made necessary by the 17 February revolution" for its "success or protection", no matter whether these acts had been of a military, security-related or civil character, if they only they had been "performed by revolutionaries with the goal of promoting or protecting the revolution." This provision caused the outrage of Human Rights organizations, because it exonerated any crime (including international ones),

---

Libya: Detention abuses staining the new Libya, available at: http://www.amnesty.org. uk/resources/libya-detention-abuses-staining-new-libya#.Vd8j6cqli1E

58 M. Kersten:'Impunity Rules: Libya Passes Controversial Amnesty Law', Justice in Conflict 8.5.2012, available at: http://justiceinconflict.org/2012/05/08/impunity-rules-libya-passes-controversial-amnesty-law/ and Lawyers for Justice in Libya (a London based think tank): LFJL strongly condemns new laws breaching Human Rights and undermining the rule of law. 7.5.2012, available (in Arabic and English) at: http://www. libyanjustice.org/news/news/post/23-lfjl-strongly-condemns-new-laws-breaching-human-rights-and-undermining-the-rule-of-law

59 Art 4 of Law 35 (2012) says: "there shall be no penalty for military, security, or civil actions dictated by February 17 Revolution that were performed by revolutionaries with the goal of promoting or protecting the revolution." No English online version is available, but Human Rights Watch published selected articles of Law 38 in its report from january 2014, titled: "Priorities for Legislative Reform. A Human Rights road map for a New Libya", which is available at: https://www.hrw.org/report/2014/01/21/priorities-legislative-reform/human-rights-roadmap-new-libya.   See   also: T. Weatherall: *Jus Cogens: International Law and Social Contract*, Cambridge: Cambridge University Press 2015, 337.

solely relying on the perpetrators' intentions.[60] At the end of May, Human Rights Watch sent a letter to ICC prosecutor Luis Moreno Ocampo, urging him "to examine the crimes currently exempted from prosecution by the laws recently passed in Libya, and if appropriate, investigate them." HRW regarded the Laws 35 and 38 as an attempt to apply victor's justice by the post-revolutionary authorities in Libya.[61] When in November of the same year, Fatou Bensouda, Ocampo's successor as ICC prosecutor, appeared before the UNSC, she called upon the Libyan authorities not to grant amnesty for "international crimes and [not to grant] impunity for crimes, regardless of who is the perpetrator and who is the victim."[62] Fatou Bensouda's demand before the UNSC to prevent an amnesty for anti-Gaddafi fighters fell on deaf ears in Libya. Law no. 38 was neither revoked by parliament nor abolished by the Supreme Court, and it was never clarified whether article 4 actually comprised international crimes. Practice shows that the Libyan judiciary – no matter in which part of the country – is able and willing to judge perpetrators, who committed crimes on behalf of the Gaddafi regime, but more than reluctant to do so in the case of people who killed and tortured in the name of the revolution.

In February 2012, the NTC also promulgated Law 17 (2012) "on the rules of national reconciliation and transitional justice", which established a fact-finding and reconciliation commissions for all acts that constituted a crime or a human rights violation between 1969 "until the intended objectives of this law are achieved."[63] It also enabled the Commission to pay reparations to victims." In December of the following year, the GNC in Tripoli passed Law 29 (2013), which revoked Law 17 (2012) and specified, among others, a deadline, for the

---

60 M. Kersten: *Impunity Rules* and Lawyers for Justice in Libya (a London based think tank): 'LFJL strongly condemns new laws breaching Human Rights and undermining the rule of law', 7.5.2012, available (in Arabic and English) at: http://www.libyanjustice. org/news/news/post/23-lfjl-strongly-condemns-new-laws-breaching-human-rights-and-undermining-the-rule-of-law

61 Sarah Lea Withson (executive director for North Africa) annd Richard Dicker (director of the HRW International Justice Programm) to Luis Moreno Ocampo: Libya: Letter to the ICC Prosecutor on Libyan Amnesty Laws. HRW 25.5.2012, available at: https://www.hrw.org/news/2012/05/25/libya-letter-icc-prosecutor-libyan-amnesty-laws

62 ICC Prosecutor Statement to the United Nations Security Council on the situation in Libya, pursuant to UNSCR 1970 (2011), available at: http://www.icc-cpi.int/en_menus/icc/structure%20of%20the%20court/office%20of%20the%20prosecutor/reports%20and%20statements/statement/Pages/4reportToUNSCRlibya.aspx

63 Law 17 (2012) is available at: http://www.security-legislation.ly/sites/default/files/files/lois/311-Law%20No.%20%2817%29%20of%202012_EN.pdf

first parliamentary elections held under a permanent constitution. The subject matter jurisdiction of the Commission was then specified to "severe and systemic violations of Human Rights through murder, abduction, physical torture or confiscation or damage of funds" committed out of political motives. From that moment on, the law also included actions committed by revolutionaries "which were necessary to reinforce the revolution and which were accompanied "with some behaviour that did not adhere to the principles." It is worth mentioning that the law does not in any way penalize such deeds and it stated in art. 4 that its first objective was "the legal recognition of the just character of the 17 February Revolution."[64] It also empowered a committee that was to be created by the GNC president to revoke the nationality of people who had obtained Libyan citizenship for "political and military" reasons. That was a clear indication of Law 29's target: people who had committed crimes under Gaddafi (even if these crimes had taken place before the revolution) and people who had been recruited abroad in order to work as mercenaries or agents of the regime.[65] The timely jurisdiction of Law 29 (2013) was larger than the one pursued by the ICC, which had jurisdiction only from the start of the revolution. Both jurisdictions overlapped during the revolution, but since Law 29 (2013) did not grant amnesty or otherwise exempt suspects from ICC prosecution, there was no conflict between the Rome Statute and Law 29 (2013).

The situation became even more complicated when the country split and the two rival governments (and parliaments) started to make contradictory decisions. In September 2014, when General Haftar prepared the attack against Benghazi, his troops offered amnesty to Benghazi fighters if they laid down their arms. Such an amnesty could potentially lead to impunity for international crimes committed earlier. However, the ICC did not react to the amnesty offer (which would not have been binding anyway) and there are no reports indicating that the defenders of the town ever accepted the offer.[66]

The next time amnesty became an issue was when the House of Representatives in Tobruk passed an amnesty law forgiving crimes committed by all Libyans after 15 February 2011. The vote took place immediately after the sentencing of Senussi and Said Al-Islam by a court in Tripoli, which inclined observers to assume a link between the verdict and the law.[67] Media reports quoting HoR

---

64 Law 29 (2013) can be available at http://www.security-legislation.ly/node/32096
65 Art. 29 of Law 29 (2013).
66 Libya Herald 9.9.2014.
67 At the time of writing this chapter, the text of the law was unavailable, only a preview in Arabic could be retrieved.

members alleged that certain crimes had been excluded from the amnesty, like terrorism, murder, kidnapping, torture, drug trafficking, sex crimes, assault, smuggling, corruption, and robbery. According to former Justice Minister Salah El-Marghani, the law was neither a response to the Tripoli verdict, nor to the ICC intervention. "Now, as things are beyond our control, we don't have any issues with the ICC", he said. The Tobruk amnesty law's objectives were to enable reconciliation with Libyans, who had committed minor offences during and after the revolution, to facilitate the return of refugees from abroad and to win over former soldiers and officers of Gaddafi's army, who had been imprisoned. Crimes which involved direct victims, such as murder and robbery, could not be included, because according to Libyan legal values and traditions, they can only be amnestied if the victims (or the descendants in cases of murder) agree and forgive the perpetrator.[68] The law also revoked Law no. 35 (2012). The ICC did not respond to the Tobruk amnesty law, at least not in public.

3.4. Penalizing Sexual Violence

If the NTC and the subsequent governments had intended to react to the ICC's judicial intervention by passing legislation, it would have made a possible ICC intervention obsolete or, at least, served as an argument in an admissibility challenge, and one of the main topics for legislative change would have been the criminalization of sexual violence. Rape and similar crimes were part of the Criminal Code, but the latter lacked concepts of sexual violence as elements of international crimes, for example in the context of an armed conflict or a crime against humanity.[69] No such provisions were included in the Criminal Code after 2011. Sexual violence was implicitly mentioned in the legislation establishing the Fact-Finding and Reconciliation Commission[70], but not as a count of an international crime.

---

68 Interview with Salah El-Marghani, former Justice Minister, by Klaus Bachmann in Leiden in September 2015.

69 For the definition of sexual violence as a count of genocide, crimes against humanity and war crimes, see, among others, the ICTY decisions in the Foca case and the ICTR judgments in the Akayesu case. For the concepts of sexual violence in the Libyan Criminal Code, see: H. M. Zawati 'The Challenge of Prosecuting Conflict-related Gender-Bases Crimes under Libyan Transitional Justice', *The Journal of International Law and International Relations* 10 (2014), p. 57–59. Available at: http://www.jilir.org/docs/issues/volume_10/10_5_ZAWATI_FINAL.pdf

70 Art 4 (2) of Law 17 and Art. 1 (3) of Law 35. See also Zawati, The Challenge of Prosecuting, 58.

There were also some minor legal changes, which can clearly be attributed to the ICC. These concern agreements with no binding force for citizens. On 29 August 2013, the ICC prosecutor met with a delegation from Libya, which comprised minister Salah Al-Marghani and Prosecutor-General Abdul Qader Juma Radwan. Both sides signed a memorandum of understanding about "burden sharing in further investigations and prosecutions."[71] In the sixth report to the UNSC, the prosecutor described this as "a positive commitment by the Government of Libya to providing justice to Libya's victims, and to cooperating with the ICC in the investigation and prosecution of additional cases against those most responsible for the most serious crimes under the Court's jurisdiction in Libya." The formula used in the report leaves it open whether the burden sharing only includes investigations against suspects outside Libya (as Minister Salah Al-Marghani claimed)[72] or also suspects within Libya, alleged of having committed crimes on behalf of the anti-Gaddafi opposition. Prosecuting them seemed rather unlikely as the wording of the respective paragraph in the report reveals: "the Office continues with investigations, with a focus in particular on pro-Gaddafi officials outside of Libya, who the Office believes are responsible for serious crimes and whose current activities may continue to pose a security threat to civilians in Libya. The Office looks forward to working closely with Libyan partners in pursuit of these and other future cases."

The ICC and the Libyan government also concluded a confidential "ad hoc agreement" about the privileges and immunities of ICC staff, which, to some extent, substitutes the standard "Agreement On Immunities and Privileges" usually signed by signatory states to the Rome Statute and countries submitting self-referrals.[73]

---

71 Sixth report of the prosecutor of the International Criminal Court to the UN Security Council pursuant to UNSC resolution 1970 (2011), p. 2, par. 11; available at: http://www.icc-cpi.int/en_menus/icc/structure%20of%20the%20court/office%20of%20the%20prosecutor/reports%20and%20statements/statement/Documents/Report%20to%20UNSC%20Nov2013EN.pdf#search=libya%20memorandum

72 Klaus Bachmann's interview with Prof. Salah Al-Marghani in Leiden in August 2015.

73 The existence of the "ad hoc agreement" was confirmed to the authors by both the (former) minister Salah Al-Marghani orally (during the interview in Leiden) and ICC spokesperson Fadi Al-Abdallah in an e-mail message later. Authors were unable to access the precise content of the agreement. There are strong arguments in the literature emphasizing Libya's obligation to cooperate (and grant immunity to ICC staff) as stemming from art. 48 of the Rome Statute and the wording of UNSC 1970 (2011) rather than from any separate agreement on immunities. From this point of view, the above mentioned ad hoc agreement would have only been necessary if its scope was wider than the obligations arising from art. 48. See: D. Akande, 'The Effect of Security

3.5. The Creation of New Bodies

Some countries, which were affected by ICT decisions, decided to create special bodies, whose task it was to cooperate with the respective tribunal or to coordinate efforts to sideline the tribunal's initiatives. As long as the main suspects, whom the NTC and later the interim government wanted to prosecute, were beyond the reach of the Libyan authorities, cooperation with the ICC was imperative and wished for. During that period, Libya signed and ratified the agreement on the immunities and privileges of the ICC, hoping the ICC would get hold of suspects who had escaped abroad. During that period, the NTC also appointed a team of lawyers, whose task it was to cooperate with the ICC. After the arrest warrants were issued, a special committee at the Ministry of Justice was created (with three to five members) as technical support for Ahmed El Gehani, a law professor who was charged with representing Libya's interests at the ICC. Gehani was not employed by the Ministry. The official communication between the ICC and the Libyan authorities went from the ICC prosecution to the Attorney General and from the ICC pre-trial (and later appeals) chamber to El Gehani.[74] The General National Congress later confirmed El Gehani's mandate. He was supported by an international team of lawyers, which included Philippe Sands and Michelle Butler, both from the British law firm Matrix Chambers, which specializes in Human Rights cases, and Payam Akhavan, an Iran-born law professor at McGill University in Montreal.

When the *Libya Dawn* movement conquered the Libyan capital in July 2014, it also took over the Ministry of Justice (including many confidential documents, which could not be evacuated in time) and established its own committee for relations with the ICC, called "the follow-up committee on the ICC".[75]

In December 2011, the NTC also established the "National Council of Human Rights and Fundamental Freedoms" as an independent body with the aim to investigate violations of Human Rights[76], and in February 2012, passed

---

Council Resolutions and Domestic Proceedings on State Obligations to Cooperate with the ICC', *Journal of International Criminal Justice*, Vol. 10, Issue 2, May 2012, available also at: http://papers.ssrn.com/sol3/papers.cfm?abstract_id=2038217

74 Klaus Bachmann's interview with Salah El-Marghani, who was Minister of Justice in Libya between November 2012 and August 2014. The interview took place in Leiden in September 2015.

75 The documents about the creation of the Tripoli-based follow-up committee are available online (but only in Arabic) on: www.aladel.gov.ly.

76 Law 5 / 2011 is currently unavailable as an English online version.

law 17 "on the rules of national reconciliation and transitional justice", a fact-finding and reconciliation commission.[77] There were also several laws containing articles which criminalized actions undertaken before the ICC's temporal jurisdiction, but they usually had one feature in common: they only penalized crimes committed by the regime and its followers.[78] Among these laws was Law 35 (2012) which excluded members of the Revolutionary Committees and members of Gaddafi's family from any amnesty and reconciliation process that might otherwise apply to them.[79] A vetting law that was also passed is not relevant here for several reasons: the ICC's gravity standard and the complementarity principle would make an ICC intervention unlikely against people who had been members of the political establishment under Gaddafi but had not committed international crimes; and the temporal jurisdiction, which the ICC had been given by the UNSC referral, excluded the investigation and prosecution of crimes committed before February 2011. The transitional justice legislation passed by the NTC had two overarching features. First, it tended to exclude or frankly exonerate crimes committed by those who had fought against Gaddafi, while penalizing supporters of his regime retroactively. And second, it was much broader in scope and with regard to their temporal reach than the ICC's temporal jurisdiction. One of the most atrocious crimes committed under Gaddafi, which remained beyond the ICC's jurisdiction, was the Abu Salim prison massacre, during which Gaddafi's security services killed more than 1,200 prison inmates. The massacre – and the families of many of the victims – played an important role triggering anti-Gaddafi protests in 2011.

3.6. New Budget Allocations

Shifts in budget allocations did not play a major role in the Libyan case. Due to the fact that the representation of interests at the ICC was outsourced to Ahmed El-Gehani and his team of international lawyers, the government in Tripoli and later in Tobruk had to pay remuneration, which it would not have needed to pay without the ICC arrest warrants. The amounts transferred for these purposes are confidential and could not be established.

The 200 million USD allegedly paid by the NTC to Mauretania are also of interest here, because they would have been unnecessary if Libya had not

---

77 English translation is available at: http://www.security-legislation.ly/sites/default/files/files/lois/311-Law%20No.%20%2817%29%20of%202012_EN.pdf

78 Zawati, The Challenge of Prosecuting 54–56.

79 Art 7(4) of Law 35 (2012).

competed with the ICC over Senussi's extradition. One must not forget that the ICC request was not the only one, and that even without it, Libya would have had to counter the French extradition request. One may assume that the price for overcoming the French competition would have been less expensive than competing with two rivals, but it would have required the Libyan government to make a budget allocation for this purpose anyway.

4. The Efficacy of Institutional Reform

Libya's transition took place under extremely unfriendly conditions. After the discovery of large oil reserves in Libya, the Gaddafi regime had evolved into a clientelist system in which traditional institutions were sidelined and marginalized and the decision-making process was dominated by Gaddafi's immediate entourage. At the same time, the exploitation of the oil reserves caused strong social tensions, as the former elite of the country was replaced by a new ascending group of managers and businessmen who were linked to the oil industry, to foreign trade, and to businesses that took to rent seeking through oil-connected corruption.[80] After Gaddafi's fall, it appeared as if Gaddafi's most problematic legacy was the lack thereof – his rule did not leave behind any stable or effective institution that could be taken over by the new rulers. Transition took place in an institutional vacuum, which the NTC tried to fill by creating new interim institutions, out of which a democratic infrastructure was to emerge.

This process was not only risky and often contradictory, it also created extremely vulnerable institutions and exposed them to threats and dangers, which were typical for a transition period. These problems were further exacerbated by the civil war that followed and forced the conflict parties to dedicate resources to military, rather than civilian, purposes. Libya gained institutions which were – as one can observe in the short period between the creation of the NTC and the outbreak of the civil war – quite efficient under transitional conditions, but were overwhelmed by the task of navigating through a transitional period tormented by civil war. The fate of the National Council for Civil Liberties and Human Rights (NCCLHR) is a good illustration of these challenges. It was created by a NTC law in order to become a government-independent Human Rights body that could evaluate legislation according to international Human Rights standards and initiate Human Rights legislation. As its 2015 report to

---

80 Similar patterns can be observed with regard to the gas industry and gas transit in Ukraine. See Igor Lyubashenko's chapter in this volume.

the office of the UN Human Rights High Commissioner states, "NCCLHR has enjoyed total autonomy to work on its mandate of promoting Human Rights, monitoring practices and intervening to prevent abuses", but it was nevertheless inefficient, because "2013 and 2014 Fiscal Budgets did not include provisions for the NCCLHR despite repeated requests submitted by the NCCLHR. The GNC failed the NCCLHR, the lack of funds has limited its ability to promote and protect Human Rights."[81]

The state of the judiciary provides a similar picture. Courts and judges are largely independent and the latter are appointed by a self-governing body, which is isolated from both the executive and the legislative (in Tobruk and in Tripoli), but judges are exposed to corruption, violence, retaliation, courts are understaffed and lack resources, and in the long run, it will be impossible to maintain the coherence of jurisprudence if the division of the country into rivalling centres of influence is not overcome quickly.[82]

But this is the general picture of Libya's post-revoutionary institutions. Since the ICC did not trigger much institutional change, the few institutions whose creation can be attributed to its influence are relatively stable: Interest representation through the legal team at the Ministry of Justice has proven quite efficient, although the choice of an external law professor working with an international team of lawyers may seem rather unusual. Libya's institutions (first the NTC, then the GNC and now the GNC's successor in Tripoli and the House of Representatives in Tobruk) passed an impressive amount of legislation, much of which was dedicated to transitional justice issues. The majority of the new legislation in this field aimed at delegitimizing the Gaddafi regime and its (leading) followers, whereas amnesties often had the purpose of emptying overcrowded prisons, winning over file-and-rank Gaddafi supporters for one of the rivalling factions in the civil war and exonerating supporters of the revolution against Gaddafi, who had committed atrocities during the liberation struggle and were then taking part in the civil war. The latter purpose often clashed with the aims of international NGOs and UN agencies, which opposed such blank amnesties.

---

81 National Council for Civil Liberties and Human Rights (NCCLHR): Universal Periodic Review Submission
State of Libya. 22 nd Session (Apr–May 2015), available at: https://uprdoc.ohchr.org/Account/Login.aspx?ReturnUrl=%2f
82 See, for example the report to the African Union's Peace and Security Council (presented at the 500th meeting of the Council in April 2015 in Addis Ababa: *Report of the Chairperson of the Commission on the situation in Libya*, PSC/PR/3(D), available at: http://www.peaceau.org/uploads/auc.rpt.libya.psc500.27.04.2015.pdf

At the moment it is difficult to evaluate how efficient these amnesties actually were, since many prisons are beyond the reach of the legislative that issued the amnesty and are controlled by militias, which report to neither the Tobruk nor the Tripoli government. Judicial review is weak, because the independence of the judiciary is not bolstered by robust instruments, which would allow judges to execute their decisions.

The few legislative acts that can be traced back to ICC influence appear to have been implemented in practice. Paradoxically, the Tripoli trial against Senussi, Saif Al-Islam and 35 other defendants was a show trial with numerous violations of fair trial rights (including Human Rights violations committed on some of the detainees during the pre-trial period), but also showed the ability and willingness of the court to use the concept of command responsibility that had been introduced into the Criminal Code. Although the indictment was not made public, Human Rights Watch investigators were able to review it and found a whole number of charges, which described actions undertaken by superiors to direct their subordinates to commit crimes, such as "creating armed tribal groups and providing them with weapons and logistical support", "inciting arbitrary shelling on cities that rose against the regime", "creating killing squads" and "planning and deciding to kill demonstrators in Tripoli".[83]

5. Was it the ICC's Influence?

Libya treated the Senussi and Saif Al-Islam cases as elements of nation building, similarly to the government of Kosovo with regard to *the prosecutor v. Haradinaj et al.* But there was also one important difference.[84] Whereas the Kosovo government's policy was directed at getting the accused acquitted in order to be able to present the struggle for independence as untainted by crimes and the

---

83 Human Rights Watch (no author), "Libya: Gaddafi Son, Ex-Officials, Held with Due Process", 13.2.2014, available at: https://www.hrw.org/news/2014/02/13/libya-gaddafi-son-ex-officials-held-without-due-process
It should not go unnoticed that the above-mentioned charges only describe a part of what has become command (or superior) responsibility. They describe orders to commit crimes. Under modern International Criminal Law jurisprudence, a leader needs not to order crimes in order to be held accountable, it is enough if he failed to prevent them (if he had the power to do so) or failed to punish the perpetrators in cases where he was later informed about crimes which took place before he was able to prevent them. The omission part of command responsibility apparently did not play a role in the Tripoli trial, despite being part of the Criminal Code.

84 See Vjollca Krasniqi's chapter on Kosovo in this volume.

whole nation as a victim, the Libyan government's objective was to prosecute and judge both accused in order to demonstrate – to its own citizens as well as to the outside world – the ability of the new Libya to cut off the Gaddafi past and to function as a nation state on an equal footing with others. Therefore, exonerating Haradinaj became an important element of Kosovo nation building and judging Saif Al-Islam and Senussi became an important step in Libya's state-building process.

In both processes, the international tribunals appeared as an obstacle to state and nation building, although the ICTY and the ICC had first been regarded as facilitators of the national independence struggle. Already in October 2011, before Saif Al-Islam had been captured, Colonel Ahmed Bani, the spokesman for military affairs at the NTC, rejected ICC interference as a violation of Libya's sovereignty: "We will not accept that our sovereignty be violated like that. We will put him on trial here. This is where he must face the consequences of what he has done. We will prove to the world that we are civilized people with a fair justice system. Libya has its rights and its sovereignty and we will exercise them."[85]

Confronted with such a position, the ICC prosecution seemed to be ready to leave the cases of Senussia and Saif Al-Islam to the Libyan judiciary. In the following, it was the OCPD and the defence that tried to fight off the inadmissibility motions of the Libyan government, together with Human Rights organizations, which wanted the ICC to take over the cases in order to ensure a fair trial. But the judges had another view about the ICC's role in Libya, as the pre-trial decision in the case against Senussi showed and as the appeals decision confirmed. According to them, the ICC's role was to make sure that perpetrators were prosecuted and judged in their home countries, even if this involved possible violations of their rights. In the light of these decisions, the ICC would not become an actor of domestic change and refrain from trying to trigger or stimulate reforms of the judiciary in countries under its jurisdiction.

Under these conditions, it was unlikely, that the ICC would trigger domestic reform. In Libya, such an influence was marginal. The UNSC referral did not even trigger the creation of a new, autonomous institution, it only caused minor budget allocations, the formation of a small team at the Ministry of Justice responsible for coordinating contacts with the ICC and outsourcing the inadmissibility challenge to external lawyers.

The Libyan example can quickly lead to false conclusions. At a first glance, many transitional justice institutions emerged after the UNSC referral, and legal

---

85 Quoted according to Kersten, *Justice after the War*, 191.

change was frequent, but far from consistent. But this was not due to the influence of the ICC on the Libyan judiciary and legislation; instead, the fact that the UNSC referral had taken place at a very early stage of the transition, when the revolution was in full swing and crimes were still being perpetrated by both sides, can create a false impression, according to which ICC decisions triggered domestic change in Libya just because this change sometimes took place after, rather than before, ICC decisions. This is true for decisions which were likely to trigger compliance with ICC requirements, but it is also true for ICC decisions which one might expect to trigger attempts to sideline the ICC or minimize its influence. Probably the most important action to sideline the ICC were Libya's efforts to get Senussi back from Mauritania.

If Libya had taken its inadmissibility challenges seriously and henceforth amended legislation in a way that was likely to bolster its case before the ICC, it would have incorporated international crimes into its Criminal Code and adopted the concept of command responsibility earlier than 2013. Libya's reluctance to incorporate international crimes suggests that even the numerous amnesties and amnesty proposals that were issued after 2011 were not aimed at minimizing or preventing ICC influence on Libya's judiciary, but had entirely domestic objectives, which are better explained by the post-revolutionary situation in the country and the balance of power among different actors. It was not necessary to shelter anyone from charges involving international crimes if that person could not be prosecuted for international crimes under Libyan law. And if such a person was sought by the ICC, a national amnesty would not have prevented the ICC from stepping in. But in view of the prosecution's hesitance to refute the inadmissibility challenges and to press charges against other actors involved in the revolution in Libya, there was and is no need for sheltering potential defendants from the ICC through a national amnesty – which would not be binding for the ICC anyway.

There is an additional argument which bolsters the claim that legislation was not passed and institutions were not built by the NTC in order to comply with or circumvent ICC decisions. This argument points to the lack of consistence of lawmaking after February 2011. When the NTC drafted the bill whose purpose was to enshrine international crimes in the Criminal Code, Libya had already long before ratified the Genocide Convention and the Convention on the non-applicability of statutory limitations to war crimes and crimes against humanity.[86] This created a paradoxical situation, which abolished statutory limitations for (among others) crimes against humanity, whose perpetrators

---

86 According to the amici curiae report to the ICC, submitted by Redress and Lawyers
    for Justice in Libya, Libya had ratified both conventions in 1989. See: Lawyers for

could not be punished, because the Criminal Code did not contain those crimes. This paradox had existed for more than twenty years under the Gaddafi regime. The bill drafted by the NTC in 2011 in order to include international crimes in the Criminal Code forbade the death penalty. But if adopted, the bill would have created a two-tier system, according to which a rank-and-file perpetrator of a war crime would face the death penalty under domestic law, whereas a commander who had ordered mass atrocities would be sheltered from capital punishment.[87] Transitional lawmaking was not only often inherently contradictory and clashed with international norms, it was also often incompatible with constitutional law, that is with the Constitutional Charter, which the NTC had solemnly promulgated. Numerous provisions in the transitional justice legislation (e.g., on vetting of former elite members) contradicted the fair trial and equality commitments of the Constitutional Charter.[88] All this leads to the conclusion that legislative and institutional change in Libya after the UNSC referral was a response to pressing problems in an unpredictable and arcane post-revolutionary situation, which overlapped with a power struggle among the revolutionaries rather than a meticulously planned and carefully designed response to the ICC intervention.

To cut a long story short: the ICC did not trigger domestic change in Libya, because the chambers never saw this as their role and cut off the prosecution attempts going in such a direction. And it did not trigger domestic change, because the post-revolutionary conditions in Libya rendered the Libyan governments unresponsive to such attempts. Instead of trying to sideline ICC actions (as, for example, the Kenyan or Sudanese governments did), Libya prefered to ignore the ICC.

This is true for the NTC and the Tobruk government, but it is even more true for the *Libya Dawn* government in Tripoli. In July, it brought Senussi and Saif

---

Justice in Libya and Redress Trust's observations persuant to rule 103 of the rules of procedure and evidence, ICC-01/11-01/11, 8 June 2012, p. 16, available at: http://www.icc-cpi.int/en_menus/icc/situations%20and%20cases/situations/icc0111/related%20cases/icc01110111/court%20records/filing%20of%20the%20participants/amicus%20curiae/Pages/172.aspx,

87 This was also criticized by the amici report. Lawyers for Justice in Libya and Redress Trust's observations persuant to rule 103 of the rules of procedure and evidence, ICC-01/11-01/11, 8 June 2012, p. 17–18, available at: http://www.icc-cpi.int/en_menus/icc/situations%20and%20cases/situations/icc0111/related%20cases/icc01110111/court%20records/filing%20of%20the%20participants/amicus%20curiae/Pages/172.aspx,

88 Zawati: The Challenge of Prosecuting, 54–58.

Al-Islam Gaddafi together with 7 other high-ranking accused from the former Gaddafi establishment to trial. Saif al-Islam was tried in absentia and could follow the trial through a videolink, which often broke down. Defence lawyers of both called the trial a show trial, during which witness statements were heard, which had been extracted by torture. Observers, including a UN officer monitoring the trial, were arrested and harassed during the trial. The Tobruk government distanced itself from the trial and international Human Rights organizations condemned it.[89] In the end, nine defendants, including Senussi and Saif Al-Islam, were convicted and sentenced to death and to a financial fine, 23 others received prison terms, four were acquitted and one referred to medical treatment.[90]

Similarly to Kosovo, where the UN mission UNMIK had undermined ICTY proceedings in the case of *the prosecutor v. Haradinaj et al.*, a conflict arose between the ICC prosecutor, Fatou Bensouda, and the UN support mission in Libya. Bensouda had denied that *Libya Dawn*'s conquest of Tripoli would affect the trial, whereas the UN support mission, which tried to foster democratization and the rule of law, found that the trial had "failed to meet international standards".[91]

The Tripoli convictions still have to be confirmed by the Supreme Court. If the judges of the ICC chambers, who accepted the Libyan inadmissibility challenge, now change their minds under the impression of the Tripoli trial, it would be too late anyway. The *Libya Dawn* judiciary in Tripoli brought Senussi to justice and intends to punish him the harshest way possible. Libya's judiciary enjoys independence from the executive and the legislative, in the Tripoli of 2015 no less than at the time when the ICC left Senussi to Libya. Threats against judges' independence usually come from militias, criminals and corruption, but not from the government. For the defence and for Human Rights organizations, the Tripoli

---

89 Amnesty International: Libya, 'Flawed trial of al-Gaddafi officials leads to appalling death sentences', 28.7.2015 available at: https://www.amnesty.org/en/latest/news/2015/07/libya-flawed-trial-of-al-gaddafi-officials/

90 C. Stephen, 'Gaddafi's son Saif al-Islam sentenced to death by court in Libya', The Guardian 28.7.2015, available at: http://www.theguardian.com/world/2015/jul/28/saif-al-islam-sentenced-death-by-court-in-libya-gaddafi-son and Human Rights Watch, 'Libya: Flawed Trial of Gaddafi Officials', HRW 28.7.2015, available at: https://www.hrw.org/news/2015/07/28/libya-flawed-trial-gaddafi-officials

91 C. Stephen: 'Gaddafi's son Saif al-Islam sentenced to death by court in Libya', The Guardian 28.7.2015.

trial may have been a sham trial, but it more or less fulfilled the low standards set in the ICC's Senussi decisions. The example of Libya makes it overly clear: the ICC is not a Human Rights court, and its role is neither to ensure that defendants are judged fairly in domestic courts, nor to shelter them from the death penalty, nor to advance the rule of law in transition countries.

Gerhard Kemp

The ICC and Institutional Reform in Kenya

1. Kenya's Post-Election Violence and its Aftermath

27 December 2007 marked Kenya's ninth general election since independence from Britain.[1] The outcome of the election turned out to be controversial. Allegations of election fraud were made. Worse, still, were the many instances of violence.[2] The levels of violent crime raised the spectre of possible crimes under international law,[3] notably crimes against humanity.[4]

The narrative of the post-election violence (commonly referred to in literature as PEV) must be understood against the background of Kenya's complex ethnic makeup. There are more than 70 distinct ethnic groups. Five of the groups have fairly large populations while the rest are quite small. The larger groups, together accounting for about 70% of the total population, are: Kikuyu (20%), Luhya (14%),

---

1   A general election combines the presidential, parliamentary and civic elections.
2   European Union Election Observation Mission, *Final Report on Kenya, General Elections 27 December 2007* (3 April 2008), 36, available at: http://www.eods.eu/library/ FR%20KENYA%2003.04.2008_en.pdf; Internal Displacement Monitoring Centre (IDMC), *Speedy reforms needed to deal with past injustices and prevent future displacement* (10 June 2010), available at: http://www.internal- displacement.org/countries/ Kenya>; Commission of Inquiry into the Post-Election Violence (CIPEV) *Final Report* (15 October 2008) 472-475, available at: http://www.dialoguekenya.org/index.php/ reports/commission-reports.html.
3   For a detailed account and legal analysis of the PEV, see S. F. Materu, *The Post-Election Violence in Kenya* Asser Press, The Hague 2015.
4   Unlike genocide (Genocide Convention of 1948) and war crimes (Geneva Conventions of 1949), crimes against humanity as a group of crimes are not yet the subject of an international convention. The Apartheid Convention of 1973 can be viewed as one form of crimes against humanity that became the subject of a UN convention. The Rome Statute of the International Criminal Court, 1998, which is a multilateral treaty, comes closest to an *international framework* on crimes against humanity. Article 7 of the Rome Statute provides for a definition of crimes against humanity, the material elements of which require the commission of one of the individual acts listed in Article 7(1). An individual act then becomes a crime against humanity when committed in a certain context, namely in the course of a widespread *or* systematic attack on a civilian population. See further, G. Werle and F. Jessberger, *Principles of International Criminal Law* Oxford, Oxford University Press (3ed) 2014, pp. 333–389.

Luo (13%), Kalenjin (11%), and Kamba (11%).[5] It is notable that Kenya's elections since independence have always to some degree been characterised by ethnic mobilisation and affiliation. The 2007 election was no exception to the general trend. Indeed, two coalitions – the Orange Democratic Movement (ODM) and the Party of National Unity (PNU) – were broadly configured around ethnic groups. The ODM received backing from the Kalenjin, Luo and Luhya groups, with geographic concentrations in the Nyanza and Western Provinces as well as the Rift Valley. The PNU received support from the largest ethnic group, the Kikuyu, with geographic concentrations in the Central and Eastern Provinces, the Coast Province, Rift Valley and in the capital Nairobi.

On 30 December 2007, the incumbent President Kibaki was declared the winner by Kenya's Electoral Commission. This result was rejected by the ODM, which objected to the electoral process. Even external observers, including the European Union observers, agreed that the election had not been free and fair.[6] The contested results soon prompted "widespread and systematic violence".[7] The ensuing violence also took on an ethnic dimension with targeted killings. Underlying tensions in the Kikuyu-dominated Rift Valley were a further contributing factor. These tensions were caused by land claims and land inequity, notably amongst the Kikuyu and Kalenjin communities. After calm returned, it emerged that the PEV was not a spontaneous outburst of violence and frustration but rather the result of planning at the local and even national level by politicians. The Kenyan national police force was also implicated in the violence.[8] The international reaction was swift. The African Union, the European Union, the United Nations, individual countries and prominent individuals like Archbishop Emeritus Desmond Tutu of South Africa expressed concern. However, diplomacy and mediation attempts initially proved to be fruitless.

It was the Kenya National Dialogue and Reconciliation Committee (KNDRC)[9] that paved the way for the power-sharing agreement that was eventually signed by

---

5 For further background and relevant documentation, see reports by the International Coalition for the Responsibility to Protect, available at http://www. responsibilitytoprotect.org/index.php/crises/crisis-in-kenya.

6 Ibid.

7 Ibid. The characterisation of "widespread and systematic violence" has significance in terms of the contextual element of crimes against humanity.

8 Ibid.

9 The Kenya National Dialogue and Reconciliation Committee (KNDRC) was established as an *ad hoc* response. Its composition reflected both governing and opposition membership, as well as some prominent international figures, including Benjamin Mkapa,

the two important role-players, namely the incumbent President Mwai Kibaki and the opposition groups. In terms of the agreement Kibaki would stay on as President and the opposition leader, Raila Odinga, of the ODM, would become Prime Minister. In addition to the political agreement, three transitional, post-conflict institutions were created, namely the Commission of Inquiry on Post-Election Violence (CIPEV), the Truth, Justice and Reconciliation Commission, and the Independent Review Commission on the General Elections.[10] The process for fundamental legal, constitutional and related institutional reform also received attention.[11]

The establishment of CIPEV,[12] also known as the "Waki Commission"[13], for the investigation of PEV incidents and with the task to make recommendations in terms of appropriate redress represented an important institutional and transitional moment. One of the most important recommendations by CIPEV was that a special tribunal should be created for the prosecution of those individuals responsible for the PEV-related crimes. However, the Special Tribunal for Kenya Bill of 2009 was never enacted. Consequently, and as a result of this failure to implement a key recommendation of CIPEV, a list of names of individuals who were thought to be most responsible for the PEV-related crimes was sent to the Chief Prosecutor of the ICC.[14] This paved the way for the first *proprio motu* investigation[15] by the Office of the Prosecutor (OTP) of the ICC in terms of Article 15 (1) of the Rome Statute, which provides: "The Prosecutor may initiate investigations *proprio motu* on the basis of information on crimes within the jurisdiction of the Court."

Graća Machel and Jakaya Kikwete. The former United Nations (UN) Secretary General, Kofi Annan, held the chair of the committee.

10 KNDRC, *Agreement on agenda item three: How to resolve the political crisis* (14 February 2008), p. 3, available at: http://www.dialoguekenya.org/index.php/agreements.html.

11 Ibid.

12 *Kenya Gazette* Notice 4473, 23 May 2008.

13 Named for the chair of CIPEV, Judge Philip Waki.

14 CIPEV set certain timelines for the creation of the Special Tribunal. CIPEV furthermore mandated Kofi Annan, the former UN Secretary General and who also chaired Kenya's mediation process, to hand over to the ICC Prosecutor an envelope containing the so-called 'secret list' of individuals who were thought to be most responsible for the post-election violence. For more detail, see Africa Centre for Open Governance, *Report by the Kenyans for Peace with Truth and Justice (KPTJ)*, Nairobi, ACOG 2014), pp. 5–6, available at http://kptj.africog.org

15 All the other situations before the ICC were all either referred to the ICC by states party to the Rome Statute (e.g. the situations in the Democratic Republic of Congo, Uganda and the Central African Republic), or were referred to the ICC by the UN Security Council (e.g. Sudan and Libya).

It has to be noted that, apart from the initial regional and international interest in Kenya's response to the PEV, the possibility of domestic prosecutions of the alleged perpetrators of the violence was always a key item in the post-election public discourse. But the possibility of transitional justice mechanisms, coupled with domestic prosecutions, was soon overshadowed by the involvement of the International Criminal Court (ICC) in the PEV matters.

2. Kenya as a State Party to the Rome Statute of the ICC

Against the background of what was sketched above by way of introduction, a few observations regarding Kenya's legal and institutional relationship with the International Criminal Court need to be made.

Kenya ratified the Rome Statute on 15 March 2005.[16] Indeed, despite its prominent current opposition to the ICC and its stated threat to withdraw from the Rome Statute, Kenya was, at the time of writing, still a state party to the Rome Statute of the ICC. In fact, Kenya is one of a small group of African states that followed through on the ultimate aim of the Rome Statute, namely to implement the treaty and to provide for the criminalisation of the core crimes and for co-operation with the ICC.[17] The Implementation of the International Crimes Act 16 of 2008 gives effect to Kenya's obligations under the Rome Statute, and provides for the incorporation of three Rome Statute crimes, namely genocide, crimes against humanity, and war crimes.[18]

The Commission of Inquiry into the PEV noted the importance of holding those responsible for the acts of violence accountable.[19] However, it became clear that the domestic criminal justice system in Kenya was not up to the task.

---

16 E. Owiye Asaala, 'The International Criminal Court factor on transitional justice in Kenya', in: K. Ambos & O. Maunganidze (eds), *Power and Prosecution*, Göttingen, 2012, 120.

17 The other African states include: South Africa, Mauritius, Senegal, and Uganda. For a discussion, see G. Kemp, 'The Implementation of the Rome Statute in Africa', in: G. Werle, L. Fernandez and M. Vormbaum (eds), *Africa and the International Criminal Court*, The Hague 2014, 61–77. For a general overview, see M. du Plessis, *African Guide to International Criminal Justice*, Pretoria 2008.

18 For an overview, see G.Kemp 'The implementation of the Rome Statute in Africa' in Gerhard Werle, Lovell Fernandez and Moritz Vormbaum (eds) *Africa and the International Criminal Court* (2014) Asser Press/Springer. The Hague. 73–74.

19 Commission of Inquiry into the Post-Election Violence (CIPEV), *Final Report* (15 October 2008), pp. 472–475 available at: http://www.dialoguekenya.org/index.php/reports/commission-reports.html.

Jurisdictional issues, inadequate police investigations, lack of legitimacy, as well as national and international political dynamics impacted the quest to bring to justice those responsible for the PEV in one way or another.

In terms of the possible domestic prosecutions of PEV (focussing on crimes against humanity), it is relevant to note that while the Implementation of the International Crimes Act adopts the Rome Statute definition of crimes against humanity, the Act came into force only on 1 January 2009, thus postdating the alleged PEV crimes. This legal fact posed an important obstacle, namely the legality principle – *nullum crimen nulla poena sine lege* – which provides *inter alia* that crimes cannot be prosecuted and punished retroactively. Of course, this may or may not be persuasive from an international criminal law perspective, but the legal reality in Kenya was that the PEV crimes could not be prosecuted as crimes against humanity in the domestic courts of Kenya.

Given that reliance on the Implementation Act was not possible, the next possibility was to look at the incorporation of international law via Kenya's foundational document.[20] The Constitution of 2010[21] explicitly states that general international law[22] and treaties ratified[23] by Kenya form part of the law of Kenya. The problem is that the Constitution could arguably also not be considered to have retroactive application.[24]

The Constitution of 2010 came into force on 27 August 2010 after ratification by the people of Kenya in a popular referendum.[25] But the Constitution could not

20 Article 2(1) of Constitution of Kenya says: "This Constitution is the supreme law of the Republic and binds all persons and all State organs at both levels of government."
21 See further below a more detailed discussion of the constitutional reforms that resulted in the adoption of the Constitution of 2010.
22 Article 2(5) of the Constitution: "The general rules of international law shall form part of the law of Kenya."
23 Article 2(6) of the Constitution: 'Any treaty or convention ratified by Kenya shall form part of the law of Kenya under this Constitution.'
24 Article 263 of the Constitution: 'This Constitution shall come into force on its promulgation by the President or on the expiry of fourteen days from the date of the publication in the Gazette of the final result of the referendum ratifying this Constitution, whichever is the earlier.' In *Rodgers Ondiek Nyakundi & two others v State* [2012] eKLR it was determined by the court that the Constitution of 2010 does not have retroactive application.
25 More than 67% of the total valid votes in the referendum were in support of the new Constitution. The Constitution came into force upon its promulgation by the President on 27 August 2010. L. G. Lumumba & Luis Franceschi, *The Constitution of Kenya, 2010 – An Introductory Commentary*, Nairobi 2014, 686.

reach into the past[26] to create a legal reality in which Kenyan institutions of law enforcement and administration of justice could retroactively apply the material provisions of the Rome Statute (already ratified by Kenya in 2005). Indeed, such a retroactive application of the new Constitution, which follows in the monist tradition of international law, would go counter to the legal tradition. Kenya, like many other Anglophone countries in Africa, generally adhered to the dualist approach to international law. That means that treaties (like the Rome Statute of the ICC) must first be incorporated into domestic law via an Act of Parliament before they can be applied by the courts.[27]

The net result of all this was that while Kenya was a state party to the Rome Statute of the ICC at the time of the alleged PEV crimes, Kenya did not have in place the necessary legal mechanisms to investigate, prosecute and ultimately punish the acts of violence as crimes under international law. The monist Constitution of 2010 changed the legal paradigm; and so did the Implementation of the Rome Statute Act. But the new paradigm could not have retroactive application. The PEV crimes thus had to be treated as ordinary (domestic) crimes like murder,[28] rape,[29] and possession of stolen goods[30].

---

26 There is another dimension here: The Constitution of 2010 was never meant to be a transitional justice instrument as was, for instance, the Interim Constitution of South Africa (1993). For more on this point, see M. Akech, *Institutional Reform in the New Constitution of Kenya*, New York, 2010, 16. The Interim Constitution in South Africa specifically provided for transitional justice mechanisms to deal with past Human Rights violations in South Africa via the TRC-process and qualified and conditional amnesty. For an historical account, see A. Sparks, *Tomorrow is Another Country: The inside story of South Africa's Negotiated Revolution*, Chicago 1995.

27 J. O. Ambani, 'Navigating past the "Dualist Doctrine": The Case for Progressive Jurisprudence on the Application of International Human Rights Norms in Kenya", in: M. Killander (ed) *International Law and Domestic Human Rights Litigation in Africa*, Pretoria 2010, 25, 30.

28 See for instance the case of *R v Stephen Kiprotich Leting and others*, Nakuru High Court Criminal Case No 34 of 2008 (in this case the accused were charged, jointly with others not before the court, with the murder of about 35 people who were burnt in a church at Kiambaa, Uasin Gishu District, Rift Valley Province). See also *R v John Kimita Mwaniki*, Nakuru High Court Criminal Case No 116 of 2007; *R v Eric Akeyo Otieno*, Criminal Appeal No 10 of 2008; and *R v Peter Kipkemboi Rutto alias Saitoti*, Nakuru High Court Criminal Case No 118 of 2008.

29 See for instance the case of *R v Philemon Kipsang Kirui*, Kericho High Court Criminal Appeal No 59 of 2009.

30 See for instance the case of *R v James Wafula Khamala*, Bungoma High Court Criminal Appeal No 9 of 2010.

Given the above-mentioned legal situation, the prospect of holding individuals accountable for crimes against humanity premised on PEV and related atrocities could, practically and legally, only occur at the international level. The international/domestic crime binary opened up some anomalies, notably in terms of punishment. For instance, under Kenyan law at the time, a conviction for a crime like murder (i.e. an 'ordinary' domestic crime) could be visited with capital punishment, while the same act of killing (and assuming all the contextual elements were present), constituting a crime against humanity under international law, does not carry the death sentence at the International Criminal Court.[31]

The incidences and scope of PEV in Kenya were – simply by the numbers – all but ordinary. According to the Report of the Commission of Inquiry into Post-Election Violence, there were about 1,200 murders, 3,000 instances of rape, 350,000 incidents of forceful removals, 117,216 cases of damage to or destruction of property and 41,000 incidents of destruction of houses and residential dwellings.[32] It is common cause that Kenya failed to institute criminal proceedings under domestic criminal law against the alleged perpetrators. This fact prompted the ICC Prosecutor's *proprio motu* investigation[33] (the first such intervention by the ICC Prosecutor) in terms of the powers granted to the OTP under the Rome Statute, and with reference to an agreement that was reached between the OTP and Kenya.[34]

3. The Relations Between the ICC and Kenya

The authority to commence the formal investigation into alleged crimes against humanity was granted to the OTP by the ICC Pre-trial Chamber on 30 March 2010.[35] This was followed in December 2010 by the OTP

---

31 Penal Code of Kenya (Cap 63 Laws of Kenya) sections 204 and 296(2) provide for the death sentence for crimes like murder and robbery with aggravated violence. The Rome Statute of the ICC, Article 77, on the other hand, provides for a maximum of life imprisonment for crimes of extreme gravity.

32 CIPEV Report (2008) 345–352; S. F. Materu, "A strained relationship: reflections on the African Union's stand towards the International Criminal Court from the Kenya experience" in: G. Werle, L. Fernandez & M. Vormbaum, *Africa and the International Criminal Court*, The Hague, Asser Press/Springer, p. 219.

33 Article 15(3) Rome Statute of the ICC.

34 Materu, *a strained relationship*, 219.

35 Decision Pursuant to Article 15 of the Rome Statute on the Authorization of an Investigation into the Situation in the Republic of Kenya, *Kenya Situation* (ICC-01/09-19), Pre-trial Chamber II, 31 March 2010. See also the corrected version of the decision, 1 April 2010 (ICC-01/09-19-Corr.).

applications for warrants of arrest for a number of individuals, including William Ruto and Uhuru Kenyatta.[36] Kenyatta is a son of a former president of Kenya and member of the Kikuyu community, and Ruto is from the Kalenjins community. Both of them allegedly played instrumental roles in the post-election violence. Both were prominent political operatives in their respective movements before the election of 2007. Ruto was eventually charged as an indirect co-perpetrator with various crimes against humanity[37] for his involvement in PEV-related crimes in various locations in Kenya from December 2007 to January 2008.[38] Kenyatta was charged, also as an indirect co-perpetrator, for alleged crimes against humanity in the forms of murder, rape, persecution, forcible transfer of people, and other inhumane acts. The crimes were allegedly committed to ensure that the PNU remained in power. Kenyatta was suspected of being instrumental in the mobilisation of a Kikuyu-led gang that formed an integral part of the attacks that led to the alleged crimes against humanity.[39]

In 2013, after the transitional period following the PEV, Kenyatta and Ruto were elected president and deputy-president, respectively, in the elections of that year.[40] Some commentators see the ICC indictments as a winning factor that contributed to the Kenyatta and Ruto election victory. Indeed, they were not shy to campaign on the issue, accusing the ICC of being disruptive and of meddling in the domestic politics of Kenya.[41]

36 Prosecutor's Application Pursuant to Article 58 as to William Samoei Ruto, Henry Kiprono Kosgey and Joshua Arap Sang, *Kenya Situation* (ICC-01/09-30-RED2), 15 December 2010; Prosecutor's Application Pursuant to Article 58 as to Francis Kirimi Muthaura, Uhuru Muigai Kenyatta and Mohammed Hussein Ali, *Kenya Situation* (ICC-01-/09-31-RED2), 15 December 2010.
37 Including murder, persecution and forcible transfer of persons.
38 Pre-TrialChamber I, Decision on the Confirmation of Charges Pursuant to Article 61(7)(a) and (b) of the Rome Statute, ICC-01/09-01/11-373, 23 January 2012, available https://www.icc-cpi.int/iccdocs/doc/doc1314535.pdf.
39 G. Lunch, M. Zgonec--Rožej, *The ICC Intervention in Kenya*, London, Februar 2013, p. 6, available at https://www.chathamhouse.org/sites/files/chathamhouse/public/Research/Africa/0213pp_icc_kenya.pdf).
40 Materu, *The Post-Election Violence in Kenya*, 241.
41 For more background, see S. Mugera, 'Uhuru Kenyatta: Kenyan President in Profile', BBC Africa, 5.12. 2014, available at http://www.bbc.com/news/world-africa-21544245).

4. Domestic Responses to the ICC Intervention: Judicial and Constitutional Institutions and Their Practice

Apart from the political response to the OTP investigation, the ICC Pre-Trial Chamber authorisation of the OTP investigation was also legally challenged quite soon after the start of the investigation. In *Joseph Kimani Gathungu v The Attorney-General and Others*[42] the High Court of Kenya heard an application for an order to declare the OTP investigation of the PEV matters to be unconstitutional and invalid. The gist of the legal argument centred on the fact that the Constitution of Kenya at the time did not provide for a judicial organ in the form of the ICC. According to the applicants, the ICC and related bodies like the OTP could not exercise lawful authority in Kenya and could not conduct investigations on the territory of Kenya. The respondents submitted the preliminary technical point that the High Court of Kenya lacked the necessary jurisdiction to pronounce on matters relating to the exercise of legitimate ICC powers. The case clearly exposed the many complexities of the application of an international legal regime in the domestic legal system of an essentially dualist state.

The application before the High Court provided Kenyan courts with an opportunity to consider some fundamental issues pertaining to the role of domestic courts in the emerging international criminal justice system. At the time, of course, the fact that Kenya had not yet domesticated the ICC Statute turned out to be a real legal obstacle. In this regard the High Court observed that:

> ...international tribunals such as the ICC is well recognized to have *compétence de la compétence* – an initial capacity to determine whether or not it has the jurisdiction to hear and determine a case coming up before it... the ICC, acting within the terms of the Rome Statute, has already determined that it indeed has jurisdiction. The ICC has gone further to determine the second jurisdictional question: whether the special facts of post-election violence in Kenya (2007–2008) render the matter justiciable before that Court. The ICC has determined that, on the facts, it has jurisdiction to investigate, hear and determine the cases arising from the post-election violence.[43]

Thus, according to the High Court, the ICC has the inherent capacity, emanating from the Rome Statute, to determine whether or not it has the necessary jurisdiction to hear and determine a particular matter. It is through the exercise of this power that the ICC determined its jurisdiction over the Kenyan cases. Furthermore,

---

42 *Joseph Kimani Gathungu v The Attorney-General and Others*, High Court of Kenya at Mombasa, 23 November 2010; (2010) eKLR (available at http://kenyalaw.org/caselaw/cases/view/72570/).

43 *Joseph Kimani Gathungu v The Attorney-General*, para h.

"Kenya was a member of the community of nations and subject to the governing law bearing upon states as members of that community."[44]

The High Court was at pains to reiterate the constitutional significance of Kenya's international law obligations. These obligations are not in conflict with Kenya's sovereignty; indeed, they are functions and expressions of Kenya's ability to engage with the international community and to subject itself to certain international frameworks. The court stated:

> …the Constitution of 2010 is not to be regarded as rejecting the role of international institutions such as the ICC. Indeed, from the express provisions of the Constitution, "the general rules of international law shall form part of the law of Kenya"; and Kenya remains party to a large number of multilateral international legal instruments: and so, by law, Kenya has obligations to give effect to these. One of such Conventions is the Rome Statute which establishes the International Criminal Court.[45]

The High Court thus rejected the application, first because it did not have the necessary jurisdiction but, secondly, also because the nature of the application was deemed not to be justiciable.

5. The Efficiency of Law Enforcement

The logic of the ICC as a court of last resort implies effective and bona fide national investigations into alleged crimes under international law. In the case of Kenya it became apparent that the efforts of the Kenyan law enforcement and investigatory institutions were not beyond criticism.[46] Indeed, observers labelled the efforts of the Kenyan police in their investigations of the PEV-related cases to be poor and even malicious. Alleged perpetrators were allowed to effectively evade accountability. The result was few prosecutions and even fewer convictions.[47]

Exact data on the progress of domestic investigations into alleged PEV-related violence appears to be incomplete and not up to date. In 2012, Kenya's Director of Public Prosecutions (DPP) reported a total of 6,081 PEV-related cases. That number represents cases reported to local police authorities. By the end of 2012,

---

44 Ibid.
45 Ibid.
46 For a critical assessment, see E. Owiye Asaala, "Prosecuting crimes related to the 2007 post-election violence in Kenyan courts: issues and challenges", in: H. J. van der Merwe and G. Kemp, *International Criminal Justice in Africa*, Nairobi 2016, 27–46.
47 Human Rights Watch, *Turning Pebbles: Evading Accountability for Post-Election Violence in Kenya* (2011) 3–4, available at https://www.hrw.org/sites/default/files/reports/kenya1211webwcover_0.pdf).

only 366 of these have been taken to court.[48] An important aspect to keep in mind is that few of the eventual convictions in the domestic courts were for serious crimes directly linked to the PEV. Further analysis of the supposed link between domestic prosecutions and the PEV shows that some of the areas with the highest PEV related casualties recorded no eventual convictions at all.[49] The apparent unwillingness or disinterest on the side of the police to investigate serious sexual offences linked to PEV was specifically noted by commentators.[50]

Prosecuting the PEV matters as "ordinary crimes" under domestic law was necessitated due to a lack of appropriate incorporation of crimes under international law at the time, as mentioned above. That was of course rectified by the adoption of the International Crimes Act, but as we have seen, that Act could not be applied retrospectively. But Kenya's ordinary criminal laws were available options. Botched investigations and subsequent discontinuation of prosecutions due to lack of evidence became the dominant narrative of Kenya's domestic efforts to deal with the PEV.[51] The modest number of cases that made it to court is indicative of the questionable institutional response to and treatment of the PEV as a criminal justice and human rights issue of grave concern.

6. The Kenya Cases at the ICC

On 24 May 2012, the ICC Appeals Chamber cleared the way for the charges of crimes against humanity to proceed against a number of Kenyan nationals.[52] The individual charges were grouped into two cases: *Prosecutor v William Samoei Ruto and Joshua Sang* (henceforth "Ruto and Sang") and *Prosecutor v Francis Kirimi Muthaura and Uhuru Muigai Kenyatta* (henceforth "Muthaura and Kenyatta"). Ruto and Sang were alleged of having committed crimes against humanity. Ruto, currently the Deputy President of Kenya, was allegedly responsible for crimes against humanity as an indirect co-perpetrator of murder,

48 The Multi-Agency Task Force on the 2007/2008 PEV, *Report on the 2007/2008 PEV Related cases*, Nairobi 2012, p. 1.
49 CIPEV report.
50 HRW, *Turning Pebbles*, 3–4.
51 The gist of the findings can be found in in HRW, *Turning Pebbles*.
52 *Prosecutor v William Samoei Ruto, Henry Kiprono Kosgey and Joshua Arap Sang*, No ICC-01/09-01/11 OA3 OA4, Decision on the appeals of Mr William Samoei Ruto and Mr Joshua Arap Sang against the decision of Pre-Trial Chamber II of 23 January 2012 entitled 'Decision on the Confirmation of Charges pursuant to Article 61(7)(a) and (b) of the Rome Statute', 24 May 2012; *Prosecutor v Francis Kirimi Muthaura, Uhuru Muigai Kenyatta and Mohammed Hussein Ali* No ICC-01/09-02/11 OA4, Decision on

forcible transfer of people and persecution. Sang, a radio presenter, allegedly contributed to the commission of various crimes committed by the group of individuals who were led by Ruto. The context of these various offences was the political conflict for power in the northern parts of the Rift Valley Province.[53] The case against Muthaura and Kenyatta[54] also concerned crimes against humanity. Muthaura was a prominent civil servant and allied to former President Kibaki. Kenyatta, son of one of modern Kenya's founding fathers, and who is currently the President of Kenya, previously served as Deputy Prime Minister of Kenya. Both Muthaura and Kenyatta were alleged of having committed crimes against humanity as indirect co-perpetrators of murder, forcible transfers, rape, persecution as well as other inhumane acts. The context here was, again, the conflict for political power and in particular the violent efforts to ensure that the Party of National Unity (PNU) remained in power. Many of the acts of violence were aimed at the Orange Democratic Movement (ODM) supporters in the central Rift Valley.

Charges against Muthaura were withdrawn on 11 March 2013,[55] because of a combination of lack of evidence and a general lack of cooperation from the Kenyan Government, which failed to provide the Prosecutor with important evidence and also failed to facilitate access by the Prosecutor to important witnesses. Several of the potential witnesses had died before they were able to testify, while others were apparently too afraid to cooperate with the Prosecution. A key witness against Muthaura also admitted that he had accepted bribes and recanted parts of his evidence. The Prosecutor thus decided to drop this key witness against Muthaura, and this contributed to the decision to withdraw the charges against him.

On 5 December 2014, the Prosecutor filed a notice of withdrawal of the charges against Kenyatta. The basic reason for this decision by the Prosecutor was lack of evidence. On 13 March 2015, Trial Chamber V of the ICC issued a decision on the

---

the appeals of Mr Francis Kirimi Muthaura and Mr Uhuru Muigai Kenyatta against the decision of Pre-Trial Chamber II of 23 January 2012 entitled 'Decision on the Confirmation of Charges Pursuant to Article 61(7)(a) and (b) of the Rome Statute', 24 May 2012.

53 For basic case information, see https://www.icc-cpi.int/iccdocs/PIDS/publications/ RutoKosgeySangEng.pdf

54 For basic case information, see https://www.icc-cpi.int/iccdocs/PIDS/publications/ KenyattaEng.pdf

55 See statement by Prosecutor, https://www.icc-cpi.int/en_menus/icc/press%20and%20 media/press%20releases/Pages/OTP-statement-11-03-2013.aspx

withdrawal of charges against Kenyatta. The Trial Chamber noted the Prosecution's withdrawal of charges. The proceedings were consequently terminated by order of the Trial Chamber and the summons to appear was vacated.[56] The case against Kenyatta was effectively over. On 5 April 2016, Trial Chamber V(A) of the ICC decided to terminate the case against Ruto and Sang,[57] thus bringing to an end all the high profile Kenyan cases.

7. Kenya's Domestic Response to the ICC

At this stage it is necessary to take a step back and consider Kenya's interaction with the ICC, once it became clear that the more abstract investigation would become a much more concrete prosecution involving the most senior political leaders in Kenya, including, ultimately, the sitting Deputy President and the President of the country.

As a starting point for this part of the discussion, one can assume that Kenya, as a state party to the Rome Statute and as one of only a few states party on the African continent that actually incorporated the Rome Statute into domestic law, initially perceived the ICC in positive terms, or, at least, not negatively. Then again, as was noted by one commentator, the "question of how the [ICC] is perceived in Kenya did not arise prior to the ICC intervention; it only arose subsequently."[58] And in terms of perception, it is necessary to point out that there is not a monolithic view, but rather a diverse (and fluctuating) number of views that can broadly be divided into two groups: the political elite and citizens/civil society.[59]

In terms of the central theme of this chapter, namely the question of whether ICC decisions brought about or affected institutional change in Kenya, the obvious group to focus on is the political elite, because they have the immediate power and supposed inclination to bring about change. However, imperfect as it may be, Kenya is a democracy and the role of civil society and the citizenry in terms of institutional change must therefore also be considered. Below follows an assessment based on one commentator's analysis, with some additional references to relevant reports from civil society.

---

56 For the Trial Chamber Decision, see https://www.icc-cpi.int/iccdocs/doc/doc1936247. pdf
57 Decision on Defence Application for Judgment of Acquittal, *Prosecutor v William Samoei Ruto and Joshua Arap Sang* ICC-01/09-01/11, 5 April 2016.
58 Materu, *A strained relationship*, 220.
59 Materu, *A strained relationship*, 220–222.

In terms of elite reaction to the PEV, it is necessary to note that there was broad agreement that individuals should be held accountable for the PEV. It was noted above that the CIPEV Report suggested the creation of a special tribunal to deal with the PEV cases. So the principle of individual responsibility was on the table right from the start, but it also became clear that the political elite was not in agreement as to the best way to go about individual responsibility for the PEV cases. It was pointed out that important legal limitations existed in terms of domestic prosecutions in the courts of Kenya (safe for prosecuting the PEV as 'ordinary crimes', as discussed earlier). So the two remaining options were the special tribunal (a domestic option) or the ICC (the international option).

The special tribunal option was never favoured by a majority in parliament, so the international (ICC) option got more traction. But it should be noted that even the ICC-option was supported for various reasons. One group, a minority in the pro-ICC grouping,[60] believed that the ICC-option was appropriate because the domestic institutions, including the judiciary, were simply too weak to deal with highly charged and complex matters like the PEV cases. This group also believed that there was a risk of the judiciary being manipulated. For them, the ICC presented a neutral and impartial forum that was better positioned than the domestic options (the ordinary courts and the proposed special tribunal). A second, larger, group of parliamentarians were less sanguine about the ICC-option. Their perceived reasoning was far more cynical. Indeed, it was reported that they viewed the ICC as a 'remote threat' and they hoped that the investigations and eventual trials would be so protracted and procedurally so entangled that real accountability would be delayed and ultimately abandoned.[61] This grim view of the ICC as an external option was formed even before the Prosecutor had the opportunity to name any specific suspects. Ironically enough, Uhuru Kenyatta (Deputy Prime Minister at the time) and William Ruto (a member of parliament) were part of the group of politicians who supported the ICC. It is speculated by some that Kenyatta and Ruto advocated for immediate ICC intervention in the PEV cases in the hope that the ICC investigation would provide political ammunition against some of their prominent rivals, most notably Raila Odinga, the 2007 presidential candidate.[62] Of course, as we

---

60 See report by the International Crisis Group, *Impact of the ICC Proceedings, ICG Africa Briefing* No 84, 9 January 2012, available at http://www.crisisgroup.org//media/Files/africa/horn-of-africa/kenya/B084%20Kenya%20-%Impact%20of%20the%20ICC%20 Proceedings.pdf).

61 Materu, *A strained relationship*, 220.

62 Materu, *A strained relationship*, 221.

know, Odinga was not indicted, while Ruto and Kenyatta both became high profile indictees before the ICC. Unsurprisingly, Ruto and Kenyatta subsequently
changed their support for the ICC-option. Indeed, Kenya under the leadership
of President Uhuru Kenyatta became one of the leading anti-ICC voices on the
African continent and in the context of African Union debates about Africa's
relationship with the ICC.

The initial broad elite support for ICC intervention in the PEV cases in Kenya
turned into strong opposition to the ICC once Ruto and Kenyatta were indicted
and once both of them indicated their political ambitions in terms of the 2013
general elections. The rhetoric became decidedly anti-ICC. The ICC was painted
in political discourse as a "neo-colonialist ploy", a "white man's court", and as
an "imperial imposition."[63] Indeed, soon after his election as president of Kenya
in 2013, Uhuru Kenyatta addressed a gathering of African Heads of State and
Government and accused the ICC of being a tool of Western interests that are
trying to influence domestic and foreign policy in Africa.[64]

Apart from the elite positions on the ICC (shifting as they were), there appears
to have been a great schism between the dominant elite view and the detect-
able views of ordinary citizens. Materu points out that soon after the PEV, the
emerging debate had two themes: (i) the role and competence of the national
judicial system in terms of potential domestic prosecutions, and (ii) the role of
the ICC in challenging the "culture of impunity." Significantly, civil society and
organised religion (notably the Catholic Church in Kenya) pushed for the ICC
to play a leading role in the PEV cases. In terms of this view, the ICC represented
"the only hope to true justice",[65] and the only institution that had the necessary
competence and impartiality, compared to domestic institutions of justice that
were largely compromised, as also noted above.

Opinion polls from 2009 to 2011 indicated majority popular support for the
ICC, which was perceived as "trustworthy", "independent" and "reliable". Some
of the polls clearly alluded to a disconnect between citizens and the political
elite in terms of perceptions and views about the ICC as an actor in the PEV era
in Kenya. The Kenya National Dialogue and Reconciliation Monitoring Project
recorded a strong public mood against impunity in a 2011 survey.[66] There are

---

63 Ibid.
64 Ibid.
65 Ibid.
66 Kenya National Dialogue and Reconciliation Monitoring Project 2011, pp. viii–ix,
    available at: http://www.iccnow.org/documents/KNDRFinalReport12October2011.pdf

three key paragraphs[67] in the Project's 2011 report that neatly encapsulate the divide between the dominant elite opinion of the ICC and the opinion of the general population:

> *The ICC is not politically manipulated*: Allegations that the ICC process has been used to eliminate political rivals ahead of the next elections do not seem to enjoy widespread public support: a majority of respondents across the country are of the view that those supporting the ICC are doing so to get justice for the victims of violence or to protect some of the suspects rather than to eliminate political rivals.
>
> *Public support and confidence in the ICC process remains high, albeit lower than it was before the naming of suspects.* As noted in previous reports, public support for the ICC has remained high since CIPEV completed its report, but the support reduced dramatically after the naming of the suspects. The reduction may be attributed to the perception that the court failed to include all the perpetrators from regions which experienced violence, which implies failure to include leaders of other ethnic groups. The claim that four of the six suspects hail from the Rift Valley has reinforced the perception of a political vendetta against the people of the region.
>
> *A majority of respondents remain confident that investigations and prosecution by the ICC will not trigger violence.* Up to 65 per cent of the respondents believe violence is highly unlikely to occur as a result of any outcome at the ICC. This is an encouraging finding. However, unlike in previous reviews, more people are concerned that isolated incidents of violence are likely to occur if certain politicians are indicted. Only 23 per cent of respondents said they think violence is likely. This percentage is the highest recorded over the past three years. This suggests that something is going on at the community level, away from the glare of the media and the public eye.

It is important to say something here about the purpose of noting the elite and public perceptions about the Kenya cases before the ICC. The aim of this chapter is not to evaluate public perceptions about the ICC. The aim is to identify institutional change as a result of ICC decisions. In the event that there were no institutional changes, that will also be discussed by way of conclusion. But it is important to contextualise the measure of institutional change that occurred. That is why it is necessary to take note of legal and political developments in Kenya before the ICC intervention in the PEV cases, and why it is important to note the trends in perceptions about the ICC as an institutional player in Kenya.

So, having noted a divide in elite perceptions about the ICC during the early part of the ICC intervention, and having noted a remarkable disconnect between the dominant elite perception (which grew more hostile towards the ICC as it became clearer which individuals were going to be indicted), it is necessary to

---

67 Kenya National Dialogue and Reconciliation Monitoring Project, 52–53.

say something about the trends after the election of President Kenyatta in 2013 and the continuation, at that stage, of the case against him and others at the ICC.

Surveys from late 2013 (after the election of that year) started to record a decline in popular support for the ICC in Kenya. Again, context is important. First, the decline coincided with a more concerted effort from the African Union to voice a regional opposition to what it (the African Union) perceived to be "an anti-Africa bias" at the ICC.[68] Second, most of the decline in popular support for the ICC-intervention in Kenya came as a result of declining support in the areas of the country where the ICC indictees have some tribal or ethnic links (notably the Central Province and the Rift Valley). A regrettable ethnic mobilisation around the growing anti-ICC sentiment in these areas further compounded the polarisation between those who viewed the ICC as an anti-impunity institution, and those who came to view the ICC as targeting not only the political leaders of Kenya, but indeed "the entire Kalenjin community."[69] Deputy President Ruto, it will be recalled, is from the Kalenjin community. This ethnic mobilisation in turn led to the concomitant accusation that the ICC is selectively targeting certain individuals and not "known suspects" from other communities.[70]

In terms of the perceptions about the role of the ICC in Kenya, it is submitted here that one can draw some preliminary conclusions:

(i) Political elite support for the ICC intervention in Kenya, such as it were, never had a firm normative basis, but was rather premised on the assumption that the ICC would be a useful, and ostensibly impartial, institution to deal with unwanted political opposition in Kenya. This rather opportunistic support for the ICC among some of the political elite turned sour when things developed in quite the opposite direction with the indictments of Uhuru Kenyatta and William Ruto. Gradually, and with the institutional cover of the African Union, the pretence of political support for the ICC at the highest level in Kenya disappeared and was replaced by clear opposition to the ICC involvement in the PEV matters and especially against the President and Deputy President.

(ii) In terms of the general population and civil society, one can note the still relatively high levels of support for the ICC in Kenya. The unfortunate, but perhaps understandable ethnic divide on this question is noticeable. The institutions of state, and certainly the most senior government leaders, did

---

68 More on this below.

69 Materu, *A strained relationship*, 223.

70 Ibid, This sentiment was also reported by Human Rights Watch report of 2013.

nothing to counter the growing perception among certain communities that
the ICC was "selective" and "biased" in its approach to the PEV indictments
and continued prosecution. At the same time there still appears to be significant public support for the ICC in Kenya, albeit at reduced and more
ethnically partisan levels.

8. Institutional Reform in Kenya

In order to make a meaningful assessment of ICC decisions on institutional
change in Kenya, it is necessary to briefly describe some of the significant institutional developments of the past decade. The aim in this part of the chapter is not
primarily to assess, but mainly to describe. The most important ICC decisions,
and certain important contextual and related issues, were noted in the preceding
sections. We now turn to a number of institutional creations and developments.

8.1. Constitutional Reform

In 2010, Kenya experienced the most significant constitutional development
since independence from Britain in 1963. The text of the Constitution, 2010,
which was ratified by a popular referendum, was the result of a constitutional
review process that had already started in 1990.[71] The process gained much
momentum after the 2007 PEV. The Kenya National Dialogue Reconciliation
Committee proposed further comprehensive constitutional reforms as part of
the transitional efforts. The other notable transitional mechanisms proposed by
the KNDRC included the establishment of a Truth, Justice and Reconciliation
Commission (TJRC), the prosecution of the perpetrators of PEV-related crimes,
and relevant institutional reforms.[72]

Commentators make the point that as a result of the contentious nature of
domestic prosecutions (to the extent that it was possible) as well as the political
uncertainty in the post-PEV time frame and the concomitant uncertainty over
the TJRC as a transitional institution, focus and popular support shifted to the
constitutional reform process as a vehicle of change and institutional reform. Two
important legal instruments – the Constitution of Kenya Review Act (2008) and
the Constitution of Kenya Amendment Act (2008) – encapsulated the sense of
political goodwill.[73] The constitutional review process thus gained considerable

---

71 Lumumba & Franceschi, *The Constitution of Kenya*, 41.
72 Lumumba & Franceschi *The Constitution of Kenya*, 45.
73 Ibid.

traction, as opposed to the other transitional and post-PEV mechanisms and proposals which by and large remained either legally impossible (for instance the domestic prosecution of crimes against humanity) or legally very difficult for procedural and technical reasons (for instance the difficulty of cooperating with the ICC due to a lack of implementation of the Rome Statute legislation in the time frame immediately after the PEV-era).

By November 2009, the so-called 'Harmonised Draft Constitution' was published. A number of contentious issues remained, notably the provisions relating to executive powers, Human Rights, devolution of power, the position of Kadhis' Courts[74] and some of the transitional provisions. The Revised Harmonised Draft – a substantially different text – was ultimately approved by the Kenyan people in the August 2010 referendum.[75]

The aim here is of course not to analyse the Constitution of 2010. Rather, the aim is simply to situate the Constitution as a significant enabling text for institutional change. The text incorporates a Bill of Rights, an independent electoral management body, an independent judiciary, an executive with circumscribed powers, a legislative body (parliament), an essentially decentralised political system, and a framework for the regulation of devolved government. These are just some of the important features from an institutional perspective. It is too early to really evaluate the impact of the Constitution, but an early assessment held that: "The constitutional reform process has served to lay the ground for important institutional reforms of Kenya's justice and security apparatus and other governance institutions, geared to prevent the recurrence of human rights atrocities."[76]

It was pointed out that in the immediate aftermath of the PEV it was, at least from a domestic perspective, legally necessary and even politically convenient (for a while) to take the ICC-route with regards to the alleged cases of crimes against humanity. The Constitution of 2010 changed the dynamic: the government of Kenya "found a legal basis to retreat from the ICC route. Indeed,

---

74 Kadhis' Courts are established under Article 170 of the Constitution, 2010. Their jurisdiction is limited to the determination of questions of Muslim Law relating to personal status, marriage, divorce or inheritance in proceedings in which all the parties profess the Muslim Religion and submit to the jurisdiction of the Kadhis' Courts. For further information, see http://www.judiciary.go.ke/portal/page/kadhis.

75 Lumumba & Franceschi, *The Constitution of Kenya*, 47.

76 E. Asaala & N.Dicker, 'Transitional justice in Kenya and the UN Special Rapporteur on Truth and Justice: Where to from here?' *African Human Rights Law Journal* 13 / 2013, 324–355.

it was noted that the government – on various occasions – referred to the new Constitution "as its new strength to try the ICC suspects."[77]

Whether one views it as a commitment to the new Constitution or as opportunism, fact is that the government of Kenya in its challenge to the admissibility of the Kenyan situation before the ICC in terms of Article 19 of the Rome Statute, referenced the 2010 Constitution as indicative of a new capacity and willingness to prosecute perpetrators of gross Human Rights violations at the national level. The ICC was called upon to essentially follow the complementarity imperative and to take note of the institutional reforms prompted and made possible by the Constitution of 2010. But as we know, the Pre-trial Chamber rejected the admissibility challenge by Kenya.[78]

8.2. Judicial Reform and the Creation of an International Crimes Division in the High Court

A precondition for any functioning domestic criminal justice system is the existence of a credible and independent judiciary. The CIPEV report noted that in the aftermath of the PEV there existed a serious trust deficit and a lack of confidence in the judiciary. The perception was that the judiciary was not independent as an institution.[79]

The Constitution of 2010 provides for a framework that aims to protect the institutional independence of the judiciary. The independent Judicial Service Commission[80] is tasked with the constitutional function of making recommendations to the President on the appointment of judges. More than that, it is also tasked with the continuing education and training of judges and judicial officers. In addition, the Judicial Service Commission is required to promote diversity, especially gender equality, on the bench. The latter aspect should thus be reflected in the Commission's appointment recommendations to the President.

Apart from the Judicial Service Commission, one can also note some of the other provisions in the Constitution aimed at fostering an independent judiciary.

---

77 Asaala, Dicker, *Transitional justice in Kenya*, 349.

78 *Prosecutor v Francis Kirimi Muthaura, Uhuru Muigai Kenyatta and Mohammed Hussein Ali*, Decision on the Application by the Government of Kenya Challenging the Admissibility of the Case pursuant to Article 19(2)(b) of the Statute, 30 May 2011 ICC-01/09-02/11-96 (available at https://www.icc-cpi.int/iccdocs/doc/doc1078823. pdf).

79 CIPEV Report, 460.

80 See Article 172 Constitution of Kenya 2010.

For instance, article 173 of the Constitution creates a Judiciary Fund that aims to insulate the judiciary from executive interference by making it financially autonomous.

An independent and impartial judiciary is of course essential for any legal system. The Rome Statute of the ICC, of which Kenya is a state party, gives further credence to this principle via the complementarity imperative. The Rome Statute sets out a number of factors the ICC will consider when determining the unwillingness of a state to prosecute at the domestic level individuals suspected of committing one or more of the crimes within the jurisdiction of the ICC. Thus, where the domestic proceedings were not or are not being conducted independently or impartially and they were or are being conducted in a manner which, in the circumstances, is inconsistent with the intent to bring the person concerned to justice the ICC may step in to adjudicate the matter on the basis of the principle of complementarity.[81]

In terms of constitutional intent and design, then, one can say that Kenya's Constitution of 2010 provides for a solid institutional regime for the protection of judicial independence as well as continuing training and capacity building.[82] The creation of an International Crimes Division within the structures of the High Court in 2012[83] should be seen as a concretization of the complementarity imperative. The International Crimes Division also gives effect to the aims of the International Crimes Act of 2008, which provides that the crimes[84] proscribed in the Act shall be prosecuted in the High Court of Kenya.[85] It should be noted that, while the initial proposal by the Judicial Service Commission was to create the International Crimes Division to focus on the crimes of genocide, crimes against humanity and war crimes (the "ICC crimes"), the eventual proposal was more expansive in terms of the substantive jurisdiction of the Division so that it

---

81 Article 17(2)(c) Rome Statute of the ICC.
82 For an assessment, see I.Ndungu 'Cautious optimism over judicial reforms in Kenya' (2012) Institute for Security Studies, available at https://www.issafrica.org/iss-today/cautious-optimism-over-judicial-reforms-in-kenya.
83 *Report of the Committee of the Judicial Service Commission on the establishment of an International Crimes Division in the High Court of Kenya* (JSC Report), 30 October 2012, available at: http://nation.co.ke/blob/view/-/2197994/data/682588/-/io86tn/-/JSC+Report.pdf
84 Notably genocide, crimes against humanity, and war crimes.
85 Section 8(2) International Crimes Act 16 of 2008.

can also hear cases of transnational crimes like human trafficking, money laundering, piracy, and terrorism.[86]

A specialised division of the judiciary to deal with international and transnational crimes goes a long way to fulfil some of Kenya's important international, constitutional and statutory obligations. In order to enhance the effective domestic adjudication of international crimes, the Judicial Service Commission also recommended the establishment of a specialised prosecution unit within the Office of the Director of Public Prosecutions (DPP). The specialised prosecution unit deals exclusively with international crimes.[87]

Laudable though the creation of an International Crimes Division in the High Court and a specialised division of the DPP may be, the general assessment is that there is a reluctance to prosecute PEV-related cases at domestic level. There are of course legal reasons, as pointed out above (PEV cases cannot retroactively be prosecuted as international crimes before the courts of Kenya).[88] But there also seems to be a general lack of institutional and political will that prevents the effective and impartial prosecution and adjudication of the PEV-related crimes, even as ordinary crimes under the criminal laws of Kenya.[89]

An important compounding issue – the apparent lack of adequate witness protection – is further explored below.

8.3. Witness Protection

When the OTP first started the investigations in Kenya for purposes of possible prosecutions at the ICC, there were some concerns about the safety and security of potential witnesses. In reaction to these concerns, the Government of Kenya introduced changes to the Witness Protection Act of 2006, in order to create an independent and autonomous Witness Protection Unit. This was regarded as a step in the right direction, but lack of adequate funding bedevilled the effective functioning of the Unit. As a result, the Witness Protection Programme administered by the ICC still elicited more trust among ordinary Kenyans compared to

---

86 Africa Centre for Open Governance, *A real option for justice? The International Crimes Division of the High Court of Kenya,* Nairobi ACOG 2014, p. 7, available at http://dspace.africaportal.org/jspui/bitstream/123456789/34936/1/a_real_option_for_justice_the_international_crimes_division%5B1%5D.pdf?1

87 *The International Crimes Division of the High Court of Kenya* (supra) 8.

88 *Report on the International Crimes Division of the High Court of Kenya,* 11–12.

89 *Report on the International Crimes Division of the High Court of Kenya,* 9.

the underfunded, albeit autonomous Witness Protection Unit.[90] After the indictment of the senior politicians, trust in the Witness Protection Unit deteriorated
further. The Kenya National Dialogue and Reconciliation Monitoring Project
noted as follows in their report:

> The low level of confidence in the government programme may be attributed to the fact
> that some of the accused are senior government officials. The apparent determination
> by the government to save the six creates the impression that it is most unlikely to coop-
> erate with the ICC or any other programme that could lead to prosecutions. Besides,
> reports on extra-judicial killings have shown that police hit squads have been able to
> trace and kill persons under civil society witness protection programmes. The fact that
> police officers are suspected perpetrators of the post-election violence means victims
> or their families might find it difficult to seek protection from the police. A regional
> analysis shows that respondents in the Rift Valley have the least level of confidence in
> witness protection programmes.[91]

Apart from the apparent lack of trust in the Kenyan government programme for
the protection of ICC witnesses, it should also be noted that by 2015 it became
clear that the OTP investigation itself had become adversely affected by the systematic interference with and intimidation of ICC witnesses in Kenya. There
were also reports of intimidation and even killing of witnesses.[92] During 2015,
the Chief Prosecutor of the ICC acted to counter the systematic interference with
ICC witnesses. On 10 September 2015 the Chief Prosecutor issued the following
statement:

> On the 10th of March 2015, Pre-Trial Chamber II of the International Criminal Court
> [...] issued two arrest warrants under seal for Paul Gicheru and Philip Kipkoech Bett,
> respectively, on charges of interfering with ICC witnesses in the Kenya Situation, con-
> trary to Article 70(1)(c) of the Rome Statute. Following the arrest of these two suspects
> in Nairobi, and the notification of this fact to the Office of the Prosecutor by the Kenyan
> authorities on 24 August 2015, the Pre-Trial Chamber II of the ICC unsealed these
> warrants of arrest earlier today.
> The Chamber's decision to issue these warrants is significant. The integrity of witnesses
> is essential for the Court's determination of the truth. Interfering with the attendance or
> testimony of ICC witnesses, or retaliating against them are serious crimes under Article
> 70 of the Rome Statute.
> In its decision to issue the arrest warrants against Messrs Gicheru and Bett, the Chamber
> found that the evidence submitted by the Prosecution demonstrated, to the standard

---

90 Kenya National Dialogue and Reconciliation Monitoring Project, 57.
91 Kenya National Dialogue and Reconciliation Monitoring Project, 58.
92 Al Jazeera, Kenya's dark path to justice, available at: http://america.aljazeera.com/
    articles/2015/8/24/kenyas-dark-path-to-justice.html

required at this stage in the proceedings, that Messrs Gicheru and Bett were involved in an organised and systematic criminal scheme, aimed at approaching and corrupting Prosecution witnesses through bribes and other inducements, in exchange for their withdrawal as witnesses and/or recantation of their prior statements to the Prosecution."[93]

Neither the ICC nor the Kenyan authorities seemed to have been able to protect the safety of witnesses in Kenya or to provide for conditions conducive to the protection of the integrity of a proper witness protection programme. But it is particularly unfortunate that Kenya's own Witness Protection Unit not only failed the ICC investigation, but ultimately also the broader Kenyan society and criminal justice system, which should have been a key institution of the new constitutional era.

8.4. Police Reform

Allegations of violent acts, including fatal shootings and sexual assaults perpetrated by the Kenyan police in the context of the post-election violence, formed an important part of the factual matrix of the PEV-situation. A lack of convictions of police officers fed the narrative of a police force that was institutionally and systematically instrumental in PEV cases and in the cover-up of PEV cases.[94]

In order to remedy the dire image and institutional weakness of the police, the National Task Force on Police Reforms was established in 2009. The recommendations[95] of the Task Force included the creation of an independent National Police Service Commission. CIPEV, in its final report, also noted the

---

93 Statement of the Prosecutor of the International Criminal Court, Fatou Bensouda, regarding the unsealing of Arrest Warrants in the Kenya situation, https://www.icc-cpi.int/en_menus/icc/press%20and%20media/press%20releases/Pages/otp-stat-10-09-2015-2.aspx. For the charges of offences against the administration of justice (articles 25(3)(a) and 25(3)(f) of the Rome Statute of the ICC) against a number of individuals, see *The Prosecutor v Walter Osapiri Barasa* ICC-01/09-01/13 (https://www.icc-cpi.int/en_menus/icc/situations%20and%20cases/situations/situation%20icc%200109/related%20cases/ICC-0109-0113/Pages/default.aspx); *The Prosecutor v Paul Gicheru and Philip Kipkoech Bett* ICC-01/09-01/15 (https://www.icc-cpi.int/en_menus/icc/situations%20and%20cases/situations/situation%20icc%200109/related%20cases/ICC-01_09-01_15/Pages/default.aspx).
94 Asaala, Dicker, *Transitional Justice in Kenya*, 351.
95 Report of the National Task Force on Police Reforms – Abridged Version, December 2009, ICC-01/09-02/11-91-Anx3, available at https://www.icc-cpi.int/iccdocs/doc/doc1072888.pdf.

need to create a single national police force that can be governed as a professional force.[96]

Section 243 of the Constitution of 2010 provides for the single National Police Force. There is no explicit constitutional mandate or framework for civilian oversight of the police force. However, one must read section 243 with section 59 of the Constitution, which provides for the Kenya National Human Rights and Equality Commission. The latter body can monitor, investigate and report on the observation of human rights by national security organs. While the constitutional and institutional mechanisms to hold the police to account for Human Rights violations seem to be available in principle, it is also necessary to point out that the National Commission of Human Rights found it very difficult in the past to deal with complaints against the police.[97]

Although the Constitution does not provide for a formal civilian oversight structure, following on the report by the National Task Force on Policing, a Police Civilian Oversight Board was established in 2009. The Board functions in terms of a legislative framework provided for in the Independent Policing Oversight Authority Act 35 of 2011. The creation of this civilian body was greeted with cautious optimism for greater public trust in the police as a vital institution.[98]

9. Kenya's Institutional Relationship with the ICC: Contradictions, Contrariness and the Emerging Continental View

At the 14th Session of the Assembly of States Parties to the Rome Statute of the ICC, held in The Hague in November 2015, Kenya's Minister of Foreign Affairs addressed the assembled delegates[99] and pointed to a number of issues that are revealing in terms of Kenya's complex relationship with the ICC. The Minister reminded the assembled delegates that Kenya was one of the founding states of the ICC; a state party who helped to create the ICC as we know it. The Minister also noted that Kenya is (still) interested in making the ICC stronger.[100] Having

---

96   CIPEV Final Report, 434.

97   Lumumba, Franceschi, *The Constitution of Kenya*, 632.

98   Asaala, Dicker, *Transitional justice in Kenya*, 352.

99   Statement by Amina Mohamed, Minister of Foreign Affairs of Kenya, at the 14th Session of the Assembly of States Parties to the Rome Statute of the ICC, 18 November 2015, The Hague, the Netherlands, available at https://www.icc-cpi. int/iccdocs/asp_docs/ASP14/GenDeb/ASP14-GenDeb-Kenya-ENG.pdf

100 Ibid.

noted Kenya's commitment to the ICC, the Minister proceeded to highlight a number of issues of concern, including ICC jurisprudence on the evidentiary threshold, developments regarding complementarity, and the problematic instances of re-characterization of charges.[101]

Taking a broader view of developments in international criminal justice, the Minister alluded to the proposed expansion of the jurisdiction of the African Court on Human and Peoples' Rights to include international criminal jurisdiction.[102] Significantly, the Minister did not present these developments as in conflict with the Rome Statute of the ICC, but rather as a manifestation of the principle of complementarity and as the African continent's contribution to international jurisprudence and "in recognition of the ICC as a Court of last resort."[103]

Having sketched the broader context of Kenya's relationship with the ICC and some developments regarding international criminal justice on the African continent, the Minister proceeded to raise some specific requests from Kenya to the Assembly of States Parties.[104] These requests can indeed be seen as emblematic of Kenya's critical and qualified support for the ICC; even as indicative of an intention to improve the ICC as an institution and to better the co-operation between Kenya and the ICC. The Minister noted Kenya's "unprecedented co-operation with the ICC" in the past. Furthermore, the Minister asserted that, for purposes of the investigations into the alleged crimes against humanity in the context of the PEV in Kenya, the Prosecutor of the ICC was

---

101 Statement by Amina Mohamed, Minister of Foreign Affairs of Kenya, 2.

102 See also Protocol on Amendments to the Protocol on the Statute of the African Court of Justice and Human Rights, the so-called Malabo Protocol, that was adopted on 27 June 2014. This Protocol provides for an International Criminal Law Section of the African Court of Justice and Human and People's Rights. The Criminal Law Section will have jurisdiction over the most important international and transnational crimes, including but not limited to the so-called 'core crimes' of genocide, war crimes, crimes against humanity and aggression. It will furthermore have jurisdiction over a number of transnational crimes like terrorism, corruption and money laundering. It will also have jurisdiction over peculiar crimes like the crime of 'unconstitutional change of government'. For more on the Malabo Protocol, see https://www.amnesty.org/download/.../AFR0130632016ENGLISH.PDF

103 Statement by Amina Mohamed, Minister of Foreign Affairs of Kenya, 3.

104 Kenya proposed a text to clarify the application of Rule 68 of the Rules of Procedure and evidence, as well as the appointment of an ad hoc mechanism of 5 independent jurists to audit the Prosecutor's witness identification and recruitment processes in the case of *Prosecutor v William Ruto and Joshua Arap Sang*. See submission made

granted "unfettered access into Kenya" and an ICC field office was established to enhance co-operation and assistance regarding the Kenya situation. However, the Minister also remarked that the field office "has been operating without any interference, although regrettably it does so without adhering to agreed protocol with the host Government."[105]

Apart from the observations regarding Kenya's general relationship with the ICC and its continued co-operation with the ICC, the Minister also pointed to certain domestic developments as concrete examples of Kenya's commitment to the aims of international criminal justice generally and the Rome Statute specifically. For instance, the Minister noted that the President of Kenya has directed that 100 million US dollars be set aside as restorative justice funds for purposes of reparations for the victims of the PEV. To this end, a multi-sector committee has been established in order to spearhead the Presidential initiative regarding reparations for the victims of PEV.[106]

As we know, by March 2015, the case against President Kenyatta of Kenya was terminated by the ICC. But this in itself did not stop the negative rhetoric against the ICC. At the same time, it is evident from Kenya's participation in the session of the Assembly of States Parties at the end of 2015 that there was at the time no drastic move to unilaterally withdraw from the Rome Statute structures. Kenya was clearly unhappy about a number of things, as highlighted above. But there was still commitment to reform the ICC rather than to abandon it. Having said that, it must further be pointed out that the trajectory does not seem to be good in terms of Kenya's long-term participation in the ICC. This should not be seen in isolation. Kenya's legal and institutional relationship with the ICC is not a product of the ongoing investigations and cases at the ICC alone; it is also part of a broader narrative about the relationship between the ICC and the African Union.

The Kenyan government and the African Union have, on various occasions and on various platforms, expressed concerns, reservations, and later on open hostility towards the ICC.[107] This was not always the case but became so for

---

by Kenya on 3 November 2015 for the inclusion of two supplementary items in the agenda of the 14th Session of the Assembly of States Parties, available at https://www. icc-cpi.int/iccdocs/asp_docs/ASP14/ICC-ASP-14-35-Add2-ENG.pdf

105 Statement by Amina Mohamed, Minister of Foreign Affairs of Kenya, 5.
106 Ibid.
107 For more on this, see T. Murithi, 'The African Union and the International Criminal Court: An embattled relationship?' *Institute for Justice and Reconciliation, Policy Brief,* March 2013, available at http://www.ijr.org.za/publications/pdfs/IJR%20Policy%20Brief%20No%208%20Tim%20Miruthi.pdf; M. Swart and K. Krisch, 'Irreconcilable

mainly two reasons: (i) a growing narrative of "anti-African bias" pushed by the African Union and by the African political elite; and (ii) the growing sense that the ICC acted unfairly by indicting and continued with proceedings against sitting heads of state or government in Africa, notably President Al Bashir of Sudan and President Kenyatta of Kenya.

By January 2016, the uneasy relationship between the AU and the ICC, and between Kenya and the ICC, took a turn for the worse. It was reported that the AU has adopted a proposal by President Kenyatta of Kenya for the development of a so-called "road map" for the withdrawal of African states from the Rome Statute.[108] If this more radical stance seems to contradict Kenya's stance of critical engagement with, rather than abandonment of, the ICC as expressed at the November 2015 meeting of the Assembly of States Parties, then it is because it is in fact a contradiction. Only time will tell what the road map will ultimately look like. Rhetoric aside, from a legal point of view it should be noted that it is not so easy or straightforward for a state party to withdraw from the Rome Statute, which is a multilateral treaty. And Kenya's Constitution of 2010 is also clear on the role of international law, including treaties, in the domestic legal context. At any rate, even in the event that Kenya would withdraw from the ICC in terms of Article 127[109] of the Rome Statute, such withdrawal from the Rome Statute will not legally affect any cooperation with the ICC in connection with criminal investigations and proceedings in relation to which Kenya had a duty to cooperate and which were commenced prior to the date on which the withdrawal becomes effective.

While Kenya's official stance vis-à-vis the ICC hardened, developments at the trials of the remaining Kenyan accused further strengthened those critical of the role of the ICC in terms of efforts to seek justice for the victims of the post-election violence. As noted earlier, on 5 April 2016 Trial Chamber V(A) of the ICC decided

---

differences?', *African Journal of International Criminal Justice*, Issue 0 2014 (no pagination), available at http://www.elevenjournals.com/tijdschrift/AJ/2014/0/AJ_2352-068X_2014_001_000_003/fullscreen; A. Aidoo, 'Africa and the International Criminal Court: Moving the narrative forward', Humanity United 8 April 2015, available at https://humanityunited.org/africa-and-the-international-criminal-court-moving-the-narrative-forward/; S. Materu, *A strained relationship*, 211–228.

108 "Kenya: AU Adopts President Uhuru's Proposal for ICC Mass Withdrawal", Allafrica 31.1.2016, available at: http://allafrica.com/stories/201601310166.html

109 Article 127 of the Rome Statute of the ICC provides: "1. A State Party may, by written notification addressed to the Secretary-General of the United Nations, withdraw from this Statute. The withdrawal shall take effect one year after the date of receipt of the notification, unless the notification specifies a later date. 2. A State shall not be discharged, by reason of its withdrawal, from the obligations arising from this Statute

to terminate the case against Ruto and Sang.[110] The majority of the Chamber (per judges Fremr and Eboe-Osuji, each providing separate reasons; judge Carbuccia, in the minority, dissenting) essentially found that the Prosecution did not provide the Chamber with sufficient evidence on which a reasonable Trial Chamber could convict the accused. However, this finding by the majority does not amount to an acquittal, with the implication that a future re-institution of charges against the accused would in principle be possible.[111] The detailed reasoning of the judges will not be repeated here. Suffice to note that the majority were of the opinion that a reasonable trial chamber would not be able to convict Mr Ruto or Mr Sang on the basis of the evidence presented by the Prosecution. In this regard one can also note that the majority of the trial chamber differed from both the CIPEV report's main conclusions and the case for the Prosecution, namely that there was a signif-icant degree of centralised planning that preceded the post-election violence, and that both Ruto and Sang were linked to these actions.[112]

In Kenya, in some quarters a triumphant reaction emerged with respect to the decision by the ICC Trial Chamber in the matter of Ruto and Sang. Media reported[113] on the historic nature of the decision, namely that it was the first time that the ICC dismissed a case after the presentation of the Prosecution's case and without the defence case been presented (a procedure which in some national criminal justice systems is known as discharge at the end of the state's case[114]).

---

while it was Party to the Statute, including any financial obligations which may have accrued. Its withdrawal shall not affect any cooperation with the Court in connection with criminal investigations and proceedings in relation to which the withdrawing State had a duty to cooperate and which were commenced prior to the date on which the withdrawal became effective, nor shall it prejudice in any way the continued con-sideration of any matter which was already under consideration by the Court prior to the date on which the withdrawal became effective."

110 Decision on Defence Application for Judgment of Acquittal, *Prosecutor v William Samoei Ruto and Joshua Arap Sang* ICC-01/09-01/11, 5 April 2016.

111 Para 1 of the Decision reads as follows: "The charges against the accused are vacated and the accused discharged without prejudice to their prosecution afresh in future".

112 See Decision on Defence Application, para 123–131.

113 See, for instance, the assessment in The Nation, 26 April 2016, http://www. nation.co.ke/news/How-Bensouda-case-against-Ruto-fell-apart-before-it-began/-/1056/3176694/-/rnufe1z/-/index.html.

114 The procedure (quite common in Anglophone countries) has its origin in procedures governing trials by jury. See J.J. Joubert (ed), *Criminal Procedure Handbook* 10th ed Cape Town, 2011, 295–296; J. Doak and C. Mcgourlay, *Criminal Evidence in Context*, London, 2009, 6.

10. Constitutional Reform Instead of Domestic Change of the Judiciary

Institutional change in Kenya in the context of ICC decisions and ongoing ICC investigations must be evaluated with due regard to a number of narratives. There is the narrative of Kenya as a state party to the Rome Statute of the ICC; a state party that has fully implemented the Rome Statute into domestic law. This narrative reveals a number of important legislative and institutional developments that resulted from Kenya's membership of the ICC from the implementing legislation. The second narrative can be seen as a cruel challenge to and disruption of the first: The PEV which not only disrupted Kenya's political stability but also put to the test the domestic institutions such as the judiciary, the police and the government in general. Kenya's commitment to (international) criminal justice was put to the test. The third narrative concerns the drafting and acceptance of a new Constitution, together with transitional mechanisms that were aimed at dealing with the aftermath of the PEV. The Constitution of 2010 did not come about only as a transitional mechanism – the process of constitutional renewal started much earlier, already in the 1990s, but the Constitution of 2010, as a result of the PEV, quickly became a vehicle to deal with the aftermath of the PEV. The fourth narrative concerns the ICC investigations into the PEV, and the (now collapsed) cases against senior political leaders. Kenya's domestic constitutional commitments, its international commitments, and its relationship with the ICC were all put to the test. In this context, one should also note the role of regional politics via the African Union.

The narratives reveal that institutional change did occur in Kenya; and much of it can, in large part but not exclusively, be attributed to the fact that Kenya was not only a passive state party to the ICC but indeed subject to ICC investigations. So one can clearly see practical steps, for instance with regard to witnesses, that were required by the ICC. But other instances of domestic change, for instance the implementation of the Rome Statute legislation, came about as a result of treaty and constitutional considerations, and not because of any ICC decisions or because of the dynamics of co-operation in the context of ICC investigations. Some of the instances of domestic institutional change, for instance those concerning the judiciary and the police, came about because of constitutional imperatives, quite independent of any ICC decisions.

It is perhaps prudent to note that the Kenyan government's reaction against the ICC, as briefly discussed in this chapter, may yet turn out to be the most consequential domestic change, or, at least a catalyst for change. It will impact on an important commitment to international law in the Constitution of 2010. It may very well affect Kenya's domestic incorporation of international crimes and down the road, also Kenya's ability to deal with mass Human Rights violations. In that sense it may very well affect institutions such as the Specialised Division in the office of the Director of Public Prosecutions, and the International Crimes Division of the High Court. If Kenya is going to make good on the political threat to leave the ICC, and at the same time keep the institutions associated with the domestication of international criminal justice (such as the specialised unit in the office of the DPP or the International Crimes Division of the High Court), it will at least show some commitment to the quest to end impunity for crimes under international law, and if it can be done without the assistance or member-ship of the ICC, then in an important sense it will be a fulfilment and a validation of the complementarity rationale. But the latter scenario seems unlikely, at least for the foreseeable future.

The ICC was not exclusively responsible for important institutional change in Kenya concerning international criminal justice imperatives, but it certainly contributed in a very substantial way.

Vjollca Krasniqi

War, Law, and Justice in Kosovo

At a first glance, Kosovo provides a shining example of how international criminal tribunals can trigger domestic legal and institutional reform in countries
under their jurisdiction. In recent years, transitional justice institutions have
spread like mushrooms in Kosovo and legal change has been frequent. The
result is that Kosovo hosts a whole number of new institutions – from specialized courts and prosecutors who are empowered to investigate, prosecute and
judge perpetrators of Human Rights abuses and war-related atrocities to a hybrid
court that deals with very specific crimes. Kosovo has incorporated international
crimes, which are under the jurisdiction of the ICTY, into its legislation and it
has ratified a whole range of international criminal law concepts and Human
Rights conventions. However, as the following chapter will show, this was not
due to pressure from the ICTY, which Kosovo, its institutions, media and public
opinion withstood or even openly defied, but to other factors, which have
nothing to do with the ICTY.

1. The Yugoslav Wars, Kosovo and the ICTY

The ICTY was the first institution after the Nuremberg War Crimes Tribunal to
prosecute violations of international law. UN Security Resolution 808,[1] which
led to the creation of the court in May 1993, entrusted the ICTY with targeting
humanitarian law breaches—from 1 January 1991 on[2]—by Serb military and
paramilitary forces in Croatia and BiH, who had engaged in large-scale atrocities. Yet, the ICTY was also established as an ad hoc subsidiary body of the UN
Security Council, serving as a legal and political framework for the maintenance
and restoration of international peace and security.[3] This two-fold mission—the

---

1   United Nations Security Council Resolution 808, 22 February 1993, available at: http://
     www.icty.org/x/file/Legal%20Library/Statute/statute_808_1993_en.pdf.
2   United Nations Security Resolution827, 25 May 1993, available at: http://www.icty.
     org/x/file/Legal%20Library/Statute/statute_827_1993_en.pdf.
3   M. Futamura and J. Gow, 'The strategic purpose of the ICTY and international peace
     and security', in: James Gow, Rachel Kerr and Zoran Pajić (eds.), *Prosecuting War
     Crimes: Lessons and Legacies of the International Criminal Tribunal for the Former
     Yugoslavia*, London and New York, 2014, 20.

prosecution of individuals suspected of war crimes and maintaining political stability[4]—constituted in Kinglsey Chiedu Moghalu words, "a bundle of contradictions, a showcase of the tensions between liberal legalism, realism, and the international society perspective."[5]

The practical implementation of the ICTY's jurisdiction was initially limited to Croatia and BiH, because the crime scenes were in these countries. Until 1998, no international crimes (in the sense of the ICTY's subject matter jurisdiction) were committed on the territory of the other Yugoslav republics. There was no war in Kosovo, but the Serbian government had established an apartheid-like political order with mass violations of Kosovo Albanians' Human Rights. The Kosovo Albanians opposed the regime of Slobodan Milošević by engaging in peaceful resistance and organizing parallel structures of state institutions and civil society.[6] The non-violent resistance approach was challenged in 1996 with armed resistance groups taking hold in Kosovo. The Kosovo Liberation Army (KLA) entered into guerilla fighting against Serbian security forces, which resulted in severe reprisals. In early 1998, the ICTY claimed jurisdiction in Kosovo,[7] as the war-like situation in Kosovo was then underway and because of the increasing violence that had prompted NATO military intervention—with an aerial bombing campaign lasting 78 days—from March to June 1999.

2. An Overview over Kosovo's Legal System

The legal system in Kosovo is built on the legal tradition of the former Yugoslavia. With the federal constitutional changes enacted in 1974, Kosovo received its own constitution, assembly, Supreme Court, and constitutional court. It shared criminal and civil procedure codes with the rest of the former Yugoslavia; it had its

4 Futamura and Gow, *The strategic purpose*, 25. See also M. I. Khan, 'Historical Record and the legacy of the International Criminal Tribunal for the former Yugoslavia' in: J. Gow, R. Kerr and Z. Pajić (eds.), *Prosecuting War Crimes: Lessons and Legacies of the International Criminal Tribunal for the Former Yugoslavia*, London and New York 2014, pp. 88–102.

5 K. C. Moghalu, *Global Justice: The Politics of War Crimes Trials*, Westport, Connecticut, London, 50.

6 H. Clark, *Civil Resistance in Kosovo*, London 2000.

7 Prosecutor's Statement Regarding the Tribunal's Jurisdiction over Kosovo, The Hague, 10 March 1998, CC/PIO/302-E, *available at:* http://www.icty.org/sid/7683.

own criminal code, augmented by federal and Serbian provisions.[8] Following the abolition of Kosovo's 1974 Constitution by the Milošević regime in 1989, the laws of Serbia trumped Yugoslav federal laws in Kosovo. This coincided with the adoption of highly discriminatory Serbian policies against Kosovo Albanians.

The practice of lawmaking in the aftermath of the Kosovo War was shaped by the legacy of socialist Yugoslavia and the administration of the international community. The mandate of the United Nations Mission in Kosovo (UNMIK), which took over the administration of Kosovo in 1999, was set out in UN Security Council Resolution 1244.[9] The main purpose was to ensure the establishment and efficient functioning of Kosovo institutions.[10] UNMIK had executive power, which permitted it to issue legislative acts framed as regulations. The UN exercised its power to enforce legal provisions in Kosovo well beyond the time the Kosovo parliament was established following the first national elections in the fall of 2001. Indeed, UNMIK regulations were made into laws. Moreover, new laws approved by the Kosovo parliament had to be sanctioned by the Special Representative of the Secretary General of the United Nations (SRSG). Thus, UNMIK was the final legal authority until Kosovo's independence in 2008.[11]

The decision to vest supreme authority in UNMIK—and to allow it to dominate other social domains, political processes and institution-building—opened the UN up to various criticisms. It was pointed out that there was a serious lack of ownership by Kosovars in policy making and that such a political system, which had more in common with a dictatorship than democracy, ran counter to the international community's democratization agenda. The vast powers of the

8   American Bar Association, 'Judicial Reform Index for Kosovo' October 2010, available at: http://www.americanbar.org/content/dam/aba/directories/roli/kosovo/kosovo_jri_vol_iv_12_2010_en.authcheckdam.pdf, p. 17.
9   UN Security Resolution 1244 (1999), available at: http://daccess-dds-ny.un.org/doc/UNDOC/GEN/N99/172/89/PDF/N9917289.pdf?OpenElement.
10   UNMIK administration was organized along four main areas encompassing: 1) police and justice; 2) civil administration; 3) institution building, and 4) economic reconstruction.
11   After independence, the two EU missions – the International Civilian Office (ICO) and the European Rule of Law Mission (EULEX) replaced UNMIK to supervise the transition to Kosovo's full independence. Indeed, as set out in the Comprehensive Proposal for Kosovo States Settlement known as the Ahtisaari Plan – the foundational document for the independence of Kosovo, the role of the ICO was to supervise the implementation of the status settlement of Kosovo. EULEX is part of European Security and Defence Mission also part of the Ahtisaari settlement charged with work on the judiciary, law, and customs.

SRSG[12] and later the Special Representative of the European Union were specifically mentioned as being anti-democratic and smacking of neo-colonialism. The immunity of the international personnel employed by UNMIK, even when faced with serious crimes, was also faulted on the grounds that it sanctioned impunity.[13]

It is true, as Mark Baskin has stressed, that the reconstruction of the justice system in Kosovo was a gargantuan undertaking: it entailed a transformation from "socialist legal precepts to one rooted in rule of law as well as from one rooted in discrimination and exclusion to one rooted in heterogeneity and inclusion."[14] But the initial UNMIK approach to the restoration of the justice sector in Kosovo was met with objection and opposition. UNMIK's decision to endorse as applicable laws those that were in force on 24 March 1999, or the date on which the NATO bombing campaign began, was severely criticized by Kosovo Albanians who viewed them as discriminatory. Such a move by UNMIK was more than a tactical error in the post-war reconstruction and institution building in Kosovo. It signified that the international protectorate was devoid of any historical perspective and the lived experiences of discrimination and violence induced under that body of law. To address this criticism, UNMIK subsequently adopted a new regulation, endorsing the legal framework that existed before Kosovo's autonomy was abolished in 1989 as applicable laws.[15]

3. Kosovo and the ICTY: Enacting Institutional Reform

The vested power on law enforcement in post-war Kosovo, with the UNMIK administration and the SRSG at the helm, was known as "reserved competence." It included the prosecution of war crimes and— as referred in the framing of UNMIK—war and ethnic crimes. Among the first UNMIK

---

12 V. Ingimundarson, "'The Last Colony in Europe': The New Empire, Democratization and Nation-Building", in: V. Ingimundarson, K. Loftsdóttir, I. Erlingsdóttir (eds), Topographies of Globalization: Politics, Culture, Language, Reykjavik 2004, 67–91.

13 R. Caplan, *International Governance of War-Torn Territories: Rule and Reconstruction*, Oxford 2005, 209–210.

14 M. Baskin, 'Lessons Learned on UNMIK Judiciary', *Report Commissioned by the Department of Foreign Affairs and International Trade of the Government of Canada* 2001, available at: http://siteresources.worldbank.org/INTLAWJUSTINST/Resources/lessonsKosovoJudiciary.pdf, p. 6.

15 UNMIK Regulation No. 1999/24, available at: http://www.unmikonline.org/regulations/1999/reg24-99.htm.

regulations, which *de facto* were laws, was that of 1999/6, laying the ground for the structure and administration of the judiciary and prosecution service in Kosovo.[16] The Technical Advisory Commission on Judiciary and Prosecution Service which was appointed on the basis of this regulation "urged the establishment of a special court, to be known as the Kosovo War and Ethnic Crimes Court (KWECC) to hear cases involving breaches of international humanitarian law or ethnically based crimes."[17] The KWECC was envisaged as an intermediary between the ICTY and national/local courts. This proposal did not materialize, as political stability was given primacy over justice. Indeed, the authority for the investigation and prosecution of war crimes in Kosovo rested with UNMIK, or more precisely, the UNMIK Department of Justice and the UNMIK police along with the ICTY. The KWECC may have been viewed as a small ICTY and hence a duplication of it. But it was the budgetary concerns about the high start-up costs and salaries of the international judges, which resulted in the rejection of the proposal in September 2000. In fact, UNMIK had already embraced a hybrid approach to criminal justice, with special panels comprising two international judges and one Kosovo judge, and an international persecutor/investigator.[18]

The ICTY's field office in Kosovo was closed down at the end of 2012, as part of the court's Completion Strategy. Its mandate was to reach out to the communities affected by the work of the Tribunal and to act as a liaison between the ICTY and national authorities on case related and other matters. It also engaged in "capacity building" of the judiciary and extended cooperation with civil society organizations.[19] The Kosovo Albanians had high initial hopes about the ICTY for the persecutions of war crimes by the Yugoslav, Serb military and paramilitary forces. They believed the ICTY was not just an instrument of justice but also could become an instrument of the nation and state building project.

However, the high public support for the ICTY faded away with the trials against Kosovo Albanian suspects, especially those of the ex-KLA

---

16 UNMIK Regulation No. 1999/6 On Recommendations for the Structure and Administration of the Judiciary and Prosecution Service, available at:, http://www. unmikonline.org/regulations/1999/re99_06.pdf.

17 M. C. Bassiouni, 'Mixed Models of International Criminal Justice', in: M. CherifBassiouni (ed.), *International Criminal Law*, vol. 3, International Enforcement, Leiden, Brill 2008, 162.

18 Ibid.

19 ICTY press release, "Tribunal Closes Offices in Croatia and Kosovo", (31.12.2012), available at: http://www.icty.org/sid/11180.

commanders, Fatmir Limaj[20] and Ramush Haradinaj.[21] Not only did the ICTY indictees enjoy the public support among the Kosovo Albanians, but also of the Kosovo government, which provided full political backing. Kosovo Albanian elites and the government expressed their solidarity with those indicted by the ICTY in both political and moral terms. This support related broadly to the defence of the KLA's armed resistance as part of fighting a just war of liberation. Yet, the Kosovo institutions did not provide any financial support for those indicted by the ICTY. In the cases of the ICTY trials of Limaj and Haradinaj, various private organizations raised money for their defence. Thus, the Limaj and Haradinaj legal defence funds were created, which were subsequently criticized for their lack of transparency.[22]

4. Judicial Reform in Kosovo 1999–2015: International Criminal Law in the National Legislation

International law has gained increasing importance within the international system and politics since the end of the Cold War. Many states have incorporated it into national laws or extended domestic criminal law to accommodate such concepts.[23] This has also been the case in Kosovo. Kosovo's statehood is envisioned in the Comprehensive Proposal for Kosovo Status Settlement—the Ahtisaari Plan[24]—which was adopted after the failed negotiations on Kosovo's futures status between Kosovo and Serbia under the auspices of the UN.[25] The Ahtisaari Plan set out the principles for an independent and accessible judiciary. It dealt with the structural changes in the justice system, foreseeing a transition

---

20 See ICTY Case Information Sheet IT-03-66 Limaj et al., available at: http://www.icty.org/x/cases/limaj/cis/en/cis_limaj_al_en.pdf.
21 Prosecutor v. Haradinaj, Balaj, and Brahimaj, Case No. IT-04-84-I, Indictment Decision, 64 (4 March 2005) [hereinafter Haradinaj et al. ICTY indictment], available at: http://www.icty.org/x/cases/haradinaj/ind/en/har-ii050224e.pdf.
22 E. Peci, 'Kosovo: Shadowy Funds Raise Corruption Fears', Balkan Investigative Reporting, 23.12.2013, available at: http://www.balkaninsight.com/en/article/kosovo-shadowy-funds-raise-corruption-fears.
23 Moghalu, *Global Justice*, 33–34.
24 See: The Comprehensive Proposal for Kosovo Status Settlement, available at: http://www.unosek.org/unosek/en/statusproposal.html .
25 The status talks that began in 2006 between the Albanians and Serbs as part of a UN-led negotiating process resulted in non-agreement between both parties. A UN plan ensued, calling for supervised Kosovo's independence. The Kosovar Albanians declared independence on 17 February 2008.

from UNMIK to Kosovo authorities.[26] Furthermore, it ensured representation of ethnic minorities in the institutions of justice.

In Kosovo, the law related to violations of international law is a combination of both the Criminal Code of socialist Yugoslavia and the Criminal Code of Kosovo, which was adopted in 2003. Chapter XV of the Criminal Code embeds the values protected under international law.[27] It outlaws genocide, crimes against humanity, war crimes (grave violations of the Geneva Conventions concerning international and internal armed conflicts) and provisions against the recruitment and use of child soldiers. In addition, the Criminal Code bans the employment of prohibited means or methods of warfare, unjustified delay in repatriating prisoners of war or civilians, unlawful appropriation of objects from those killed or wounded on the battlefield, endangering negotiators, the organization of groups to commit genocide, responsibility of commanders and other leaders, and instigating war of aggression or armed conflict.[28]

5. The Court System and Institutional Reform

The highest judicial authority in Kosovo is the Supreme Court. Ethnicity is an important element in its composition; 15 per cent of the judges of the court have to come from ethnic minority backgrounds. Lower courts also need to include judges coming from ethnic minorities. The Office of the Special Prosecutor has jurisdiction in cases of genocide, crimes against humanity, and war crimes.[29]

---

26 The Comprehensive Proposal for Kosovo Status Settlement.

27 Code No. 04/L-082, Criminal Code of the Republic of Kosovo, 2012, Chapter XV, available at: http://www.assembly-kosova.org/common/docs/ligjet/Criminal%20Code.pdf.

28 Criminal Code of the Republic of Kosovo, art. 148–162. The following international agreements and conventions are also directly applicable according to the Constitution: (1) The Universal Declaration of Human Rights; (2) the European Convention for the Protection of Human Rights and Fundamental Freedoms and its Protocols; (3) the International Covenant on Civil and Political Rights and its Protocols; (4) the Council of Europe Framework Convention for the Protection of National Minorities; (5) the Convention on the Elimination of All Forms of Racial Discrimination; (6) the Convention on the Elimination of All Forms of Discrimination Against Women; (7) the Convention on the Rights of the Child; (8) and the Convention against Torture and Other Cruel, Inhumane or Degrading Treatment or Punishment. Constitution of the Republic of Kosovo, *available at:* http://kryeministri-ks.net/zck/repository/docs/Constitution.of.the.Republic.of.Kosovo.pdf, art. 22.

29 Criminal Code of the Republic of Kosovo, art. 441.

European Union Rule of Law Mission in Kosovo (EULEX), which was part of the Ahtisaari Plan, has jurisdiction in cases of human trafficking, racial and/or ethnic crimes, sexual crimes, economic crimes and corruption.[30]

Two additional important laws are the Law on the Courts[31] and the Law on the Kosovo Judicial Council,[32] which were adopted in 2010. Following the 2008 independence of Kosovo along with the reconfiguration of UNMIK and deployment of EULEX, 450 sitting judges underwent an internationally-led vetting process, which was open to all interested persons. In total, 898 persons took part in the process, which was carried out by the Kosovo Judicial Council and the Independent Judicial and Prosecutorial Commission and which was supported financially by the EU and the United States.[33]

The practice of appointing local judges and prosecutors by UNMIK's executive institutions was premised on a fixed-term renewable contract. Judges are now recruited and proposed by the Kosovo Judicial Council,[34] with final appointment by the President of Kosovo. EULEX judges and prosecutors were initially appointed by the governments that took part in post-independence institution building. Unlike the UNMIK judges, who could not be dismissed or sanctioned for misconduct, the EULEX judges can be removed.[35]

6. Witness Protection

One of the major obstacles to the prosecution of war crimes in Kosovo—as well as in other parts of the former Yugoslavia—has been the lack of a witness

---

30 Criminal Code of the Republic of Kosovo, art. 442.
31 Law No. 03/L-199 On Courts, 2010, available at: http://www.assembly-kosova.org/common/docs/ligjet/2010-199-eng.pdf.
32 Law No. 03/L-223 On The Kosovo Judicial Council, 2010, *available at:* http://www.kuvendikosoves.org/common/docs/ligjet/2010-223-eng.pdf.
33 UNDP, 'Perceptions on Transitional Justice' New York, UNDP 2012, available at: http://www.ks.undp.org/content/dam/kosovo/docs/TJ/English-Web_965257.pdf, p.:36.
34 Striving for an impartiality and independence of the judicial system in Kosovo, an institution charged to ensure this, as accorded by the Constitution, is the Kosovo Judicial Council. It comprises of 13 members, elected on a five years term. See Constitution of the Republic of Kosovo, Article 108.
35 OSCE, 'Independence of the Judiciary in Kosovo: Institutional and Functional Dimensions'"OSCE report, January 2012 *available at:* http://www.osce.org/kosovo/87138?download=true, pp. 12–13.

protection laws and programmes.[36] Difficulties in securing witness testimony also characterized the ICTY trials.[37] In Kosovo, intimidation, fear, and silence have left an imprint on the justice system and its efficacy. More seriously, it has affected the fate of the witnesses themselves, even if they had entered the witness protection programme.[38]

As set out in UNMIK Department of Justice Circular 2003/5, UNMIK was responsible for witness protection. The ICTY requests for evidence as well as witness protection fell under the mandate of UNMIK's Department of Justice and police. Witness protection, however, was considered one of the weakest points in UNMIK's administration of justice. Indeed, it was only three years after this Circular was issued that UNMIK developed a legal protection programme.[39] UNMIK's Witness Protection Unit was in charge of the physical security and witness relocation of witnesses in cases of organized crime, trafficking in persons, and war crimes.[40] The reasons for weak witness protection were attributed to structural deficiencies and Kosovo's "culture" of justice. Structural deficiencies and institutional inefficiency were usually not cited as contributing factors. Yet, weak court infrastructure eventually prompted the U.S. and UK governments to start a programme designed to upgrade courts in Kosovo, for example by providing them with equipment (closed-circuit television), which are considered crucial for witness protection.[41]

Obstacles to witness protection were seen as a result of the demographic structure of Kosovo as a small country with close kinship ties. They were also regarded in connection to the legacy of oppression and discrimination of the Kosovo Albanians during the reign of Slobodan Milošević. This, it was said, resulted in a culture of distrust in the justice system and an enduring (lack of)

---

36 See: Human Rights Watch, 'Justice at Risk: Justice at Risk: War Crimes Trials in Croatia, BiH, and Serbia and Montenegro' New York, Human Rights Watch 2004, available at: http://www.refworld.org/docid/42c3bcf70.html.

37 See Prosecutor v Ramush Haradinaj, Idriz Balaj and Lahi Brahimaj, ICTY Judgment, *available at:* http://www.icty.org/x/cases/haradinaj/tjug/en/080403.pdf.

38 M. Brunwasser, 'Death of War Crimes Witness Casts Cloud on Kosovo', The New York Times, 6.10.2011, available at: http://www.nytimes.com/2011/10/07/world/europe/death-of-war-crimes-witness-casts-cloud-on-kosovo.html?_r=0.

39 OSCE, *Witness Security and Protection in Kosovo: Assessment and Recommendations*, Vienna, OSCE 2007, available at: http://www.osce.org/kosovo/28552?download=true , p. 5.

40 OSCE, Witness Security and Protection in Kosovo, 8.

41 OSCE, *Witness Security and Protection in Kosovo,* 9.

culture that does not value testifying as witnesses of crimes as a moral duty.[42] Indeed, there were also several cases in which the media violated witness protection policies. This led the ICTY to enact an indictment against journalists. The journalist Baton Haxhiu was, for example, charged with breaching the anonymity of the prosecution witnesses in the Haradinaj et al. ICTY case;[43] he was, subsequently, found guilty of contempt and fined 15,000 euros.[44] The lack of funds, expertise and a sound legal framework undoubtedly played a far greater role in hampering the witness protection programme than a culture of judicial distrust.

To increase accountability in Kosovo, a law on witness protection went into effect in 2012. This law regulates special and extraordinary measures and procedures for witness protection and justice cooperation.[45] Grounds for the application of protection measures have included criminal offences against international law.[46] The types of protection listed in the law include physical protection; temporary re-location; change of residence; change of identity; financial support; social and legal assistance; access to data and information; and protection for persons in custody and in correctional institutions.[47] The law stipulates the establishment of a committee for witness protection made up of the State Prosecutor, the head of the investigation unit of the Kosovo Police, and the Director of the Witness Protection Directorate. The Witness Protection Directorate is a specialized unit under the direct supervision of the General Director of the Kosovo Police. It is charged with the implementation of witness protection measures. The law accords the Directorate a special fund, which is managed by the Director of Witness Protection Directorate in accordance with special instructions approved by the Minister of Interior and the Minister of Finance. The funding for the implementation of the witness protection law comes from the Kosovo state budget. However, the law stipulates that it can also be financed from international resources and programs.[48]

---

42 Ibid.

43 See ICTY Press Release, Baton Haxhiu Indicted for Contempt of Court, available at: http://www.icty.org/sid/9886.

44 ICTY Press Release, Kosovo journalist found guilty of contempt, 24.7.2008, available at: http://www.haguejusticeportal.net/Docs/ICTY/Baton%20Haxhiu%20-%20 Press%20Release%20-%20Guilty%20of%20Contempt.pdf.

45 Law No 04/L-015 On Witness Protection, 2011, *available a t*http://www.md- ks.org/ repository/docs/law_on_witness_protection.pdf

46 Ibid.: Article 4.

47 Ibid.: Article 5.

48 Ibid.: Article 5; Article 15, Article 17, Article 29, Article 32.

Finally, the law allows EULEX to engage in witness protection as part of the Kosovo judiciary in its capacity of "capacity building"; training, organizational development of the directorate; and assistance in establishing contact and coop- eration agreements with witness protection units in other countries. The law also foresees the EULEX Witness Security Unit and the EULEX Security Review Group.[49] Effecting the broad scope of the law, it gives EULEX the authority to run a special witness protection programme, which is independent of that of Kosovo.

7. Prosecuting Sexual Violence and Breaking the Silence on Wartime Rape

History shows that post-war legal language, whether it involves retributive or restorative justice, is never neutral. Judicial processes need not only to take into account ethnicity but also gender. There is a built-in gender-bias when it comes to justice mechanisms, especially on sexual violence in war. In the 1990s, rape and sexual violence were specifically codified for the first time as a recognizable and independent crime by the jurisprudence of the ICTY and the International Crime Tribunal for Rwanda (ICTR). The rape camps in BiH and the widespread occurrence of rape during the genocide in Rwanda played an important role in the emergence of the respective verdicts.

The problem of rape is, of course, universal: in Kosovo, Rwanda, East Timor, and Sierra Leone, women and girls are still reeling from the aftermath of having been herded together and sexually violated in war. Women have had a hard time recounting rape experiences before the ICTY because of the court's stereotyp- ical gender framework and because they risk social exclusion at home. As Julie Mertus has observed, war crimes trials do not adequately meet the needs of survivors. With reference to the handling of testimonies of women raped in the Bosnian War, she has criticized the ICTY specifically on two grounds. First, the meta-narrative of women as victims underpins the tribunal's logic when dealing with sexual violence. Such a narrative takes away any agency from women. That preconceived notion of victimhood (read: all women are victims or possible victims whether in peace or war) places women (in this case, women who sur- vived rape) in an existing schema. Mertus argues that in such a construction, the pre-imagined victim is the actor and that the story of the raped woman is listened to but not heard. Second, Mertus argues that the tribunal is not victim-centered

---

49 Ibid.: Article 32.

and that victims' needs are never fully accommodated. In other words, the trials are de-humanizing and re-traumatizing experiences for women who testify at the ICTY.[50]

The social landscape for survival—or how wartime victims of rape overcome radical discontinuities—is rarely heard at the trial. This not only shows the need for gender-based remedies for conducting war crimes trials; it also points to the requirement of complementary processes, such as civil suits for compensation and welfare protection. Theda Skocpol has argued that the origins of social policy "reside in the political processes and ideas that mobilize constituencies to create legislation."[51] Hence, it is important to look at how war-affected categories—combatants and civilians—have been accommodated in social policies and welfare programs. During the Kosovo War, rape and the sexual assault of women were both part of a military strategy and of a political campaign aimed at ethnic cleansing. Thus, sexual crimes were a weapon of war. Gathering first-hand accounts of rape has proved very difficult. It has been estimated that around 20,000 women were raped during the Kosovo War. Kosovo women have found it impossible to reveal what they have been through (primarily because of severe traumatization, feelings of shame, lack of trust, fear of reprisals against themselves and their families, and the social stigma associated with their victimhood) and to bring their lives to some kind of normality. Hence, silence became the strategic choice of women who endured sexual violence in war until 2012, when legal recognition of war affected injuries appeared on the agenda.

The legislation that shaped the redefinition of citizenship and welfare rights—and proved to be the most controversial piece of legislation among international and local actors in Kosovo—is without doubt the law on war victims, veterans, and war invalids.[52] As the primary legislation that regulates reparations for civilian victims of war and their families, this law ignored the category of the survivors of wartime sexual violence and rape. To counter this omission—and in an act of solidarity with the women survivors of rape—the Kosova Women's

50 J. Mertus, 'Shouting from the bottom of the well: the impact of international trials for wartime rape on women's agency', *International Feminist Journal of Politics* vol. 6. No.1, 2004, 110–128.

51 T. Skocpol, *Protecting Soldiers and Mothers: The Politics of Social Policy in the United States*, Cambridge 1992.

52 The Law on the Status and the Rights of the Martyrs, Invalids, Veterans and Members of the Kosovo Liberation Army, Civilian Victims of War and their Families, 2011, available at: http://www.assembly-kosova.org/common/docs/ligjet/Law%20on%20 the%20status%20of%20the%20martyrs.pdf

Network (KWN) chose to break the silence. It staged protests and campaigned for the recognition of women survivors of rape in the legislation on war categories so that they would be entitled to social benefits. The KWN was aware of the cultural and societal risks posed by disclosures of rape and sexual assault of women survivors. Yet, they regarded wartime rape as an issue of justice and a women's rights issue, and, hence, decided to fight for legal recognition to ensure welfare provisions for women who survived sexual violence in war.

On 8 March 2012, to mark Women's International Day, the KWN engaged in protests to demand justice for survivors of wartime sexual violence. The protest manifesto stated the following:

> Thirteen years after the war in Kosovo, women who were raped still have not received the justice they deserve. There has yet to be a single conviction for this heinous crime perpetrated against hundreds of women during the war in 1998 and 1999. These women deserve respect and support from governmental institutions and civil society. Rather than giving flowers to the women they love and respect, the Kosovo Women's Network calls upon fellow citizens to stand up and demand justice for the many women for whom justice has been blind. The protest will call upon the Government of Kosovo to acknowledge the crime that was committed against women and to provide them with legal protection equivalent to that received by men who suffered war crimes.[53]

The manifesto of the protesters was directed at the Kosovo government, but it also encouraged civil society to join the Women's Movement in making visible the issue of wartime rape and for recognition of it as an issue of justice, which the state should act upon.

These protest actions brought wartime rape to the public arena and led to debates in the parliament of Kosovo. What is more, the issue created a rift between women activists and women parliamentarians on the one hand, and the political parties in power and the opposition on the other. The Women's Movement demanded that the survivors of wartime rape be recognized by law and accorded entitlement rights. Such demands were met with rejection from the women parliamentarians, especially from the *Partia Demokratike e Kosovës* (Democratic League of Kosovo – PDK), the party, which was the senior government party. Yet, the amendment to include wartime rape as a distinct category in the body of law was supported by women of one of the opposition parties, *Vetëvendosje* (Self-determination), which also pushed for an amendment of the

---

53 Kosovo Women's Network, "Forget Flowers: Women Call for Justice for War-Raped Women on 8 March" Kosova Women's Network, March 2012, available at: http://www.womensnetwork.org/documents/20130213223130717.pdf.

law in order to include rape and sexual violence in war. Kosovo's visibility in transnational initiatives such as the one launched by British Foreign Secretary, William Hague, on global action against rape as weapon of war, played a great role in bringing wartime rape to the fore in the public.

The opposition to recognition of wartime rape in Kosovo was grounded in material justifications; it was presented as a legal welfare issue, which would burden the Kosovo budget. Hence, it could not be enacted in law. The amendments to the law on war victims to include women survivors of war rape had initially foreseen a pension of 300 euros per month. This proposal was changed to 100 euros to balance it with the rest of the social schemes in Kosovo, for example, the disability pension. Finally, in March 2014, the Parliament of Kosovo adopted amendments to the law on war-affected categories to include the survivors of wartime sexual violence.[54] Indeed, women, who survived sexual violence in war, are now entitled to welfare protection. Wartime rape is not counted as a form of disability but damage affected by war. However, women are entitled to the same benefits as war veterans. This long process for legal recognition was hailed as a victory for women's groups in Kosovo.

8. International and "Internationalized" Domestic War Crimes Prosecutions

The ICTY trials related to the Kosovo War included several Serb state, military and police officials. The most notable trial—and the one that attracted much media attention, internationally and in Kosovo—was the trial of Slobodan Milošević. He was the first sitting head of state to be charged with war crimes and crimes against humanity, when the ICTY indicted him in 1999. The trial of Milošević stretched over a five-year period—from 2002 to 2006—and was finally cut short by his death in his ICTY cell.[55] Other ICTY trials dealing with war crimes committed in Kosovo have included the trial of former Serb political, military and police officials: the prosecutor v. Milutinović et. al., known as the "Kosovo six," where five out of six defendants were found guilty, except Milutinović,[56] and the Prosecutor v. Šainović et al.,[57] where three of the indicted

---

54 Law On the Status and Rights of the Martyrs, Invalids, Veterans, members of the Kosova Liberation Army, Civilian Victims and their Families, art. 5.

55 On the ICTY trial of Slobodan Milošević see T. W. Waters (ed.), *The Milošević Trial: An Autopsy*. Oxford New York 2013.

56 The Prosecutor v. Milutinović et al., IT-05-87-T.

57 The Prosecutor v. Šainović et al IT-05-87

were found guilty.[58] A number of individuals from Kosovo were tried at the ICTY. Two cases involved Kosovo Albanian ex-KLA commanders and combatants: The Prosecutor v. Limaj et al. the Limaj et al.[59] and The Prosecutor v. Haradinaj et al.[60] In the Limaj et al. case, Balaj was found guilty; Limaj and Musliu, however, were acquitted.[61] In the Haradinaj et al. case, Brahimaj was found guilty in 2008, but acquitted after a partial retrial along with Haradinaj and Balaj, who were found not guilty.[62]

8.1. From UNMIK to EULEX: Hybrid War Crimes Trials

When the UN Security Council agreed on the terms for the withdrawal of UNMIK in favour of EULEX at the end of 2008, many Kosovo Albanians strongly criticized the fact that EULEX would deploy on the basis of Security Council Resolution 1244. It refers to Kosovo as part of the Federal Republic of Yugoslavia, whose "sovereignty and territorial integrity" it reaffirmed. It was seen as a negation of the declaration of independence. Kosovo accepted limitations to its sovereignty by inviting EULEX and granting it executive powers in key areas in return for assistance in rebuilding the judicial system. In fact, the court system was paralleled by a Serb court system, indeed an extension of the Serb state institutions and governed by the Serb state.[63] Hence, Kosovo hoped that EULEX would extend Kosovo's sovereignty across the entire territory, particularly the north. The Kosovo Serbs living in northern Kosovo view Kosovo as part of Serbia, reject the Prishtina administration, and treat the state of Kosovo as non-existent.

In Kosovo, war crimes suspects have been investigated by the international investigators of the ICTY, UNMIK police, and EULEX. No Kosovo police officers took part in those investigations. Around 1,187 acts of suspected war crimes from the Kosovo War, which were identified by UNMIK, were handed over to

---

58 Sense Agency: "Joint Criminal Enterprise Confirmed, Slightly Milder Sentences" 23.1.2014, available at: http://www.sense-agency.com/icty/joint-criminal-enterprise-confirmed-slightly-milder-sentences.29.html?news_id=15661

59 The Prosecutor v. Limaj et al. IT-03-66.

60 The Prosecutor v. Haradinaj et. al. IT-04-84.

61 Case information sheet, IT-03-66 Limaj et. al. available at: http://www.icty.org/x/cases/limaj/cis/en/cis_limaj_al_en.pdf.

62 Case Information Sheet, IT-04-84 Haradinaj et. al. *available at:* http://www.icty.org/x/cases/haradinaj/cis/en/cis_haradinaj_al_en.pdf.

63 OSCE, "Parallel Structures in Kosovo 2006–2007", Vienna, OSCE available at: http://www.osce.org/kosovo/24618?download=true, p. 14

Table 1 EULEX: Handling of War Crimes 2008–2014.

Number of cases	Dismissed/Closed due to lack of evidence	Pending/ On-going	Adjudicated	Missing Persons	Wartime rape and sexual violence	War crimes Cases	On-going war crimes trials
1200	500	600	15	216	51	100	5

Source: http://www.eulex-kosovo.eu

EULEX. Of those, 50 cases have been referred for indictment.[64] As presented in Table 1 below, 500 cases have been closed or dismissed due to lack of evidence. Moreover, as trials *in absentia* are not allowed in war crimes cases in Kosovo, many cases are suspended indefinitely. There are 300 cases pending with Kosovo and EULEX prosecutors. In total, EULEX has adjudicated 15 war crimes cases, seven involved Serb defendants, and eight involved Albanian defendants. There are 216 active cases on missing persons. EULEX has initiated 51 new war crimes cases, including the first-ever investigations into cases where acts of sexual violence or rape have been assessed as war crimes. Kosovo and EULEX prosecutors are currently investigating 100 war-crimes cases. There are five on-going war-crimes trials.[65]

The crimes related to the Kosovo War and "high profile" corruption cases were tried by "hybrid panels," initially by UNMIK-appointed judges and later by EULEX and Kosovo judges. These panels have been made up of two international judges and one Kosovo judge. The "hybrid panels" require translation from from English into local languages and vice-versa (just as in the case of the ICTY trials[66]) since the international judges lack the knowledge of the local languages spoken in Kosovo. According to the Law on Use of Languages in Kosovo, the Albanian and Serbian language enjoy an equal status in Kosovo institutions. In Kosovo municipalities inhabited by at least five per cent of the total population of non-majority ethnicity, that language is regarded as an official language. Moreover, in

---

64 OSCE, "Kosovo's War Crimes Trials: An Assessment Ten Years On 1999–2009", Vienna, OSCE, 2010, available at: http://www.osce.org/kosovo/68569?download=true p. 6.

65 EULEX and War Crimes, Bernd Borchardt, EULEX Head of Mission, *available at:* http://www.eulex-kosovo.eu/en/news/000427.php

66 On politics of translation and the ICTY trials see E. Elias-Bursac, *Translating Evidence and Interpreting Testimony at a War Crimes Tribunal: Working in a Tug-of-War,* London 2015. The ICTY and the ICTR also translated from and into French.

Kosovo municipalities inhabited by a community whose mother tongue is not one of the official languages of Kosovo and which represents above three percent of the total population of the municipality, the language of the community has the status of a language in official use in the municipality.[67] In addition, the English language has been used in official communication between the Kosovo institutions and international bodies and organizations, and in all documents issued by the Kosovo institutions. The language barriers may have made the interaction of the "hybrid panels" more complex. The following example shows that the relationship between the international and Kosovo judges was not always in tune. On the contrary, it was sometimes marked by significant contradictions and disagreements:

> Upon re-trial, the accused was convicted of war crimes in front of a mixed panel comprising one local and two EULEX judges. The hearings were at times contentious, although the re-trial proceeded without significant incident. On the day following the reading of the verdict, the local judge made a statement to the press to the effect that he had been outvoted by the two EULEX judges, that the evidence against the accused was insufficient, and that the guilty verdict was, in his view, unlawful.[68]

Hence, it is not only the language barriers that make the EULEX judicial practices challenging. As the example presented here shows, it relates to a far broader issue: war crimes trials are contested and disputed because they touch the nation's social fabric. As Nicola Lacey has argued, "the instrumental and the symbolic cannot be separated neatly: the material effects of particular practices will depend on their meaning for those subject to or those observing them."[69] There is a prevalent opinion in Kosovo that the justice system is flawed and that "powerful individuals" are not held accountable. Moreover, corruption allegations have been made against EULEX itself. This made the EU appoint an independent expert to investigate EULEX whose report dismissed these charges although it found administrative shortcomings.[70] The charges against EULEX

---

67 Law No. 02/L-37 On The Use Languages, 2006, available at: http://www.assembly-kosova.org/common/docs/ligjet/2006_02-L37_en.pdf, Article 2.
68 OSCE, Independence of the Judiciary in Kosovo, 23.
69 N. Lacey, 'Criminal Justice', in: Robert E. Goodin, P. Petit and T. Pogge (eds.), *A Companion to Contemporary Political Philosophy*, Oxford, 2012, 518.
70 See "Press Conference: Allegations of Corruption against EULEX are being pursued vigorously", available at: http://www.eulex-kosovo.eu/en/news/000528. php; see also Human Rights Watch, "Letter to the High Representative of the EU for Foreign Affairs and Security Policy and Vice President of the European Commission" (15.12. 2014), available at: http://www.hrw.org/news/2014/12/15/

have diminished the hopes among the Kosovo population that the culture of impunity will be challenged and that justice will prevail. Indeed, the allegations have once again brought attention to the question of EULEX's accountability to the Kosovo population or to European publics. To many, the absence of oversight and accountability and the allegations of corruption have made a mockery of EULEX's motto "nobody is above the law"; it is seen as a rhetorical mantra, not as a sign of institutional integrity.

8.2. Seeking a New Mechanism of Justice: The Special Criminal Tribunal

Unlike BiH, which established war chambers and the special department for war crimes,[71] no such body was created in Kosovo. As noted, a proposal by an expert committee for a Kosovo criminal tribunal to deal with war and ethnically motivated crimes was made in 1999, but it never materialized[72], because of political reasons, financial concerns, and also concerns that it was deemed to parallel the ICTY.[73] A book by Carla Del Ponte, the ex-chief prosecutor of the ICTY and later the Ambassador of Switzerland to Argentina, entitled *The Hunt: Me and the War Criminals*[74] did much to redraw attention to the matter. In her book, she accuses KLA members of war crimes and of trafficking in human body parts in Kosovo and Albania after the NATO bombing of Serbia in 1999. Swiss Senator Dick Marty followed up on these accusations in a report to the Council of Europe.[75]

---

letter-high-representative-eu-foreign-affairs-and-security-policy-and-vice-president; see also A. Capussela, 'EULEX report exposes EU failure in Kosovo', EU Observer, 16.4.2015, available at: https://euobserver.com/opinion/128343.

71 O. Martin-Ortega, 'Beyond The Hague: Prosecuting War Crimes in BiH', in: J. Gow, R. Kerr and Z. Pajić (eds.), *Prosecuting War Crimes: Lessons and Legacies of the International Criminal Tribunal for the Former Yugoslavia*, London and New York 2014, 119–120.

72 OSCE, 'Kosovo's War Crimes Trials: An Assessment Ten Years On 1999–2009', Vienna 2010, 11, available at: file:///C:/Users/VK/Downloads/Report%20OSCE%20war%20 crimes%20trials.pdf.

73 Bassiouni, *mixed models*, 162.

74 C. Del Ponte (with Chuck Sudetić), *Madame Prosecutor. Confrontations with Humanity's Worst Criminals and the Culture of Impunity*. New York 2008, 273–304.

75 Council of Europe, *Inhuman treatment of people and illicit trafficking in human organs in Kosovo*, Rapporteur: Mr Dick Marty, Switzerland, Alliance of Liberals and Democrats for Europe, Council of Europe, Doc. 12462, submitted on 7 January 2011, available at: http://www.sitf.eu/images/110107CoEReport.pdf.

This report prompted the creation of the European Union Special Investigative Task Force (EU SITF), with John Clint Williamson as the lead Prosecutor.[76] In July 2014, Williamson announced that his investigations showed that there was a basis for an indictment of "certain senior officials of the KLA."[77]

Indictments presuppose a special tribunal or a war crimes court. The EU requested the Kosovo authorities to establish a special criminal tribunal whose jurisdiction would be limited to the alleged crimes committed by members of the KLA during the Kosovo War and raised in Dick Marty's report. Baroness Catherine Ashton, then the High Representative of the EU for Foreign Affairs, proposed in letters to Atifete Jahjaga, the President of Kosovo,[78] that the Kosovo parliament approve the establishment of a special criminal tribunal to try alleged war crimes and other serious crimes committed during and after 1998–1999 armed conflict. It was also suggested that the Kosovo parliament extend the EULEX mandate to allow continuation of the investigation and prosecution of serious and politically sensitive crimes in Kosovo.[79] She further proposed that the special criminal tribunal be embedded in the Kosovo court system, but with specialist chambers based in an EU member state. The Netherlands have been referred to—in many media reports—as the location of the specialist chambers. Although this special criminal tribunal will have a seat in Kosovo, its proceedings will take place in the specialist chambers abroad. The separate judicial chambers will hold filings and sensitive records and be operated by the international staff. EULEX will appoint the judges and prosecutors.[80]

---

76   See http://www.sitf.eu/index.php/en/
77   Statement of the Chief Prosecutor of the Special Investigative Task Force, 29 July 2014, available at: http://www.sitf.eu/images/Statement/Statement_of_the_Chief_Prosecutor_of_the_SITF_EN.pdf..
78   Ç'thuhet në letërkëmbimin ndërmjet Jahjagës e Ashtonit [What has been said in the letter exchange between Jahjaga and Ashton], 4 September 2012, available at: http://koha.net/arkiva/?page=1,13,113898. See also Law No. 04/L-274 On Ratification of the International Agreement between the Republic of Kosovo and the European Union on the European Rule of Law Mission in Kosovo, available at: http://www.kuvendikosoves.org/common/docs/ligjet/04-L-274%20a.pdf.
79   B. Krasniqi, "Aktakuzat, para konstituimit të Gjykatës Speciale" [Indictments before constitution of the Special Criminal Tribunal," Koha Ditore, 23.12.2014: front page.
80   Human Rights Watch, "Kosovo: Approve Special Court for Serious Abuses: Parliament Should Also Endorse EU Law Mission Extension" (Human Rights Watch, 11.4.2014), available at: http://www.hrw.org/news/2014/04/11/kosovo-approve-special-court-serious-abuses.

In April 2014, the Kosovo Parliament ratified the agreement and upgraded it to a law,[81] with 88 voting in favour, 22 against and 2 absentees. This opened the way for the establishment of what in Kosovo became known as the *Gjykata Speciale* or the Special Criminal Tribunal.[82] The Constitution of Kosovo foresees the establishment of specialized courts, when necessary, but no extraordinary courts.[83] Thus, a new legislation was required. After many delaying manoeuvers and a vote rejecting the proposal in June 2015, the Parliament reversed its stance in August 2015 and approved the constitutional changes. It also adopted a law on specialist chambers and specialist prosecutors' office and a law on legal protection and financial support for those accused before the special chambers.[84]

The Law on Specialist Chambers serves the purpose of trying criminal acts in relation to allegations of grave trans-boundary and international crimes committed during and in the aftermath of the conflict in Kosovo as reported in the Council of Europe Parliamentary Assembly Report Doc 1246 of 7 January 2011.[85] The law gives primacy to international customary law over national laws.[86] Yet, in determining customary international laws at the time the crimes were committed, it stipulates that judges may refer to other sources of international law, including subsidiary sources: the jurisprudence from the international ad hoc tribunals, the International Criminal Court, and other criminal courts.[87] The temporal jurisdiction is over crimes, which occurred between 1 January 1998 and 31 December 2000.[88] The law applies the *non-bis-in-diem*

---

81 See also Law No. 04/L-274 On Ratification of the International Agreement between the Republic of Kosovo and the European Union on the European Rule of Law Mission in Kosovo, *available at:* http://www.kuvendikosoves.org/common/docs/ligjet/04-L-274%20a.pdf (accessed 29 August 2015).

82 Kuvendi i Kosovës miratoi themelimin e Gjykatës Speciale [The Parliament of Kosovo approved the creation of the Special Criminal Tribunal], http://www.telegrafi.com/lajme/kuvendi-i-kosoves-miratoi-themelimin-e-gjykates-speciale-2-43822.html.

83 Constitution of Republic of Kosovo, Article 103.

84 See Law No.05/L-053 On Specialist Chambers and Specialist Prosecutor's Office available at: http://www.kuvendikosoves.org/common/docs/ligjet/05-L-053%20a. pdf and the Law No. 05/L -054 On Legal Protection and Financial Support, available at: http://www.kuvendikosoves.org/common/docs/ligjet/05-L-054%20a.pdf.

85 Law No.05/L-053 On Specialist Chambers and Specialist Prosecutor's Office, Article 1.

86 Ibid.: Article 2.

87 Ibid.: Article 3.3.

88 Ibid.: Article 7.

rule. Thus, persons who have already been tried by another court in Kosovo and the ICTY will not be tried for the same offences by the specialist chambers.[89]

There is no amnesty for those convicted by the specialist chambers.[90] The law grants the Specialist Prosecutor's Office, which takes over the mandate and personnel of SITF independence for the investigation and prosecution of crimes within the jurisdiction of the specialist chambers.[91] Moreover, the law sets the special chambers as mobile and transnational bodies of justice, projecting multiple locations of the specialist chambers and seats in the "host" country and Kosovo.[92] The collection of evidence admissible can come for the Kosovo Police, the ICTY, EULEX or the SITF.[93] The official languages of the specialist chambers are Albanian, Serbian, and English.[94] Neither the specialist chambers nor the Specialist Prosecutor's Office will be funded by the Kosovo government. Hence they will not be liable for any auditing purposes either.[95] However, the Kosovo state will provide legal and financial support to the accused. As stipulated in the law on legal protection and financial support for the persons to be accused before the specialist chambers, those charged will be provided with support for defence and financial assistance to their family members. Moreover, the law foresees compensation for the accused if they are proved innocent.[96]

9.3. An Uneasy Dialectic: Kosovo's Interaction with the International Community

There are no available data on public opinion on the Special Criminal Tribunal. The vast majority of Kosovars thinks it is important to discover the truth about crimes in Kosovo—whether committed by Serbs or Albanians.[97] Yet, most Kosovars regard those indicted by the ICTY or domestic courts not as

---

89 Ibid.: Article 17.
90 Ibid.: Article 18.
91 Ibid.: Article 24.2.
92 Ibid.: Articles 3.6 and 3.7.
93 Ibid.: Article 37.
94 Ibid.: Article 20.
95 Ibid.: Article 63.
96 Law No. 05/L -054 On Legal Protection and Financial Support, Article 5. This is a big difference with regard to the UN-sponsored tribunals, the ICTY and the ICTR, which do not compensate falsely accused and acquitted suspects.
97 UNDP, "Perceptions on Transitional Justice", UNDP, 2012, available at: http://www.ks.undp.org/content/dam/kosovo/docs/TJ/English-Web_965257.pdf, p. 22.

perpetrators but as heroes.[98] In fact, ICTY indictments of the KLA members as well as of those put on trial at the domestic courts in Kosovo (such as the "Dukagjini group" and the "Llap Group" and the recent case known as "Drenica Group" that ended in May 2015[99]) were followed by street protests and occasionally also with violence. The jailing of KLA members of the "Llap Group" led to a bomb attack on the district court in Prishtina.[100]

The creation of a Special Criminal Tribunal was not an easy task for the Kosovo political elite, especially the political parties close to ex-KLA structures, such as the PDK. Yet, the PDK, which—together with its new government coalition partner, *Lidhja Demokratike e Kosovës* [Democratic League of Kosovo, LDK[101]]—holds the majority of seats in the Kosovo parliament, has endorsed the proposal and legislation for the court. It is the political parties led by Ramush Haradinaj and Fatmir Limaj, *Aleanca për Ardhmërinë e Kosovës* [Alliance for Future of Kosovo, AAK] and *Nisma për Kosovën* [Initiative for Kosovo, NK] respectively, which along with *Vetëvendosje* [Self-determination], strongly oppose it on grounds that it is the crimes of the state of Serbia that should be put on trial because Serbia was a perpetrator and Kosovo a victim.

As Dov Jacobs has shown in the case of the French trials after the Second World War, the search for truth through trials is important for reconciliation,

---

98 V. Krasniqi, 'Kosovo: Topography of the Construction of the Nation', in: Pål Kolstø (ed.) *Strategies of Symbolic Nation-Building in South Eastern Europe*, London 2014, 156.

99 "The Troubled Trial of Kosovo's 'Drenica Group', Balkan Insight, 27.5.2015, available at: http://www.balkaninsight.com/en/article/kosovo-awaits-kla-guerilla-verdict.

100 A. Qirezi, 'Kosovo: KLA Trial Backlash', Institute for War and Peace Reporting, 6.9.2005, available at: http://iwpr.net/report-news/kosovo-kla-trial-backlash.

101 In the national elections of 2014, the PDK won 30.38 per cent of the votes, LDK .24 per cent, third came *Vetëvendosje* [Self-determination] with 13.59 per cent, followed by AAK with 9.54 per cent, the Srpska Lista [The Serb List] 5.22 per cent, and NISMA për Kosovën [Initiative for Kosovo] 5.15 per cent. PDK could not establish the government because LDK, *Vetëvendosje*, AAK and Nisma together outnumbered the PDK's power to elect the President of the Parliament and the Government. The opposition parties approached the Constitutional Court of Kosovo for a reading of the constitution in the light of the election results and the majority-plurality votes in the Parliament. The Constitutional Court's verdict was in favour of PDK but the opposition block rejected the verdict. Hence Kosovo was left for six months without a government. It was only in December 2014 that LDK broke from the opposition coalition to enter into government with the PDK. PDK and LDK have been rival parties although they governed jointly for one term. However, this coalition just like the previous one was only made possible after much pressure from the international community.

but the over-reliance on truth undermines the fact that rapprochement is not premised on truth but on accepted myths.[102] The language used to discuss the Kosovo War is loaded with moral meanings. The dominant ideology of the KLA in the public discourse on the armed struggle of the KLA has been that of the just war. Thus, the accepted myth in Albanian nationalist ideologies is that the KLA breached no legal bounds of war and moral laws. Hence no war crimes were committed. Therefore, there is neither moral nor legal blame.

Yet, non-action on the Special Criminal Tribunal seems to have been a non-option for the Kosovo polity. Hence, there can be no denial of responsibility, even though this move is presented by the political elite as not chosen by them but by the international community. In this shrinking sphere of state responsibility, the Special Criminal Tribunal has been represented as an intrusion by the international community in Kosovo and an unjust imposition. According to this script, there is no place for any blameworthiness. Moreover, the Special Criminal Tribunal is placed in the symbolic economy of Kosovo's friendship with, and/or accountability to, the international community. Mimicking a western type discourse on public accountability, the then Prime Minister of Kosovo and now President of Kosovo, Hashim Thaçi, stated the following:

> Kosovo institutions are facing an imposition from the international community, fully immoral and unjust [...] Our consciousness would remain stained in case we do not provide an adequate response to the request of the EU and the USA for the creation of the Special Criminal Tribunal to address allegations made in the Dick Marty's report approved by the Council of Europe in 2010.[103]

Two important aspects—which are parts of broader national narratives—flow through this quote. Criminal justice aspires to moral and political legitimacy; thus, it signifies a displacement of the responsibility for the creation of the Special Criminal Tribunal—from the Kosovo polity towards the "international community." The second aspect relates to the political importance for the Kosovo government and Thaçi personally, who posits that it was neither him nor the government that initiated or sanctioned such a project. Indeed, this position

---

102 D. Jacobs, 'A narrative of Justice and the (Re) Writing of History: Lessons Learned from World War II French Trials' in: K. J. Heller and G. Simpson (eds.), *The Hidden Histories of War Crimes Trials*, Oxford 2013, 135–136.

103 Kuvendi i Kosovës miratoi themelimin e Gjykatës Speciale [The Parliament of Kosovo approves the creation of the Special Criminal Tribunal], available at: http://www.dw.de/kuvendi-i-kosov%C3%ABs-miraton-themelimin-e-gjykat%C3%ABs-speciale/a-17587510.

became clear in the words of Hajredin Kuçi, the Minister of Justice, who stated that the "Kosovo authorities have not partaken in the creation of the Special Criminal Tribunal [...] the law is being written in Brussels and with no local input."[104] He reiterated this view after the law on the creation of the tribunal was approved by the Parliament, saying that "the Special Criminal Tribunal is in the hands of the internationals."[105]

In other words, the Special Criminal Tribunal is an externally driven institution, with the Kosovo political elite having no authorship in its making. Moreover, what these two examples represent is the dominant position held by the dominant political parties. Symbolically, the Special Criminal Tribunal occupies a space between the ideologies of KLA just war and innocence and the friendship/partnership between Kosovo and the "international community," notably, the EU and the United States. But opposing political parties regard the Special Criminal Tribunal as a colonial throwback and an attempt to absolve the state of Serbia for crimes committed in Kosovo.[106] Again, the questions of accountability and responsibility have been so thoroughly politicized that the question of justice has become a secondary concern.

10. An ICTY Impact on Kosovo?

This chapter has demonstrated that the reconstruction of the justice system in post-war and post-independence Kosovo has been shaped by a complex history and practices stemming from the legacy of socialist Yugoslavia, the apartheid-like policies of Slobodan Milošević, the Kosovo War, and international rule. It has mapped out the features of the institutional and legal reforms that have addressed violations of international law in the Kosovo War. Under an international framework, the justice system has evolved through top-down approaches

---

104 B. Krasniqi, 'Qeveria fsheh autorësinë për Gjykatën Speciale' [The Government conceals the authorship of the Special Criminal Tribunal], (Koha Ditore, 27–28 December 2014): front page.

105 'Kuçi: Gjykata Speciale tërësishtë në duart endërkombëtarëve' [Special Criminal Tribunal is in the hands of the internationals], Kosovapress, available at: http://www.kosovapress.com/sq/siguri/kuci-gjykata-speciale-teresisht-ne-duart-e-nderkombetareve-49854/.

106 Glauk Konjufca in 'Kuvendi i Kosovës miratoi themelimin e Gjykatës Speciale' [The Parliament of Kosovo approved the creation of the Special Criminal Tribunal], available at: www.telegrafi.com/lajme/kuvendi-i-kosoves-miratoi-themelimin-e-gjykates-speciale-2-43822.html.

adopted by the UNMIK protectorate and the ICTY as one of the actors within it, to the EU and EULEX post-independence structures.

When judging judicial reform in Kosovo, the representations of the impact of international law in general, and the ICTY in particular, cannot be attributed to a single author. They have to be looked at within the context of the history of the Kosovo conflict and the ideal of global justice. Rather than trying to pinpoint the ICTY's impact on the justice system in Kosovo, this chapter shows how global justice is localized and how relationships between actors involved and practices have been enacted in the case of Kosovo. Originally, the ICTY was attached to the UNMIK administration and later EULEX, and in contrast to other post-Yugoslav countries, it needed no special agreement with the Kosovo government. Moreover, because Kosovo was not a state until 2008, EULEX took over the executive power in the judiciary after the declaration of independence. When Kosovo was an international protectorate, the requests of the ICTY were well channeled through the international institutions. The ICTY may have kept a low profile in Kosovo to suit the goal of the international community for political stabilization. Hence, the ICTY did not appear to be at the centre of judicial changes in Kosovo. During the early years of the ICTY, there were no indictments involving Kosovo suspects, which could have antagonized the political establishment and public opinion in the same way the ICTY's indictments against leading politicians and military commanders did in other parts of the former Yugoslavia. This changed with the first indictments—and later verdicts—in the cases of the Prosecutor v. Limaj et al. and The Prosecutor v. Haradinaj et al. But again—the proportion of acquittals was relatively high as compared to other ethnic communities of the former Yugoslavia. And finally, when the ICTY started to implement its UNSC-imposed completition strategy, there was no need to prepare Kosovo for taking over cases from the ICTY, because the ICTY did not intend to transfer any case to Kosovo. The only crimes, which the ICTY's OTP had—according to Carla Del Ponte—deliberately set aside, were finally taken over by a special court. At that time, Kosovo was already independent and enacted the necessary legislation. But it did so not under the influence of the ICTY, but because of the pressure from the EU, the UN, and the Council of Europe. Nevertheless, the reform process has mirrored the very logic of international criminal law, of which the ICTY was an important part. Thus, the ICTY has left an imprint throughout the judicial reform in post-war and post-independence Kosovo, including the Kosovo Special Criminal Tribunal, although it was not the trigger that launched the reforms.

As has been shown here, the reconstruction of the Kosovo justice system, in general, and prosecution of war crimes, in particular, has not proven to be an easy task. Moreover, judicial reform has not assumed an important role in the Kosovo government's agenda. War crimes trials—as instruments of pursuing justice—are shaped by dominant war narratives and also how justice is interpreted. They are contested and disputed because they include notions of national identity, sentiments, and belonging. The ideology of the KLA's war was framed as a just war and with no breaches of the legal bounds of war. Hence there is no legal or moral responsibility to face. The Kosovo polity has been pushed by the international community, especially by the EU and the United States, to establish the Special Criminal Tribunal. The Tribunal has been framed by political elites to fit different nationalist discourses. In reality, it is a question of grappling with the anxieties associated with the danger of "abandonment"—or "unfriending"—of Kosovo by the international community if the court had been rejected.

Kosovo may have an advanced legislation and "internationalized" judiciary system in place. However, law enforcement—for example, with respect to witness protection—as well as welfare provisions for survivors of sexual violence leave much to be desired. The prosecution of war crimes, ethnically motivated crimes, and corruption cases involving "powerful individuals," have failed to be perceived as impartial, even if they have been conducted by international actors and enacted in domestic courts with a majority of international judges on hybrid panels. Thus, mixed EULEX and Kosovo panels of judges have proved problematic because of a lack of trust. If this systemic flaw is not corrected, justice to survivors will not be delivered; nor will such courts shed new light on crimes committed during the war. Worse still, it will not be possible to bridge the divided narratives of what happened in Kosovo.

IV) Special Cases: South Sudan, Ukraine and Russia

Amani M. Ejami

The ICC and South Sudan

It may not be immediately obvious why South Sudan is included in the analysis of this volume. The country neither signed nor ratified the Rome Statute, it has not adopted the Agreement on Privileges and Immunities of the ICC, and until the time of writing this chapter, the ICC neither investigated crimes in South Sudan, nor did it indict anyone of the country's citizens. Even the most recent violence, which erupted in the country in 2014, never became an issue for the ICC, beause in August 2015, the conflict parties signed an agreement brokered by the US and Britain, which provided for the creation of a hybrid tribunal with the task of prosecuting the crimes committed during the civil war. Once operative, it would have rendered any ICC investigation inadmissible under the complementarity principle. Only if the hybrid tribunal did not start to work, was constrained in its mission or left aside international crimes would an ICC intervention would be possible – but only as a consequence of a UNSC referral.

This has not happened so far. But nevertheless, there is a reason to include South Sudan in the analysis about the ICC's impact on domestic reform. This has to do with the protracted way, in which South Sudan as a state came into being.

South Sudan's first war with the North 1955–1972 was primarily a struggle for the South's independence led by the *Anya-Nya* movement. That war ended in 1972 with the Addis Ababa Accord, which granted the South regional autonomy, recognizing the dominant belief systems of Christianity and traditional religions. The war resumed in 1983 after President Nimeiri declared the application of Sharia Law in Sudan. This new war was under the leadership of the SPLM/A. The SPLM's objective was no longer the secession of South Sudan from the North, but the liberation of the whole of Sudan from Arab-Islamic domination and the creation of a "New Sudan", in which there would be no discrimination according to race, ethnicity, culture, religion, or gender. This new vision of the SPLM attracted other marginalized regions in the North, accordingly the Nuba of Southern Kordufan and the Ingessana or Fung of the Southern Blue Nile region, who joined the South in the struggle.[1] Thus the SPLM considered itself the representative of the South, East, the West, and the Nuba mountains.

---

1 F. M. Deng, 'Customary Law in the Cross Fire of Sudan's War of Identities', available at: http://southsudanhumanitarianproject.com/wp-content/uploads/sites/21/

In 1985, SPLA started with a small force of allies in Jabel Marra in Darfur led by Engineer Dawood Yahya Bolad, a former member of the National Islamic Front NIF. The 1991–1992 rebellion against the NIF regime led by Engineer Bolad in Darfur failed in large part due to a lack of preparation inside Darfur and the counteraction by the *Janjaweed*, and the Army.[2] The commander of the SPLA force in Darfur decided to withdraw his troops after the government and Arab militia forces had discovered the location of the SPLA force before it was ready to fight. Some government members wanted to bring Bolad back into the NIF for talks, pledging to change policies and address the concerns of the Darfurians. Bolad decided to return to engage NIF officials, but he did so against the advice of the SPLA leadership and the force commander. Upon his return he was captured, tortured, and executed, according to Sudanese sources. Eventually, the SPLA was formed in Darfur, Suliman Arcua Minawi (also called "Minnie Minawi") was appointed as its secretary general and Abdul Wahid Mohamed Nur became Chief of the movement.[3]

During the peace negotiations that led to the CPA, the government of Sudan started to accuse the SPLM/A of supporting rebels in Darfur, while John Garange denied such support. However, it was clear that Garange was following the strategy of "fight and talk" by supporting resistance not only in the three areas of Abyei, Southern Kordofan, the Blue Nile and the East, but also in the West, in Darfur.[4] Neither the government of Sudan nor the SPLM wanted to permit other rebellion groups to participate in the peace negotiations. The government insisted that the negotiations be understood solely as a North-South affair. The deal was called Comprehensive Peace Agreement, but it dealt only with the North-South war.[5] Civil society and other political parties were never allowed to participate in the CPA negotiations.[6] Thus the concept of the New

---

formidable/Deng-2010-Customary-Law-in-the-Cross-Fire-of-Sudan-%E2%80%99-s-War-of-Identities2.pdf, 289.

2   The traditional leaders in Darfur described the Janjaweed then as men who own a horse and a G-3 rifle and who commit crimes against civilians.

3   K. M. Obeid, *Darfur – The Absent Truth*, Khartoum: The Sudanese Media Center (CMC), January 2005, 1st edition, 102.

4   H. F. Johnson, *Waging Peace in Sudan: The Inside Story of the Negotiations That Ended Africa's Longest Civil War*, Eastbourne 2011, 110.

5   R. Dowden, *Africa: Altered States, Ordinary Miracles*, New York, Philadelphia 2010, 158–198.

6   J. Young, *The fate of Sudan: The Origins and Consequences of A Flawed Peace Process*, London 2012, 99.

Sudan has never been addressed by the CPA, and the sudden death of Garange in July 2005 has in fact affirmed the SPLM's shift from the New Sudan Concept. As a result, many Northern Sudanese have lost faith and defected from the SPLM.[7]

During the interim period following the implementation of the CPA (but before independence), South Sudan enjoyed autonomy for six years (2005–2011). South Sudan, which emerged from the transition period as an independent state in July 2011, was a multi-ethnic society comprised of more than 60 different ethnic communities and estimated inhabitants of 11 million people living in an area of over one million square kilometers (400,000 square miles, an area almost twice the size of France).[8] One of the roots of the conflict between the Muslim North and the Christian and animist South was quarrel about access to the South's natural oil deposits. During the transition period, two per cent (2%) of the oil revenue were allocated to the oil producing states in the South and after the payment of the oil revenue account, fifty percent (50%) of the net oil revenue derived from oil producing wells in Southern Sudan was allocated to the government of Southern Sudan (GOSS).[9] However, these funds were never utilized by the GOSS to construct or otherwise develop institutions within Southern Sudan. Instead the income from the oil business trickled away into corrupt networks.[10]

During the transition period, Sudanese laws applied in the whole country and Sudanese institutions had jurisdiction over South Sudan, too. After independence, the new state could have at least partially inherited the institutions and the laws of Sudan, including those, which the government in Khartoum had created in order to respond to the ICC's judicial intervention. This is the question this chapter intends to answer: are there any traces of the Sudanese judicial reforms in South Sudan after the declaration of independence? Can we find a kind of collateral influence of the ICC on a country that is not a signatory to the Rome Statute and not even under the influence of an UNSC referral?

---

7   P. Adwok Nyaba, *South Sudan: The State We Aspire To*, Cape Town 2013, 113, 156.
8   South Sudan Human Rights Commission (SSHRC), Interim Report on South Sudan Internal Conflict December 15, 2013–March 15, 2014; http://www.gurtong.net/LinkClick.aspx?fileticket=RO6rWq-_ogw%3D&tabid=124
9   Comprehensive Peace Agreement 2005, Chapter III, Wealth Sharing Protocol 7 January 2004.
10 Justin Ambago Ramba, "the 13 Top Corrupt South Sudanese" Who are they?, 18 September 2011, http://www.southsudannewsagency.com/opinion/editorials/the-13-top-corrupt-south-sudanese-whore-they

1. State Building and Criminal Justice in South Sudan

The Interim Constitution of Southern Sudan was mandated by the CPA 2005 and entered into force in 2005. Following the Independence of South Sudan, the Transitional Constitution 2011 was issued, including a Bill of Rights, which forms "the cornerstone of social justice, equality and democracy".[11] The Constitution makes reference to international Human Rights treaties, the ones adopted by South Sudan becoming "an integral part" of the Bill of Rights, and creates a Human Rights Commission to ensure the respect of these fundamental rights.[12] South Sudan is yet to ratify any of the major Human Rights instruments, whether global or regional (The International Covenant on Civil and Political Rights "ICCPR", Covenant on the Economic, Social and cultural Rights "CESCR", and the African Charter on Human and People's Rights "ACHPR".[13] The Human Rights Commission was established in 2009.[14]

South Sudan is bound by the four Geneva Conventions of 1949, the two Additional Protocols of 1977 (both sets of treaties ratified by South Sudan in 1912), and to give effect to these conventions, the government of South Sudan issued the Geneva Convention Provisional Order 2012.[15] According to this Order, the competent court for violations of these conventions is the South Sudan High Court.[16]

After the secession, the new nation found itself inappropriately prepared to run the affairs of the country. South Sudan was in need of infrastructure, it had no functioning telephone lines, no electricity network, lacked running water and roads. This is why GOSS decided to start from scratch – not only in terms of state-building efforts, but also with regard to the justice system.[17] During the wartime and after the secession, dispute resolution was handled within local communities

---

11 Part (11) articles 9–34 of the South Sudan Transitional Constitution 2011 available at: http://www.sudantribune.com/IMG/pdf/The_Draft_Transitional_Constitution_of_the_ROSS2-2.pdf
12 Chapter IV, articles 49–50 of the South Sudan Transitional Constitution 2011.
13 Interim Report of AU Commission of Inquiry on South Sudan, 26–27 June 2014 http://au.int/en/sites/default/files/Assembly%20AU%2019%20(XXIII)%20_E.pdf
14 Southern Sudan Human Rights Commission 2009, http://www.icnl.org/research/library/files/South%20Sudan/SSHumanRights%20CommissionAct2009.pdf
15 Provisional Order No.12/2012
16 Ibid, Art (10)
17 D. Pimentel, 'Rule of Law Reform Without Cultural Imperialism? Reinforcing Customary Justice Through Collateral Review in Southern Sudan', Hague Journal on the Rule of Law, 2/1/2010, 1–28.

by tribal authorities under principles of customary laws (unwritten traditional rules) and 90% of the legal disputes in Southern Sudan were handled by customary courts which do not always adhere to minimum standards of justice and Human Rights.[18] Accountability for war crimes was not included in the CPA, and no one was prosecuted for committing war crimes during the long conflict with the North. New laws were enacted in South Sudan during the interim period (2005–2011) including the Army Act 2009 and the Penal Code 2008. Although the SPLM has witnessed the UNSC referral of the situation in Darfur to the ICC, none of these laws contain any clause prohibiting crimes against humanity or war crimes. Two years after the independence and while state building is yet to be completed, South Sudan has been tormented by interethnic conflict, putting the world's youngest country back into a cycle of violence.[19]

The formal court system can serve only a small percentage of the population in South Sudan. Litigants in South Sudan both outside and in the towns often prefer to take criminal cases as well as civil cases to chiefs because justice is speedier, more accessible, and more likely to grant compensation. Public confidence in these courts runs significantly higher than any confidence in the statutory courts. The Local Government Act of 2009 codifies the recognition of customary law courts in South Sudan and provides that: "The Customary Law Courts shall have judicial competence to adjudicate on customary disputes and make judgments in accordance with the customs, traditions, norms and ethics of the communities".[20] The majority of the customary courts does not have court buildings, or some have appropriated neglected buildings. Customary law is not merely relevant in certain family law cases, but is an entire system for dealing with criminal as well as civil cases.[21] The operation of customary courts in Southern Sudan is therefore

18 Pimentel, *Rule of Law Reform*, 14.
19 G. Larson, P. Biar Ajak and L. Pritchett, "South Sudan's Capability Trap: Building a State with Disruptive Innovation," UNU-WIDER Working Paper No. 2013/120, October 2013, available at www.wider.unu.edu/publications/working-papers/2013/en_GB/wp2013-120/.
20 Section (98) of the Local Government Act 2009, http://mlgi.org.za/resources/local-government-database/by-country/sudan/sub-national-legislation/The%20Local%20Government%20Act%202009.pdf
21 C. Leonardo, L. N. Moro, N. Santschi, D. H. Isser, 'Local Justice in Southern Sudan', Washington, D. C.: United States Institute of Peace and Rift Valley Institute 2010, available at: http://www.usip.org/sites/default/files/PW66%20-%20Local%20Justice%20in%20Southern%20Sudan.pdf

an essential aspect of establishing and maintaining the rule of law there.[22] However, these indigenous systems do not adhere to minimum standards of justice and Human Rights. The term "Human Rights" has generally acquired negative popular connotations in Southern Sudan. Sudden, poorly coordinated, and poorly disseminated attempts to reform the courts in line with Human Rights principles have had limited effect at best, and at worst have actually set back the cause of Human Rights.[23]

There is still the cultural practice of 'bride wealth'– a custom by which a young man wishing to marry must present the bride's family with a bride price – an unmarried girl has significant economic value in certain local communities. For many families in this incredibly impoverished region, their daughters are their only significant assets. When a tort claim such as wrongful death arises between two families, the wrongdoer may have nothing to compensate the plaintiff with other than his own daughter. Customary courts in South Sudan have historically resorted to this as a remedy, ordering one family to compensate the other by giving them one of their daughters.[24]

With regard to the reform of customary law, it has been argued by Francis Deng that "there is also ambivalence about the Human Rights pressures for reform related to the status of women and children, for which traditional practices have been strongly and rightly criticized."[25] Customary law also faces the challenge of being non-recorded. What's more, the integration and the relation between the informal and formal justice system presents another challenge for customary law reform.[26] With regard to the formal laws, new laws were issued by the government of South Sudan, like the Penal Code 2008 and the Army Law 2009. These laws have been marked with the absence of any clause related to war crimes, genocide, and crimes against the humanity.

2. South Sudan and the ICC

In 2008, the SPLM was part of the national unity government. Back then, the SPLM issued a press release that declared that "the solution to the crisis is for the Government of National Unity to forge an understanding with the international

---

22 Pimentel, *Rule of Law Reform*, 13, 14.
23 Leonardi et al., *Local Justice In Southern Sudan*, 84.
24 Pimentel, *Rule of Law Reform*, 18.
25 Deng, *Customary Law in the Cross Fire*, 312.
26 ibid.

community and to co-operate with the ICC on the legal processes."[27] However, the SPLM was concerned about a possible collapse of the CPA and was preparing to fight for Southern self-determination. For its leaders, the CPA was primarily the passage to the 2011 referendum and just a cornerstone in the way to their own independent state.[28] The situation is similar to the one in Kosovo and the ICTY: the issues of international justice, impunity and accountability for past crimes became overshadowed by the state-building process.[29] Already in July of the same year, Salva Kiir, the SPLM leader, saw the ICC arrest warrant against President Al Bashir as a danger to the CPA that could affect Sudan's transition. In January 2009, Salva Kiir again warned of possible difficulties if the case against Bashir went ahead. Speaking at the CPA fourth anniversary celebrations in Malakal, he asked "what would happen to the CPA if Bashir is charged by the court? What about the outstanding items in the peace agreement? Will they be implemented afterwards? Will we have a referendum in 2011? These are urgent questions that everyone should pay attention to." In the end, the SPLM provided cautious but critical support to the ruling party in Sudan, the National Congress Party.[30]

Since the independence in 2011, life in South Sudan has been marked with ethnic conflicts which reached their peak in December 2013, when a political dispute arose between the President Salva Kiir Mayardit from the Dinka ethnic group and his former Vice President Riek Machar from the Nuer ethnic group.[31] The war quickly spread across the country, causing the deaths of an estimated 10,000 people, including many civilians. People were brutally killed inside their houses, in the streets, in police stations, in the hospital, and inside the United

---

27 T. Dagn, 'Sudan, The Crises in Darfur and the Status of the North-South Peace Agreement', Congressional Research Service Report for Congress, May 28, 2010 available at, http://fpc.state.gov/documents/organization/142785.pdf

28 International Crises Group, 'Sudan: Justice, Peace and the ICC', Africa Report N.152-17 July 2009, http://www.crisisgroup.org/~/media/Files/africa/horn-of africa/sudan/ Sudan%20Justice%20Peace%20and%20the%20ICC.ashx

29 A difference to Kosovo consists in the absence of nation-building efforts in South Sudan, due to the civil war that broke out in 2014 and put the two major ethnic affiliations, the Nuer and the Dinka against each other. Due to the much smaller presence of ethnic minorities in Kosovo, state building and nation building went hand in hand. Compare with the chapter on Kosovo, written by Vjollca Krasniqi in this book.

30 International Crisis Group, Sudan, Justice, Peace and the ICC.

31 Dinka and Nuer are the two largest ethnic groups in South Sudan among other 60 different ethnicities.

Nations Mission in the South Sudan UNMISS compounds, only because of their ethnic background.[32] There was widespread destruction and looting of personal property as well as government's institutions.[33] Almost one million Southern Sudanese were internally displaced and hundreds of thousands became refugees, fleeing to neighbouring countries.[34]

The recent and on-going war in South Sudan brought back the discussions about the ICC. The government of South Sudan has conflicting policies towards resorting to the ICC. President Kiir was on record saying that he would "never accept" the ICC, speaking during his visit to Kenya, where he met with Kenyan president and (then) ICC indictee Uhuru Kenyatta. Kiir dismissed the ICC, rejected demands to sign the Rome Statute and alligned with other African leaders, accusing the ICC as biased against Africans. "We have talked about these problems of the ICC, that the ICC, whatever has been written in Rome, has never been used against any one of their presidents or heads of states. It seems that this thing has been meant for African leaders, that they have to be humiliated", he said upon arrival in Juba after returning from Kenya.[35] During the following year, he was less intransigent. After the violence between the Nuer and Dinka had erupted and the ICC had signaled its readiness to embark on investigations, if empowered by the UNSC, Kiir said: "If they want to come, they will come. In all our areas, they will be facilitated to go there and find out [the truth]."[36]

In general, South Sudan's polices with regard to the ICC could be viewed in the context of the AU standpoint on the ICC and in light of the AU approach of solving African problems within Africa. In this context, the African Union formed a commission of inquiry on South Sudan, whose mandate is the investigation of Human Rights violations and other abuses committed during the armed

---

32 South Sudan Human Rights Commission (SSHRC), *Interim Report n South Sudan Internal Conflict*, December 15, 2013–March 15, 2014.

33 ibid.

34 Rule of Law Initiative, *Assessment of Justice, Accountability and Reconciliation Measures in South Sudan*, Rule of Law Initiative – Final Report and Recommendations – June 2014, available at: http://www.americanbar.org/content/dam/aba/directories/roli/sudan/aba_roli_sudan_assessment_final_report_0614.authcheckdam.pdf

35 Hannah McNeish, 'South Sudan's President Says 'Never' to ICC', Voice of America 23.5.2013, available at: http://www.voanews.com/content/south-sudan-president-says-never-to-icc/1667226.html

36 Times Life (South Africa), South Sudan President welcoes ICC crime investigation, 7 February 2014, http://www.timeslive.co.za/africa/2014/02/07/south-sudan-president-welcomes-icc-crime-investigation

conflict in South Sudan.[37] It can also make best-practice recommendations for ensuring accountability, reconciliation and healing among all South Sudanese communities. The PSC requested that the commission submit its report to the Council within a maximum period of three months. However, the Commission has so far failed to release its final report, despite pressure from international NGOs.[38]

3. Justice and Accountability in South Sudan

Successive peace processes in South Sudan, including the CPA in 2005, have repeatedly failed to hold perpetrators of serious abuses accountable for their actions. Peace talks in South Sudan were typically initiated with explicit or implicit amnesties and the promise of political and military appointment for belligerent parties. During the CPA peace negotiations, the Intergovernmental Authority on Development (IGAD) secretariat proposed a reconciliation component to the CPA; it was opposed by the NCP and later by SPLM. Both parties knew they had committed major crimes during the course of the civil war, which would be discussed in public forums, and they were reluctant to see that happen.[39] At some point there was an agreement between the SPLM and the NCP to give themselves a blanket amnesty for crimes committed during the civil war, but the mediators convinced them that such an agreement was illegal under international law and could not be enforced.[40]

The South Sudanese justice system suffers from various weaknesses and challenges upholding due process, and its judiciary has suffered a lack of independence from authorities in the government and army and, largely as a result of this, it lacks the capacity to try serious crimes committed during the current conflict. However, the South Sudan Human Rights Commission (SSHRC), a governmental body mandated to monitor and promote Human Rights, released an interim report on 18 March 2014 that described abuses in Juba, Malakal, Baliet

---

37 The Peace and Security Council of the African Union at its 411th meeting held at the level of Heads of State and Government on the 30 December 2013 APSC, Communiqué PSC/AHG/COMM.1 (CDX1) dated 31 December 2013.

38 Human Rights Watch, 'South Sudan's New War: Abuses by Government and Opposition Forces', HRC report, August 2014 available at: https://www.hrw.org/report/2014/08/07/south-sudans-new-war/abuses-government-and-opposition-forces

39 IGAD is a sub-regional organization, with the support of the US and the international community it helped the government of Sudan and the SPLM/A negotiate the CPA.

40 Young, The fate of Sudan, 112.

County (Upper Nile state) and in other areas. The report blamed the killings of what the commission estimated was around 600 Nuer civilians in Juba on a loss of control of troops by the army. The SSHRC called on the government to speed up investigations into the alleged perpetrators. No investigations have so far taken place.

At present, the ICC does not wield any jurisdiction over South Sudan. Even in the case of a ratification of the Rome Statute, which seems very unlikely, an ICC intervention could not be retroactive. Crimes committed before 2011 could only be investigated under a self-referral, but since at that time Sudan was still one country, such a self-referral would have to be triggered by the Sudanese government. For the crimes committed after independence, the situation is even more complicated. The civil war that broke out in 2013 ended two years later with the so-called "Compromise Peace Agreement", brokered by the Intergovernmental Authority on Development, an eight-country trade block, which includes the four countries from the Horn of Africa, Kenya, Uganda, and both Sudans. The new agreement provided for the creation of a hybrid court, which would judge the atrocities committed by the conflict parties. If the hybrid court were to become operational and cover the crimes included in the Rome Statute, South Sudan could claim inadmissibility, even if the UNSC decided to refer the situation there to the ICC. It is doubtful whether the hybrid court will ever become operational. In June 2016, the president of South Sudan, Salva Kiir, and vice president Riek Machar as the heads of both warring factions of the civil war jointly appealed in a New York Times op-ed for an amendment of the peace treaty of August 2015. The international community, and "the United States and Britain in particular", were asked to reconsider "one element of the peace agreement to which they are cosignatories: support for a planned international tribunal, the Hybrid Court for South Sudan. We call on them instead to commit to global backing for a mediated peace, truth and reconciliation process." The latter should be modelled on the South African and Northern Irish commissions.[41] In July 2016, fighting between the two warring factions erupted again.

---

41 Salva Kiir, Riek Machar, 'South Sudan needs truth, not trial', The New York Times 7.6.2016, available at: http://www.nytimes.com/2016/06/08/opinion/south-sudan-needs-truth-not-trials.html?_r=0225
    Machar later retracted the letter, claiming he had not been consulted by Kiir about it.

Igor Lyubashenko

The Ukrainian Self-Referrals and Their Institutional and Legal Consequences in Ukraine and Russia

1. Ukraine and the International Criminal Court

Ukraine was one of the most active initiators of the creation of the International Criminal Court. Its delegation participated constructively in all stages of preparation of the Rome Statute and Ukraine's position; the authorities demonstrated full support for the idea of creating the International Criminal Court.[1] On 11 December 1999, president Leonid Kuchma issued the ordinance authorizing the Permanent Representative of Ukraine to the United Nations, Volodimir Yelchenko, to sign the Rome Statute,[2] which was done on 20 January 2000. Paradoxically, about one year later, the same president Kuchma applied to the Constitutional Court of Ukraine with a request to establish whether the Statute was in line with the constitution of Ukraine, suggesting several potential points of non-compliance. On 7 July 2001, the Constitutional Court issued a verdict, according to which the Rome Statute cannot be ratified without changing the constitution. In particular, according to the Court, the Ukrainian constitution does not provide for the possibility to complement the national criminal jurisdiction, as established in the Article 1 of the Rome Statute[3] (the Court referred to article 124 of the constitution: "Justice in Ukraine is administered exclusively by the courts. The delegation of court functions, as well as their usurpation by

---

1   Igor Lyubashenko's interview with prof. Volodymyr Vasylenko, International Law Chair at the National University of "Kyiv-Mohyla Academy", former judge in the International Criminal Tribunal for the Former Yugoslavia and currently member of the Constitutional Commission established by president Petro Poroshenko to elaborate amendments to the constitution of Ukraine (Kyiv, 21 July 2015).

2   The text of the ordinance is available in the online database of Ukrainian legislation: http://zakon4.rada.gov.ua/laws/show/313/99-%D1%80%D0%BF.

3   The full text of the verdict of the Constitutional Court of Ukraine is available in the online database of Ukrainian legislation: http://zakon1.rada.gov.ua/laws/show/v003v710-01.

other bodies and officials is not allowed"[4]). Although the verdict should not be regarded as a fundamental obstacle, which made the ratification of the Statute impossible (the necessary amendment to the constitution is rather a technical issue), it has *de facto* frozen the debate on the ratification of the Rome Statute for over a decade.

The reason for a sudden U-turn of Ukraine's authorities regarding the attitude to the ICC at the beginning of the 2000s should be looked for in the specificity of the political regime of "late Kuchma" combined with a sheer lack of understanding of the essence of international justice. At the beginning of 2000s, which was also the first half of his second presidency, Leonid Kuchma started consolidating his power and sliding towards authoritarianism. In November 2000, records suggesting the president's involvement in a number of crimes were leaked. The affair became known under the name "Kuchmagate", which included the murder of opposition journalist Georgiy Gongadze and the violation of an UN arms embargo by selling "Kolchuga" radars to Iraq. Leonid Kuchma was never prosecuted for "Kutchmagate", but it is possible that he and his proxies were convinced they could be tried for it by an international tribunal,[5] and therefore were reluctant to accept such a jurisdiction.

During the mid-2000s, the requirement to ratify the Rome Statute became an element of the EU's conditionality within the framework of the European Neighbourhood Policy and the so called "acquis communitaire" of the EU and it also figured among the priorities of the EU-Ukraine Action Plans[6] and later – of the subsequent Association Agendas.[7] The Association Agreement between

---

4   The text of the Constitution of Ukraine is available in the online database of Ukrainian legislation: http://zakon4.rada.gov.ua/laws/show/254%D0%BA/96-%D0%B2%D1%80.

5   This interpretation was confirmed in Igor Lyubashenko's interviews with prof. V. Vasylenko and with Stanislav Batryn, Kyiv-based Human Rights activists and experts of the NGO "Public Commission for the Investigation and Prevention of Human Rights Violations in Ukraine" (Kyiv, 28 July 2015).

6   Action Plans were basic tools of the ENP on bilateral level. They were soft law instruments containing specific goals (reforms, introduction of new policies, adjustment of existing policies of neighbouring countries) agreed with each particular neighbouring country in order to bring it closer to the EU in terms of norms, standards and values.

7   Association Agendas are similar to Action Plans. They are aimed at accelerating the process of Ukraine's adaptation to the *acquis communautaire* as foreseen by the Association Agreement before the latter's entrance into force. Association Agendas are adopted by the EU-Ukraine Cooperation Council for a period of ca. 2 years. The respective documents were signed in November 2009, June 2013 and March 2015.

the EU and Ukraine also foresaw that "the Parties shall cooperate in promoting peace and international justice by ratifying and implementing the Rome Statute of the International Criminal Court (ICC) of 1998 and its related instruments"[8], which means that as soon as the agreement enters into force, Ukraine will eventually be obliged to ratify the Statute.

In practice, since 2001 Ukraine has not faced a political situation, in which the authorities of the state would be prone to commit actions that could be regarded as international crimes. Ukraine was also not targeted by perpetrators of international crimes. Cooperation with the ICC was not a central issue in the public debate. In the meantime, the problem was raised by Human Rights activists and experts[9], but remained rather marginal and theoretical in nature. The situation has changed fundamentally since the end of 2013. Along with a series of events that are widely referred to as the "Ukraine crisis" – mass protests resulting in a change of authorities followed by the armed conflict in the region of Donbas – the Ukrainian government was confronted with the mass murders of its citizens, many of which could be regarded as crimes against humanity and war crimes. The issue of cooperation with the ICC suddenly became imperative, because it might have an impact on urgent political problems. Ukraine's moves in this field are analyzed in the following chapter.

2. The Euromaidan Uprising

On 25 February 2014, the Verkhovna Rada[10] adopted a declaration accepting the jurisdiction of the ICC over alleged crimes committed on its territory from 21 November 2013 to 22 February 2014.[11] On 9 April 2014, the embassy of

---

8 Article 8 of the Association Agreement between the European Union and its Member States on the one hand and Ukraine on the other. The document is available in the Official Journal of the European Union: http://eeas.europa.eu/ukraine/docs/association_agreement_ukraine_2014_en.pdf.

9 For example: Amnesty International Ukraine, *Річниця підписання Україною Римського статуту: подальша затримка ратифікації є недопустимою*, 20.01.2015, http://amnesty.org.ua/bez-rubriki/p-yata-richnitsya-pidpisannya-ukrayinoyu-rimskogo-statutu-podalsha-zatrimka-ratifikatsiyi-ye-nedopustimoyu/.

10 Ukraine has a one-chamber parliament, the Verkhovna Rada (Supreme Council).

11 The full text of the document is available in the online database of Ukrainian legislation: http://zakon1.rada.gov.ua/laws/show/790-18.

Ukraine to the Kingdom of the Netherlands sent the declaration on to the ICC.[12] On 25 April 2014, the Prosecutor of the ICC opened a preliminary examination of the case.[13] The adoption of the above mentioned declaration is not the same as the ratification of the Rome Statute by Ukraine, but the *ad hoc* acceptance of the ICC's jurisdiction according to article 12(3) of the Rome Statute, which allows the ICC to investigate and prosecute specific crimes, which fall into the indicated time frame.

The time span covered by Ukraine's self-referral overlaps with the events known as the Euromaidan (or simply Maidan) uprising. Protests started in the centre of Kyiv on 21 November 2013, following the decision of Ukrainian authorities not to sign the Association Agreement with the EU. The initial protest was small-scale and gathered predominantly young people with pro-European orientations. The protest grew after the *Berkut* special police forces intervened in the night of 29–30 November 2013. The attempt to suppress the protest led to the opposite effect and inclined different social groups, including some who were skeptical or indifferent towards the idea of Ukraine's European integration, to join the protest. The culmination took place between 18 and 21 February 2014, when lethal weapons were massively used by the police[14] resulting in around 100 casualties, mainly among protesters but also among police officers (the exact number of victims of the protests remains unknown). On 21 February 2014, an agreement was reached among the authorities and the opposition, mediated

---

12 The full text of the document is available on the official website of the ICC: http://www.icc-cpi.int/en_menus/icc/press%20and%20media/press%20releases/Documents/997/declarationRecognitionJuristiction09-04-2014.pdf.

13 According to information published on the official website of the ICC: http://www.icc-cpi.int/en_menus/icc/press%20and%20media/press%20releases/Pages/pr999.aspx.

14 As the confrontation between the protesters and the authorities continued, the tension grew. For example, Anatoliy Hrytsenko, one of the opposition leaders, former Minister of Defence and the presidential candidate after the revolution, appealed those in possession of legal weapons to carry them and use them to protect of themselves as well as other unarmed protesters in accordance with the law and the right to self-defence. It is thus clear that despite the generally peaceful nature of the Maidan uprising, there were armed persons among the protesters as well. What is obvious is that the police was fully equipped, organized and prepared to suppress the protest, while armed protesters were rather an exception to the rule. What remains unclear is who started shooting on the most bloody day of 20 February. The journalistic investigation by Sonya Koshkina based on interviews with representatives of both sides reveals that there is no clear evidence of who initiated the violence. See: С. Кошкина, Майдан. *Нерассказанная история*, Киев, издательство "Брайт" 2015.

by a last minute mission of three EU foreign ministers.[15] However, during the night of 21–22 February, President Viktor Yanukovych escaped from the capital and several days later organized a live press conference from the Russian city of Rostov-on-Don, stating that an armed *coup* had taken place in Kyiv. On 22 February 2014, the parliament interpreted Yanukovych's absence as *de facto* resignation from his office and scheduled early presidential elections for 25 May 2014[16], when Petro Poroshenko was elected president.

The 25 February 2014 declaration is an important step towards cooperation between Ukraine and the ICC. However, it contains purely political elements that might help understand the motives and logic of the transitional government and the Verkhovna Rada. In particular, the declaration alleges the direct responsibility of president Viktor Yanukovych, prosecutor-general Viktor Pshonka, and interior minister Vitaliy Zakharchenko (along with "other officials who gave and executed clearly criminal orders, and who can be identified by the prosecutor of the International Criminal Court"). Undoubtedly, such a direct indication of specific persons was meant to influence the examination and investigation. The investigation of the violence during the Maidan uprising was among the main points of the above mentioned 21 February agreement between Viktor Yanukovych and the opposition. This issue remained high on the political agenda of the opposition, which had taken power. The unfreezing of Ukraine's cooperation with the ICC in the context of the "Maidan massacre" investigation could thus be interpreted, among others, as an attempt to highlight the weight of responsibility of the previous administration for the described events.

From the institutional point of view, the most important step towards improvement of the process of investigation of the "Maidan massacre" was taken as late as 18 December 2014, when the unit for special investigations was created within the structure of Prosecutor General's Office of Ukraine[17], with the

---

15 The three ministers were Frank Walter Steinmeier (Germany), Laurent Fabius (France) and Radosław Sikorski (Poland).

16 For more details on the Euromaidan protests and the uprising see: I. Lyubashenko, "Euromaidan: From the students' protest to mass uprising", in: K. Bachmann, I. Lyubashenko (eds.), *The Maidan Uprising, Separatism and Foreign Intervention. Ukraine's complex transition*, Frankfurt/M. 2014, 61–86.

17 The Prosecutor General of Ukraine heads the unified system of prosecution. According to the constitution, the Prosecutor General is appointed and dismissed by the President of Ukraine, after obtaining the proper acceptance from the parliament. The main task of the system of prosecution is defined as activities aimed at strengthening the rule of law and protection against illegal encroachments. The law on prosecution guarantees

task to coordinate all inquiries on "usurpation of power" and the whole complex of criminal activities committed during the period of Viktor Yanukovych's presidency. The unit's primary task was "to investigate mass murders among the participants of the peaceful protests on 18–20 February 2014."[18] Additionally, in order to provide transparency, a website was created by the Prosecutor General's Office containing information about ongoing criminal cases connected to the Maidan events, as well as regularly updated information about the status of trials of the most spectacular cases.[19] It is undoubtedly a step increasing general transparency, but not necessarily making the process clearer and easier to understand for the average citizen.

Although the assessment of the investigation is not the primary goal of this chapter, it is important to note that based on publicly available materials, not much progress can be noted during the first two years after the outbreak of the protests. This assessment is also supported by Ukrainian experts and commentators. For example, a survey among experts conducted in the second half of December 2014 by the Kyiv-based Democratic Initiatives Foundation has shown that the lack of consequences for those responsible for the killings as well as those who delayed investigations against members of the Yanukovych administration were mentioned among the most significant shortcomings of Ukraine's internal politics in 2014.[20]

A report published by the International Advisory Panel of the Council of Europe[21] also criticized the lack of progress. One of the conclusions states that "in certain important respects, the investigations into the Maidan cases lacked practical independence in circumstances where the investigating body belonged to the same authority as those under investigation. The Panel further considers

---

independence of the system of prosecution from public authorities, officials, mass media and social and political organizations and movements.

18 According to information published on the official website of the General Prosecutor's Office, 18.12.2014, http://www.gp.gov.ua/ua/news.html?_m=publications&_c=view&_t=rec&id=148237.

19 The address of the website is: http://rrg.gp.gov.ua/.

20 Democratic Initiatives Foundation, *2014-й рік в оцінках експертів*, available at: http://dif.org.ua/ua/polls/2014_polls/rey5yuu6.htm.

21 The International Advisory Panel was constituted by the Secretary General of the Council of Europe in order to oversee that the investigations of incidents which took place in Ukraine from 30 November 2013 onwards met all the requirements of the European Convention on Human Rights and the case-law of the European Court of Human Rights.

that the appointment post-Maidan of certain officials to senior positions in the MoI [Ministry of Interior] contributed to the lack of appearance of independence and served to undermine public confidence in the readiness of the MoI to investigate the crimes committed during Maidan."[22]

There are numerous reasons for this. First, Ukraine's law enforcement system and judiciary are generally underdeveloped and inefficient. No political revolution can change this overnight. Second, there is undoubtedly an internal resistance within the law enforcement system and the judiciary, which were directly involved in repressions during the Maidan protest. Third, despite the change of power, Ukraine's institutional frame remains the same, which is not helpful in terms of establishing the rule of law and the fight against corruption. It means that even the most well-designed policies face informal barriers during their implementation.

In November 2015, the ICC's Office of the Prosecutor found the repressions against the Euromaidan to be "rather a reaction to events [...] and aimed to limit the protests rather than being part of a deliberate, coordinated plan of violence methodologically carried out against the protest movement."[23] Thus the ICC prosecutor abolished the argumentation of the Ukrainian authorities presenting Maidan-related violence as a crime against humanity. Taking into account the low quality of Ukraine's internal investigation of these events, this decision means that the potential involvement of the ICC is no longer a motivating force for the introduction of reforms of the judiciary and the law enforcement agencies. At the same time, the mentioned decision does not inhibit further cooperation between Ukraine and the ICC.

3. Warfare in Donbas

The formation of an interim government, a new majority in the Verkhovna Rada, and the escape of Viktor Yanukovych were followed by an increase in strong centrifugal tendencies in some of Ukraine's eastern and southern regions. These separatist movements were strongly encouraged and supported by Russia. Already in March 2014, armed insurgents, supported by Russian troops, stormed the

---

22 Report of the International Advisory Panel on its review of the Maidan Investigations, 31.05.2015. The report is available online on the official website of the Council of Europe: http://www.coe.int/pl/web/portal/-/maidan-violence-investigations-fail-european-human-rights-standards.

23 International Criminal Court. The Office of the Prosecutor, *Report on Preliminary Investigation Activities (2015)*, 12 November 2015, 23.

parliament of the Autonomous Republic of Crimea and ousted the regional government. The new authorities of Crimea lodged a motion with the Russian State Duma and requested the incorporation of the peninsula into the Russian state.[24] The Duma accepted the motion. On 18 March 2014 the process of annexation of Crimea was finalized. In parallel, a separatist movement was developing in the Donbas region (the Donetsk and Luhansk provinces of Ukraine), escalating into a war-like situation in summer 2014. On 13 April 2014, the National Security and Defence Council (NSDC) of Ukraine[25] approved the beginning of the so-called anti-terrorist operation (ATO) in the east of Ukraine, thus starting the phase of active counter-measures against separatism. On 11 May 2014, unconstitutional referendums took place in the territories captured by the separatists, providing a formal basis for announcing the independence by these self-proclaimed "people's republics" of Donetsk and Luhansk. On 24 May 2014, both organizations proclaimed the establishment of a new federal "state" – Novorossiya.[26]

Attempts have been made to negotiate a peaceful resolution of the conflict. The first ceasefire was negotiated in Minsk on 5 September 2014, but did not even last for several days. The second ceasefire, negotiated on 12 February 2015,

---

24 Russia has a two-chamber parliament, the State Duma of the Federal Assembly of the Russian Federation.
25 The National Security and Defence Council is the institution headed by the president of Ukraine, which coordinates and controls activities of the executive in the field of national security and defence.
26 The cases of Crimea and Donbas are similar from the point of view of Russia's activities towards them. What differs is the historic background. Crimea was the protectorate of the Ottoman Empire since the 15th century. In 1783, it was conquered by Russia and remained part of it until 1954, when it was presented as a "gift" to Ukrainian Soviet Socialist Republic. Since Soviet times, its population was dominated by ethnic Russians. Crimea demonstrated some separatist tendencies already in early 1990s. Donbas was part of the USSR since 1922. The ethnic composition of the region became mixed in Soviet times, which resulted in the development of a specific "Soviet" identity. There were no obvious separatist tendencies in the region before 2014. What should be noted, however, is that many studies confirmed that local inhabitants in fact identified themselves as Ukrainians. Their understanding of "Ukrainianness" differs significantly from the rest of the country and tends to be based on nostalgia for old Soviet Ukraine. For more details on Crimea and its role in Ukrainian-Russian relations, see: N. Shapovalova, 'The Role of Crimea in Ukraine–Russia relations', in: K. Bachmann, I. Lyubashenko (eds.), *The Maidan Uprising, Separatism and Foreign Intervention. Ukraine's complex transition*, Frankfurt/M. 2014, 227–266. For more details on the evolution of the war in Donbas, see: A. Wilson, *Ukraine Crisis. What It Means for the West*, New Haven, Yale University Press 2014.

appeared to be more effective, but resulted in the lowering of intensity of violence rather than a complete end of it. According to the UN, at least 9,733 people were killed and 22,720 injured by the end of 2016.[27] Killings also took place outside the so-called ATO zone. The most infamous case is the death of around 37 pro-Russian activists in Odessa on 2 May 2014, when pro-Ukrainian protesters set fire to a trade union building.[28]

The described events in Donbas fit into the wide category of asymmetric warfare, which is a military confrontation between parties with a different status (e.g. states and non-state organizations) and unequal military capabilities. A lack of clear organizational structures on the side of separatists, large-scale engagement of non-governmental entities (e.g. volunteers providing material supplies for the army, the phenomenon of volunteer battalions), large-scale political and material support from the the Russian Federation, but first and foremost the lack of a formal declaration of war by any of the engaged parties have obfuscated the situation for observers and international lawyers. Ongoing fighting makes it difficult to assess actors' responsibility for Human Rights abuses and atrocities fairly. The result are mutual accusations of war crimes and crimes against humanity by the conflict parties.

Since March 2014, Ukraine has sent several communications about allegations of crimes committed in Donbas to the ICC. The ICC found these events beyond the Court's temporal jurisdiction, which Ukraine had restricted in the first self-referral until February 2014.[29]

On 4 February 2015, the Verkhovna Rada of Ukraine adopted a second declaration about a self-referral to the ICC, this time covering the period from 20 February 2014[30] for an unspecified time. The second self-referral was intended to cover the annexation of Crimea and the occupation of parts of the Donetsk and Luhansk provinces by armed separatists. Unlike the first self-referral, the

---

27 UN Office of the High Commissioner for Human Rights, *Report on Human Rights Situation in Ukraine, 16 May–15 August 2015*, 8 September 2015, available at: http://www.ohchr.org/Documents/Countries/UA/11thOHCHRreportUkraine.pdf.

28 UN Office of the High Commissioner for Human Rights, *Report on Human Rights Situation in Ukraine, 16 August to 15 November 2016*, 8 December 2016, available at: http://www.ohchr.org/Documents/Countries/UA/UAReport16th_EN.pdf

29 International Criminal Court, The Office of the Prosecutor, *Report on Preliminary Examination Activities 2014*, 02.12.2014, p. 14 available at: http://www.icc-cpi.int/iccdocs/otp/OTP-Pre-Exam-2014.pdf).

30 The full text of the document is available in the online database of Ukrainian legislation: http://zakon1.rada.gov.ua/laws/show/145-19.

second one did not set a clear time frame and, again, identifies specific suspects but without naming them. Responsibility is alleged with regard to "the highest officials of the Russian Federation" for crimes against humanity and war crimes on the territory of Ukraine. The Ukrainian Ministry of Foreign Affairs lodged the self-referral on 8 September 2015.[31] According to the report on preliminary examination activities published by the ICC's Office of the Prosecutor, "[t]he information available suggests that the situation within the territory of Crimea and Sevastopol amounts to an international armed conflict between Ukraine and the Russian Federation."[32] The OTP also admitted that "direct military engagement between Russian armed forces and Ukrainian government forces that would suggest the existence of an international armed conflict [...] in parallel to the non-international armed conflict".[33] There are no final conclusions on whether the ICC accepts the admissibility of the case at the time of writing the chapter.

4. Domestic Change in Ukraine

During the period between the Verkhovna Rada's resolution to accept the jurisdiction of the ICC over the Donbas case and the official submission of the self-referral to the ICC, Ukrainian authorities made several steps that could be regarded as legal reform with a potential impact on further cooperation with the ICC. In particular, in April 2015, a new law was adopted, which increased the punishment for the abuse of power by military officials.[34] On 9 June 2015, the Ukrainian government informed the Council of Europe about its derogation from the European Convention on Human Rights under Article 15 of the Convention.[35] It is an important legal step which shifts the responsibility for the protection of Human Rights

---

31 The full text of the document is available on the official website of the ICC: http://www.icc-cpi.int/iccdocs/other/Ukraine_Art_12-3_declaration_08092015.pdf.

32 International Criminal Court, The Office of the Prosecutor, Report on Preliminary Examination Activities 2016, 14.11.2016, p. 35, available at: https://www.icc-cpi.int/iccdocs/otp/161114-otp-rep-PE_ENG.pdf.

33 Ibid., p. 37

34 The full text of the law is available in the online database of Ukrainian legislation: http://zakon4.rada.gov.ua/laws/show/290-19.

35 Art. 15 of the Convention reads as follows: "In time of war or other public emergency threatening the life of the nation, any High Contracting Party may take measures derogating from its obligations under this Convention to the extent strictly required by the exigencies of the situation, provided that such measures are not inconsistent with its other obligations under international law."

in the ATO zone to Russia, which is directly referred to as an invader occupying integral territory of Ukraine.[36]

Furthermore, the General Prosecutor of Ukraine started a number of investigations following the most brutal cases of shelling of civilian objects (qualified as terrorist attacks) and killings of Ukrainian servicemen. Presumably, this step was taken under the erroneous assumption that Ukraine could keep the ICC investigations under control by eventually claiming its ability and willingness to deal with the crimes in Donbas and thus prevent the ICC from intervening against crimes committed by Ukrainian forces. As parliamentary debates and public speeches by government members have shown, there seems to be a widespread conviction about Ukraine being able to challenge admissibility of ICC investigations and invoke the complementary principle under the conditions of a self-referral. Subsequently to the launch of investigations into the Donbas violence, the General Prosecutor of Ukraine opened an investigation against the Investigative Committee of the Russian Federation in September 2014 for the alleged support of terrorists.[37]

5. Domestic Change in Russia

As in every case of self-referral, the probability of institutional and legal reform in the self-referring country is very low, as such self-referrals are usually used in situations, where the judiciary of a country is unable to investigate, or, where investigations are possible, it is unable to prosecute suspects, because they are beyond the reach of the authorities, either because they are acting in a part of the national territory, which the central government no longer controls, or they have escaped abroad and are protected by a friendly government.

The Ukrainian self-referrals were therefore unlikely to trigger domestic change in Ukraine, but they could be expected to unleash domestic change collaterally in Russia. Similarly to Ukraine, Russia signed the Rome Statute in 2000, but never ratified it. It is therefore not covered by the ICC's territorial jurisdiction.

---

36 The text of Ukraine's notification on derogation from the ECHR is available on the website of the Council of Europe: http://conventions.coe.int/treaty/Commun/ ListeDeclarations.asp?PO=U&NT=005&MA=999&CV=1&NA=15&CN=999&VL= 1&CM=5&CL=ENG.

37 According to information published on the official website of the General Prosecutor's Office, 29.09.2014, http://www.gp.gov.ua/ua/news.html?_m=publications&_c=view&_ t=rec&id=144823. The Investigative Committee of the Russian Federation will be explained below.

Nevertheless, the ICC's personal jurisdiction could extend to Russian citizens as far as they are suspects of crimes committed on the territory of Ukraine within the time frame of the Ukrainian self-referrals. This could have either been the case with respect to the Maidan sniping massacre, where Ukrainian politicians and investigators used to talk about a "Russian trace", or with respect to repressions following the annexation of Crimea by Russia (e.g. against Ukrainian citizens and especially members of the Tatar community in Crimea) and to war crimes committed in Donbas.

Although at the moment of writing there was no clear evidence of any direct institutional impact of the Ukrainian self-referrals on Russia, there are signals that could be interpreted as counter-actions aimed at preventing potential negative consequences for Russian officials.

Russian authorities often used claims about war crimes and crimes against humanity when referring to the crisis in Ukraine. According to the dominating Ukrainian narrative, the Maidan protests constituted the will of Ukraine's society to get rid of corrupted political elites, which hampered the development of the country and prevented it from getting closer to a western-style model of liberal democracy and capitalist economy. The Russian counter-narrative presented the same events as an armed *coup d'etat*, dominated by radical far-right forces. The emergence of separatist movements was thus interpreted (by the Russian government and the separatist leaders themselves) as an uprising of the Russian-speaking populations against a nationalist, or even fascist, government. ATO was interpreted as a punitive action against the insurgent Russian population.[38] Both leaders of the self-proclaimed "people's republics" of Donetsk and Luhansk and Russian authorities started to use the term "genocide" in order to describe ATO.

These rhetorics were soon accompanied by legal measures, whose aim was to support the Russian narrative. The most important role here was played by the Investigative Committee of the Russian Federation, a specific federal organ created in 2011, whose aim was to increase the efficiency of criminal investigations. The activities of the Investigative Committee are supervised by the president of the Russian Federation. A special investigative unit dealing with international crimes committed on the territory of Ukraine was created within the structure of the Committee. According to information published on the Committee's website,

---

38 A comprehensive overview of the Russian narrative is presented in the 2015 documentary by A. Kondrashov 'Крым. Путь на Родину' (Crimea. A Way Back to the Motherland). The movie is published on the official YouTube channel of "Rossiya 24" TV channel: https://youtu.be/t42-71RpRgI.

the work of the unit will continue until all Ukrainian military servicemen as well as other persons involved in committing crimes against civilians are prosecuted.[39] A number of investigations of particular incidents were launched. On 29 September 2014, the Investigative Committee opened a criminal case about an alleged genocide of the Russian-speaking population living on the territory of the Donetsk and Luhansk people's republics. According to the preliminary investigation, after 12 April 2014 unidentified persons from the highest political and military leadership of Ukraine, the Ukrainian Armed Forces, the National Guard of Ukraine and the "Right Sector" issued orders whose aim was the complete annihilation of the Russian-speaking inhabitants of the above mentioned territories.[40] On 13 January 2015, an additional case was opened in order to investigate new incidents of this alleged genocide during the period from 1 December 2014 to 12 January 2015, when the massive shelling of cities and towns in Donbas took place.[41] Along with such general investigations, the Investigative Committee opened criminal cases against representatives of Ukrainian state authorities, in particular interior minister Arsen Avakov and businessman Igor Kolomoyskyi.[42] Both are suspected of such crimes as murder, the use of prohibited means and methods of warfare, kidnapping, and the obstruction of lawful activities of journalists.[43] Furthermore, in several cases individual Ukrainian citizens were arrested for war crimes during ATO. The case of Nadia Savchenko[44] is probably the most prominent one.

The second dimension of Russia's activities that could be regarded as countermeasures against possible outcomes of ICC investigations could be observed in the wave of rhetoric presenting skepticism towards the idea of international

---

39 According to information published on the official website of the Investigative Committee, http://sledcom.ru/press/cases/item/1168/.

40 According to information published on the official website of the Investigative Committee, 26.03.2015, http://sledcom.ru/news/item/908156/.

41 According to information published on the official website of the Investigative Committee, 13.01.2015, http://sledcom.ru/news/item/886833/.

42 One of the most influential Ukrainian so-called oligarchs, allegedly supporting several volunteer battalions fighting in Donbas and governor of the Dnipropetrovsk province in March 2014–March 2015.

43 According to information published on the official website of the Investigative Committee, 18.06.2014, http://sledcom.ru/news/item/522788/.

44 Ukrainian military helicopter pilot, captured in summer 2014 by the pro-Russian separatists and transported to the territory of Russia, where she was sentenced to 22 years in prison, but in May 2016 was pardoned by President Putin and exchanged for two Russian intelligence officers sentenced for imprisonment in Ukraine.

justice as it exists nowadays. In February 2015, Aleksandr Bystrykin, the head of above-mentioned Investigative Committee of the Russian Federation, prepared a report containing a proposal to abolish the principle of supremacy of international law over national law. This principle was characterized as a "legal diversion" that undermines the efficiency of national criminal proceedings.[45] Bystrykin's report does not amount to a policy change. Still, the principle of supremacy of international law is defined in the first chapter of the constitution of the Russian Federation, which cannot be changed. Its elimination or modification would require the adoption of a new constitution. Furthermore, Dmitry Peskov, press secretary of President Vladimir Putin, did not confirm that president Putin intended to consider abolishing the principle.[46] Nevertheless, Russian authorities continued moving in this direction – on 14 July 2015, the Constitutional Court of the Russian Federation issued a decision, according to which verdicts of the European Court of Human Rights may be not obligatory on the territory of Russia in cases when there is a conflict with basic values of the constitution.[47]

This rhetoric can be used to discredit international law in the eyes of Russian public opinion, presenting it as a tool used by a hostile West to undermine Russia's international position. Indeed, on 24 March 2015, Vyacheslav Nikonov, head of the committee for education of the State Duma of the Russian Federation proposed the creation of Russia's own tribunal specializing in war crimes. According to him, the ICC lost its credibility because it is allegedly controlled by the countries that are at the same time patrons of the "regime of war criminals"[48] in Ukraine. Furthermore, Russian experts indicated that taking into account the political flexibility of the Constitutional Court, there is no actual need to introduce far-reaching legislative changes to react to eventual decisions of the ICC in

---

45 The report itself was not published, but it was widely cited by the media. For example: *Бастрыкин: национальные законы надо ставить выше международного права*, "Ria Novosti", 26.02.2015, available at: http://ria.ru/politics/20150226/1049768155. html.

46 *Пескову неизвестно о планах по отмене приоритета международного права*, Forbes.ru, 27.02.2015, http://www.forbes.ru/news/281449-peskovu-neizvestno-o-planakh-po-otmene-prioriteta-mezhdunarodnogo-prava.

47 According to information published on the official website of the Constitutional Court of the Russian Federation, http://www.ksrf.ru/ru/News/Pages/ViewItem. aspx?ParamId=3244.

48 *В ГД призывают подумать о своем трибунале по военным преступлениям*, „Ria Novosti", 24.03.2015, http://ria.ru/politics/20150324/1054138247.html.

accordance with the actual wishes of the Russian authorities.[49] An example of such a "politically flexible" approach was presented in an article by Valery Zorkin[50], the head of Russia's Constitutional Court. Referring to the annexation of Crimea, the author justified it as lawful, presenting, however, a specific understanding of international law that is based primarily on its "spirit" rather than literal understanding. Undoubtedly, such an approach could open nearly limitless possibilities to interpret it in accordance with the current political logic and denies the very sense of law as such. The final accord of Russia's steps aimed at preventing potential negative consequences for its officials took place on 16 November 2016, when President Putin signed a decree on his state's withdrawal from the Rome Statute.[51] It should be noted that in the statement accompanying the decree, Russian MFA mentioned its dissatisfaction with the quality of investigation in the Georgian case, it did not refer to the situation in Ukraine.[52] Taking into account that the decree was issued two days after the mentioned publication of the OTP report classifying the annexation of Crimea as an act of occupation, there are grounds to assume that the ICC's preliminary investigation of the Ukrainian case was not without meaning for the Russian president's decision.

6. The ICC's Institutional Impact on Ukraine and Russia

At the time of writing this chapter, the ICC stated that it "will continue to engage with the Ukrainian authorities, civil society and other relevant stakeholders such as the Russian Federation, on all matters relevant to the preliminary examination of the situation in Ukraine."[53] In the Maidan case, the ICC's preliminary examination found the available evidence too weak to prove the existence of a crime against humanity. It is much more difficult to imagine that the ICC could also reject the subject-matter jurisdiction with respect to the war in Donbas, especially because a large number of reports from international Human Rights

---

49 I would like to thank Sergey Utkin, Head of Department of Strategic Assessment, Russian Academy of Sciences, for drawing attention to this hypothesis.

50 В. Зорькин, *Право – и только право. О вопиющих правонарушениях, которые упорно не замечают*, "Российская газета", №6631 (60), 23.03.2015, http://www.rg.ru/2015/03/23/zorkin-site.html.

51 The document is available on the website of the Ministry of Foreign Affairs of the Russian Federation: http://www.mid.ru/documents/10180/2523446/распоряжение.pdf/d1674f8d-b331-43ca-9216-2023cec0c050.

52 Заявление МИД России, 16.11.2016, available at: http://www.mid.ru/ru/foreign_policy/news/-/asset_publisher/cKNonkJE02Bw/content/id/2523566.

53 *Report on Preliminary Investigation Activities (2016)...*, op.cit., p. 42.

organizations have been published, which show the commission of war crimes by both sides. The downing of the Malaysian airplane MH17 in July 2014 attracted additional attention to the fighting there. With the development of the ICC investigations there, one might well observe domestic change in Ukraine (e.g. in order to prevent investigations and/or prosecutions of Ukrainian perpetrators of war crimes and crimes against humanity) as well as in Russia (in order to curb ICC activities against Russian citizens and/or Ukrainian separatists involved in war crimes).

Both Ukrainian self-referrals have so far contributed to a renewal of the debate about Ukraine's final ratification of the Rome Statute. The need for ratification not only comes from the fact that the Ukrainian government once signed the Rome Statute; it is now also part of the political part of the Association Agreement with the EU. The EU is pushing Ukraine in this direction, as the presidency's conclusions of the January 2015 European Council meeting reiterates: "The Council encourages the Ukrainian authorities to swiftly take the intended legal steps enabling the International Criminal Court to examine the alleged crimes against humanity, committed on the territory of Ukraine in 2014–2015. The Council reiterates the importance of moving forward with the ratification of the Rome Statute by Ukraine, as it has committed to in the Association Agreement."[54] In their rhetoric, representatives of Ukrainian authorities speak enthusiastically about international justice when referring to the prosecution of Viktor Yanukovych and his entourage as well as the case of war in Ukrainian Donbas.[55] But at the same time, the Ukrainian authorities do not seem to have a full understanding of international criminal justice's functioning.[56] This was demonstrated when Ukraine submitted evidence of crimes in Donbas at a time, when the ICC did not yet have jurisdiction over the conflict in Donbas and when

54 Council of the European Union, *Council conclusions on Ukraine*, 29.01.2015, http://www.consilium.europa.eu/en/press/press-releases/2015/01/council-conclusions-ukraine/.

55 For example, Ukraine's Prime Minister Arseniy Yatsenyuk proposed to send the above-mentioned documentary 'Crimea. A Way Back to the Motherland' directly to the ICC as evidence of crimes committed by President Vladimir Putin. See: *Яценюк поручил отправить в Гаагу трейлер российского фильма о захвате Крыма*, "UNIAN", 11.03.2015, http://www.unian.net/politics/1054097-yatsenyuk-poruchil-otpravit-v-gaagu-treyler-rossiyskogo-filma-o-zahvate-kryima.html.

56 Prof. V. Vasylenko said about the "legal incompetence" in the field of international justice of Ukrainian authorities that came to power after the Maidan uprising as well as unwillingness to provoke Russia (Igor Lyubashenko's interview, Kyiv, 21 July 2015).

the Rada submitted a list of suspects for the ICC to prosecute thus preempting the work of the ICC prosecutor.

Confusion about the working of international criminal justice seems to be an important factor in shaping Ukraine's response to crimes as well as to the legal challenges the country faces. The National Security and Defence Council of Ukraine has expressed doubts about the advantage of ratifying the Rome Statute, arguing that it would open a possibility for the representatives of the rebellious regions to accuse Ukraine of war crimes. Therefore, the NSDC argued, the ratification might make sense only in the case of a similar step being taken by the Russian Federation.[57] Similar arguments were publicly expressed by MP and the leader of the party "Petro Poroshenko's Bloc", Yuriy Lutsenko. In a short interview he labelled the self-referrals a "partial ratification of the Rome Statute".[58] These reservations neglect the fact that the ICC prosecutor can investigate crimes and bring to trial suspects for international crimes committed in Donbas no matter whether the Russian Federation or the separatist leadership ratify the Rome Statute or not, because it is the territorial and timely jurisdiction, not the subject matter or personal jurisdiction, which the Ukrainian self-referrals conferred to the ICC. Very often, politicians question the need to ratify the Rome Statute arguing that it would expose Ukrainian forces to the ICC's prosecution, ignoring the fact that the Ukrainian self-referrals already opened an avenue for the ICC prosecutor to investigate crimes committed by both sides, if he wishes to do so. Therefore, Ukrainian civil society activists and lawyers dealing with Human Rights law usually refute these arguments against ratification.[59]

Some of them argue, however, that Ukrainian authorities may be reasonably afraid of an ICC investigation into ATO[60], not only because of the knowledge

57 В. Полевий, *Чи потрібен Україні Міжнародний кримінальний суд як відповідь на російську агресію?*, Information and Analytical Centre of the NSDC, 02.02.2015, http://mediarnbo.org/2015/02/02/chi-potriben-ukrayini-mizhnarodniy-kriminalniy-sud-yak-vidpovid-na-rosiysku-agresiyu/.

58 The interview is available on the website of Kyiv-based NGO "Human Rights Information Centre": http://humanrights.org.ua/material/zaraz_mi_majemo_vojuvati_a_ne_jizditi_v_gaagu__lucenko.

59 According to a brief survey of experts conducted by the NGO Human Rights Information Centre. Opinions of experts are published on the website of the International Renaissance Foundation. Микола Мирний, *Україна в позиції страуса щодо ратифікації Римського статуту*, 04.02.2015, http://www.irf.ua/knowledgebase/news/ukraina_v_pozitsii_strausa_schodo_ratifikatsii_rimskogo_statutu/.

60 For example, such an idea was expressed in the author's interview with the above mentioned S. Batryn (Kyiv, 28 July 2015).

about crimes committed there by Ukrainian forces, but also because of the loss of reputation among Western donor countries, which might be the result of the mere investigation. From this perspective, the situation is similar to the one Kutchma faced back in 2000 and 2001, when the ratification of the Rome Statute was on the agenda for the first time.

But full access to the Rome Statute is currently also difficult for another reason, also relating to the situation in 2001. Back then, the Constitutional Court declared the Rome Statute as being in contradiction with some provisions of the Ukrainian constitution. A partial solution to this problem was achieved on 2 June 2016, when the Rada adopted an amendment to the constitution concerning the reform of the judiciary. Among other things, the amended constitution clearly states now that Ukraine can accept jurisdiction of the ICC on conditions specified in the Rome Statute. But the amendment which allows to ratify the Rome Statute will come into force only after three years (that is in 2019). The rationale for this delay, as it was presented by the representative of the President (who is the formal author of the adopted amendment) at the public hearing held by the Constitutional Court of Ukraine,[61] is the (misplaced) fear that an immediate ratification during an ongoing conflict would expose the Ukrainian military to harassment by the ICC.[62] This can happen immediately (and with no regard to the constitutional three-year delay) based on the self-referrals alone. Actually, as demonstrated by the experience of other countries described in this volume, by fully acceding to the Rome Statute, preventing ICC investigations of crimes committed by one's own forces would even be easier after ratifying the Rome Statute than under a self-referral. As a full member state, Ukraine would have the opportunity to challenge the admissibility of cases brought before the ICC more convincingly than if it were only backtracking on its own self-referral.

There are some steps undertaken by the Ukrainian government and the Rada in order to advance the ratification of the Rome Statute, and these steps can be clearly traced back to the self-referrals. The constitutional amendment is probably the most important one among them. Other cases of domestic change, like the lingering domestic investigations into the Maidan massacre and the delay of the Rome Statute ratification, are adaptation to rather than compliance with ICC requirements. Both, however, can hardly be seen as triggered by the ICC's

---

61 The procedure of constitutional amendment requires acceptance of the proposed amendment by the Constitutional Court followed by two readings in the parliament.
62 The recording of the hearing is available online: http://youtu.be/r_5-Jq4S6p0.

actions. The latter have so far been rather disappointing from the perspective of the Ukrainian authorities (the preliminary finding about the Maidan sniping not being a crime against humanity). Ukraine's rapprochement with the ICC is therefore rather a result of EU conditionality than a reaction to an ICC intervention.

This is different with regard to Russia. There, we can clearly see adaptive steps only. Confronted with the possibility of having its own citizens and its Ukrainian allies (the separatists) investigated, the Russian government and the pro-governmental media embarked on a counter-blaming campaign, which seeks to spread allegations about an alleged Ukrainian genocide against the Russian-speaking population of Ukraine's East. At the same time, existing international criminal justice is being discredited and references to ICL notions are used as elements of information warfare against Ukraine and an allegedly hostile West in general. But Russia did not undertake specific steps toward the creation of new institutions or legislation which could counter the pereived threat of an ICC investigation into its role in the Ukrainian crisis. The Russian government rather seems to rely on the flexibility of its Constitutional Court with regard to the domestic situation. In other words: the Russian government is likely to respond to an ICC challenge by mounting legal obstacles under domestic law. However, Russia as a non-contracting state can hardly influence the ICC's activities outside Russia, and Russian citizens may expect to be interrogated, investigated and maybe even indicted for crimes committed on the territory of Ukraine (including Crimea, whose adherence to Ukraine can hardly be challenged under international law). Whether they will also be extradited to the ICC by their host countries is an issue that goes far beyond this chapter and will depend mostly on the diplomatic and military leverage of Russia over these host countries rather than legal considerations.

Conclusion and Outlook

Broadly two types of ICTs were considered in this publication, namely ad hoc international criminal tribunals, created by the UN, and the treaty based, permanent International Criminal Court (ICC). It can be said that Africa – with an abundance of case studies at hand – is as good a laboratory as any other to examine the question that is focused on in this volume, namely the measure of domestic change effected by ICTs in the selected jurisdictions. The African case studies each have their own nuances and measure of change, not to be repeated here in detail. In addition to the individual conclusions with respect to Rwanda, Sudan, Libya, Kenya, and South Sudan, which will be referenced here where appropriate, there is one aspect that warrants a more detailed exploration and shall serve as a kind of critical epilogue: *regionalization* and domestic change.

We have noted in the Introduction that the phenomenon of "Europeanization" is a relevant concept to (help) explain domestic change with regards to the ICTY. It was also noted that there is no equivalent driving force with respect to the African *ad hoc* tribunal case study, Rwanda, for the simple reason that there was no coordinated effort between the ICTR, as an international actor, and the relevant regional body, the African Union (and its predecessor, the OAU). There was a degree of political and moral support for the ICTR, of course, but nothing approximating the conditionality regime imposed by the EU with respect to domestic changes in Serbia and Croatia, and with respect to their relationship with the ICTY. Regarding domestic change and the relationship between ICTs and states, we postulated that the African regional impact (via the AU) on member states was much weaker than the above-mentioned EU conditionality regime.

Looking to the future, however, the impact of regionalization of international criminal justice in Africa may yet play a far more prominent role, certainly compared to the role that regional dynamics have played in the African case studies that we have examined. With regards to anticipated and projected domestic change caused by ICTs in Africa, we can point to four important areas. First, the relationship between the AU and the ICC; second, the evolving notion of complementarity; third, the future of the proposed Multilateral Treaty for Mutual Legal Assistance and Extradition in Domestic Prosecution of Atrocity Crimes; and, fourth, developments concerning the adoption of the Malabo Protocol on the creation of an African regional criminal jurisdiction. It is not the aim here to analyse all these aspects in detail. Rather, we want to link these developments to our most pertinent conclusions regarding the African case studies that we have examined in this publication in order to put forward some thoughts about the future of domestic institutional change resulting from the existence of ICTs.

The first, and arguably most contentious, development in international criminal justice in recent years has been the growing animosity between the AU and the ICC. It is prudent to note that there is a sizeable body of literature on this topic, and not all the writings on this are very sober or balanced. But it is fair to say that while African states were some of the earliest to sign, ratify, and implement the Rome Statute of the ICC, and while it is a fact that African states form one of the largest blocs in the Assembly of States Parties, there is at present a real institutional rift between the AU and the ICC. This is true also with regards to individual African states party to the Rome Statute in terms of their bilateral relationships with the ICC, as we have for instance noted in the chapter on Kenya. The picture is, however, not so binary as many would want to project it. There is not a monolithic African stance on the ICC. Even AU decisions reflect nuance and debate. It is worth recalling that 34 African states (more than two-thirds of the members of the AU) are states parties to the Rome Statute.[1] Within this group there is also diversity of views regarding the AU-ICC relationship. To add to the complexity, one should also note the evolving and fluctuating views of individual states. A case in point is South Africa. In 2010, when the institutional relationship between the AU and the ICC had started to deteriorate, South Africa insisted that African states party to the Rome Statute cannot ignore their obligations under the Rome Statute, and that these obligations must be balanced with their obligations to the AU. At that stage, a number of African states called on AU members to take a stance of non-cooperation with the ICC, but the initial absolutist call was watered down, as reflected by South Africa's efforts that resulted in a more balanced AU decision.[2] We know, of course, that the calls for African states to withdraw from the Rome Statute and to stop cooperating

---

1   For more analysis, see M. du Plessis, T. Maluwa and A. O'Reilly, *Africa and the International Criminal Court* Chatham House Occassional Paper 01/2013, 2, available at www.chathamhouse.org).

2   Decision on the Progress Report of the Commission on the Implementation of Decision Assembly/AU/Dec.270(XIV) on the Second Ministerial Meeting on the Rome Statute of the International Criminal Court (ICC), July 2010, Doc. Assembly/AU/10(XV), par 6. See also comments and background information by Dire Tladi 'The duty on South Africa to arrest and surrender President Al Bashir under South African and international law' *Journal of International Criminal Justice* 13 (2015) 1027–1047, at 1030.

with the ICC only intensified as a result of cases like the Kenyan case as well as the arrest warrant against President Al Bashir of Sudan. And yet, despite the heated rhetoric, by July 2016, on occasion of the 27th AU Summit, there was still no official AU call for a collective withdrawal of African states parties from the Rome Statute. Indeed, observers noted that there was considerable pushback from some state parties (notably Nigeria, Senegal, Ivory Coast, and Tunisia), as well as Algeria, which is not a member state of the ICC. These states (correctly) pointed out that the AU as an institution is not (and cannot be) a member of the ICC.[3] Membership of, and thus legal and institutional relationships with, the ICC is a matter for sovereign states. Given this state of affairs, it is assumed that for the foreseeable future there will be a significant number of African states that are members of the ICC. Some of these states (for instance Nigeria, Senegal, and Botswana) will presumably be more enthusiastic than others. Some, like South Africa, which has one of the most comprehensive domestic implementation regimes, will, at least for the short to medium term be ambivalent, or worse, schizophrenic, in terms of its relationship with the ICC. The saga surrounding the South African government's failure to arrest President Omar Al Bashir on occasion of his visit to South Africa during the 2015 AU Summit in Johannesburg[4] illustrated the regrettable lack of legal and political conviction on the side of South Africa, in stark contrast with the more principled stance that the country took in 2010, as noted above.

---

3   E. Keppler 'Dispatches: Governments defend ICC at African Union Summit' Human Rights Watch, 20 July 2016, available at www.hrw.org/print/292277.

4   For factual background and a chronology of events surrounding Al Bashir's visit to South Africa, see Manuel Ventura 'Escape from Johannesburg – Sudanese President Al Bashir visits South Africa, and the implicit removal of head of state immunity by the UN Security Council in light of Al-Jedda' *Journal of International Criminal Justice* 13 (2015) 995–1025. See also the decision by South Africa's Supreme Court of Appeal in *Minister of Justice and Constitutional Development & others v Southern Africa Litigation Centre & others* 2016 (3) SA 317 (SCA), where the Court held that the South African government failed to uphold its obligations in terms of the Rome Statute of the ICC, South Africa's domestic implementation legislation, as well as South Africa's Constitution. For a discussion of the decision by the Supreme Court of Appeal, see G. Kemp 'International and transnational criminal procedure' in Du Toit et al *Commentary on the Criminal Procedure Act* (Revision Service 57) Appendix B, B59.

In September 2016, it was reported that the Republic of Gabon, a state party to the Rome Statute, had referred the post-election violence[5] situation in that country, starting from May 2016 with no end-date, to the ICC Prosecutor for further investigation and consideration.[6] Whatever the ICC organs may ultimately decide with regards to the admissibility of the Gabon situation, at a minimum it can be regarded as a rebuttal of the proposition that there is an African consensus to withdraw from the ICC.

A second important aspect affecting the future of domestic change as a result of or caused by ICTs is the evolving notion of complementarity. This only really applies to the ICC, and not the ad hoc tribunals, because, as we know, the ad hoc tribunals were established on the basis of primary, not complementary, jurisdiction. Complementarity is at the heart of the Rome Statute of the ICC. This principle essentially entails that the ICC should be a tribunal of last resort, only taking on cases where states are either unwilling or unable to investigate or prosecute crimes that are within the jurisdiction of the ICC. It is worth recalling that the Preamble of the Rome Statute puts the emphasis on effective prosecution at the national level as well as enhanced international cooperation. Furthermore, it is noted that it is each state's duty to exercise its criminal jurisdiction over those responsible for international crimes.[7] It is worth restating the legal and policy effects of the principle of complementarity as embodied in the Rome Statute: "It serves to ensure state sovereignty and takes advantage of the benefits of decentralized prosecution by states closest to the crime and most directly affected by it. At the same time, it bestows *de jure* oversight powers upon the Court that reach far into the core areas of domestic criminal law. The ICC Statute thus regulates the relationship between international and domestic criminal jurisdictions through a carrot-and-stick mechanism. Ideally, the state parties will fully discharge their obligation to prosecute and thereby make intervention by the International Criminal Court unnecessary."[8] At present, there is not a lot of jurisprudence on the practical meaning and implications of complementarity, given the fact that the first number of situations before the ICC

---

5   For background, see 'ICC opens preliminary probe into Gabon unrest', 29 September 2016 (available at www.france24.com/en/20160929-icc-opens-preliminary-probe).

6   Statement of the Prosecutor of the ICC concerning referral from Gabonese Republic, 29 September 2016 (available at www.icc-cpi.int//Pages/item.aspx?name=160929-otp-stat-gabon).

7   Rome Statute of the ICC, Preamble paras 4 and 6.

8   G. Werle and F. Jessberger, *Principles of International Criminal Law* Oxford, 3ed, 2014, 95.

came about because of so-called self-referrals (Central African Republic, the Democratic Republic of Congo, and Uganda). Naturally, the issue of complementarity did not have any prominence because the states involved evidently did not wish to pursue the investigations and prosecutions at the national level, hence the involvement of the ICC. In this volume we considered two situations where the principle of complementarity did receive some substantive attention – the situations in Libya and Kenya. In the Libya matter, we have noted the pre-trial chamber's decision concerning the admissibility of Saif al-Islam's case, and Libya's ability and willingness to conduct his trial. It was also noted that a considerable part of the pre-trial chamber's decision concerned the question of whether the Libyan indictment covered the same conduct and events as the ICC warrant. In the case of Saif al-Islam Gadaffi, the Appeals Chamber determined the crucial issue to be whether the criminal proceedings at the national level 'sufficiently mirrors' the case of the ICC prosecutor.[9] In a number of decisions, including the *Ruto* Admissibility decision,[10] the relevant Pre-Trial Chamber held that the proceedings at the national level and the corresponding case before the ICC must involve the 'same conduct'. However, this standard is different from the one articulated by the Appeals Chamber in the Kenya cases (including the *Kenyatta* case). Indeed, in the latter case, the Appeals Chamber viewed the matter less restrictively, and held that it would be enough for the national criminal proceedings to involve 'substantially the same conduct' as the proceedings before the ICC.[11] The differentiation between 'same conduct' and 'substantially same conduct' goes beyond semantics. Commentators have criticised the Prosecutor's interpretation and justification (and the Appeals Chamber's acceptance of the interpretation) of 'same conduct' that should be understood as 'substantially the same conduct' for purposes of admissibility challenges of specific cases before the ICC.[12] As Heller

---

9   Judgment on the appeal of Libya against the decision of Pre-Trial Chamber I of 31 May 2013, 'Decision on the admissibility of the case against Saif al-Islam Gaddafi', *Gadaffi and Al-Senussi* (CC-01/11-01/11), Appeals Chamber, 21 May 2014 (*Gadaffi* Appeal Judgment), par 73.

10   Decision on the Application by the Government of Kenya Challenging the Admissibility of the Case Pursuant to Art 19(2)(b) of the Statute, *Ruto, Kosgey, and Sang* (ICC-01/09-01/11), Pre-Trial Chamber II, 30 May 2011, par 55.

11   Decision on the Application by the Government of Kenya Challenging the Admissibility of the Case Pursuant to art 19(2)(b) of the Statute, *Muthaura, Kenyatta, and Ali,* (ICC-01/09-02/11 OA), Appeals Chamber, 30 August 2011, par 39.

12   C. Stahn 'Admissibility challenges before the ICC from quasi-primacy to qualified deference?' in C. Stahn (ed) *The Law and Practice of the International Criminal Court*

noted, there is a clear textual basis in the Rome Statute for the 'same conduct' test (referencing Articles 20(3) and 90(1) in particular), whereas the 'substantially the same conduct' standard simply does not appear in the Statute. It seems as if the Appeals Chamber borrowed the language from the European Convention on Human Rights, but as a matter of treaty interpretation the method of the Appeals Chamber seemed curious, indeed unprincipled.[13] Having said that, and without going into the minutiae of treaty interpretation, we can agree with Heller that the *practical* consequences of the differentiation between 'same conduct' and 'substantially the same conduct' for purposes of admissibility in the context of complementarity seem less important.[14] The degree of flexibility will be determined by the facts of the specific case. In the matter of Saif-Al Islam Gaddafi, the Appeals Chamber noted that the real issue is "the degree of overlap required as between the incidents being investigated by the Prosecutor and those being investigated by a State – with the focus being upon whether the conduct is substantially the same." And further, it will be hard to envisage a "situation in which the Prosecutor and a State can be said to be investigating the same case in circumstances in which they are not investigating any of the same underlying incidents".[15] Even though there seems to be a significant degree of flexibility as a result of the Appeals Chamber's interpretation of 'substantially the same conduct' requirement, making the practical difference between 'same conduct' and 'substantially the same conduct' less obvious, commentators like Heller have criticised this approach and have come to the conclusion that the Appeals Chamber's interpretation unjustifiably imposes significant costs on both states and the ICC. We will not repeat Heller's whole argument here, but we briefly note his solution in the form of 'radical complementarity'; a notion that can potentially contribute to the conceptualisation of a more realistic division of labour between the ICC and national criminal justice systems.

When articulating the concept of 'radical complementarity', the point of departure is the ICC Appeals Chamber's acceptance of the meaning of complementarity to include the possibility that states can, at the national level, prosecute individuals for ordinary crimes (for instance murder, assault, or rape) instead of the applicable international crimes (for instance war crimes or crimes against

---

(2015) OUP 242; K. J. Heller 'Radical Complementarity' *Journal of International Criminal Justice* 14 (2016), 646–648.

13 Heller, *Radical Complementarity*, 647.
14 Heller, *Radical Complementarity*, 647.
15 *Saif al-Islam Gaddafi* Appeal Judgment par 72.

humanity).[16] It is the alleged conduct, and not so much the legal characterisation, that matters for purposes of admissibility in the context of complementarity. However, as Heller sees it, "there will be many situations in which a prosecution based on different conduct will be much more likely to succeed than one based on the same conduct." Thus, he argues that "the Appeals Chamber's mechanical insistence on using the [substantially same conduct] requirement to determine whether a state is 'active' is both counterproductive and indefensible."[17] How can radical complementarity help in this regard? At the heart of the matter is the quest to end impunity. Heller notes that, "as long as there is no reason to believe the state is trying to shield the suspect from criminal responsibility, the state should be permitted to investigate the different conduct without the case becoming admissible"[18] before the ICC. Importantly, in terms of the purview of our focus in this publication Heller's proposal may also lead to better capacity building and the strengthening of domestic institutions. In terms of Heller's proposal there would be a move away from the ICC-centric view of the admissibility of cases. The elimination of the 'substantially the same conduct' requirement, which is rather restrictive, would permit states to prosecute *different conduct* within the general scope of a situation that would otherwise fall within the purview of the ICC; the potential number of domestic investigations and cases will thereby be increased, thus strengthening the domestic investigative, prosecutorial, and judicial systems.[19] The end-result will be a more state-centric approach to complementarity. A critical question is, of course, the issue of resources and resource allocation, especially in post-conflict societies. While a state like post-conflict (PEV) Kenya may have been regarded as relatively capable of conducting domestic investigations and prosecutions of complex factual situations, the situation in countries like post-conflict Libya and South-Sudan clearly would have impacted negatively on the domestic criminal justice systems, such as they were. In terms of radical complementarity, with an emphasis on smaller investigations, even investigations focussing on 'ordinary' crimes and not necessarily the complex international crimes, the negative impact on domestic capacity would be minimised.[20] Heller's conclusion is intriguing – and relevant for our purposes: He assumes that Kenya might have been more cooperative with the ICC, if the

---

16 Decision on the admissibility of the case against Abdullah Al-Senussi, *Gadaffi and Al-Senussi* (ICC-0I/II-0I/II OA 6), Appeals Chamber, 24 July 2014 par 119.

17 Heller, *Radical Complementarity,* 650.

18 Heller, *Radical Complementarity,* 651.

19 Heller, *Radical Complementarity,* 657.

20 Heller, *Radical complementarity,* 658.

Pre-Trial Chamber "had bent over backwards (as it did in the Libya situation) to avoid finding the Kenya cases admissible".[21] Ultimately, according to Heller, the solution to the problems surrounding complementarity rests on two legs: first, the 'same person'[22] requirement needs to be relaxed, and secondly, the 'substantially the same conduct' requirement needs to be eliminated as a matter of law. The latter aspect will probably require an amendment of the Rome Statute. There also needs to be a policy shift – deference to national proceedings, where at all possible.[23]

While the debate about the perceived tension between the AU and the ICC has received a great deal of attention, both in academic circles and in popular media, there is a potentially important initiative that exists, albeit somewhat under the radar. In November 2013, a number of states party[24] to the Rome Statute of the ICC (including four African states) issued a statement on an International Initiative for Opening Negotiations on a Multilateral Treaty for Mutual Legal Assistance and Extradition in Domestic Prosecution of Atrocity Crimes (crimes of genocide, crimes against humanity, and war crimes).[25] By November 2015, at the Fourteenth Session of the Assembly of States Parties of the ICC, held in The Hague, the number had grown to 48 states that supported this initiative. The initiative is primarily, but not exclusively, aimed at states party to the Rome Statute. The aim is to find ways to overcome some of the legal obstacles to practical interstate cooperation in national investigation and prosecution of the most serious crimes of international concern. Indeed, the underlying idea is to expand the legal and practical avenues at the interstate level to fight impunity for international crimes. It is premised on the commitment of states to provide

---

21 Heller, *Radical Complementarity*, 664.
22 It will be recalled that, in the Kenya cases, the Appeals Chamber held that for an admissibility challenge to succeed it has to be shown that the state is actively investigating the same individual suspect as the Prosecutor of the ICC. See Decision on the Application by the Government of Kenya Challenging the Admissibility of the Case Pursuant to Article 19(2)(b) of the Statute, *Muthaura, Kenyatta and Ali* (ICC-01/09-02/11 OA), Appeals Chamber, 30 August 2011, par 40.
23 Heller, *Radical Complementarity*, 664–665.
24 Albania, Andorra, Argentina, Austria, Belgium, BiH, Bulgaria, Chile, Costa Rica, Cyprus, Czech Republic, Finland, Georgia, Greece, Hungary, Ireland, Liechtenstein, Lithuania, Luxemburg, the Netherlands, Malawi, Republic of Macedonia, Moldova, Mongolia, Norway, Panama, Paraguay, Peru, Samoa, Senegal, Serbia, Seychelles, Slovenia, Slovak Republic, South Africa, Suriname, Sweden, Trinidad and Tobago, Uruguay.
25 Assembly of States Parties to the Rome Statute, Twelfth session, 20–28 November 2013.

for the necessary laws and institutions at the domestic level in order to be able to investigate and prosecute atrocity crimes. If states are able to effectively cooperate in criminal investigations of atrocity crimes, and successfully extradite suspects for trial in domestic courts, it will supplement and even make redundant investigations and prosecutions by international tribunals, if, of course, the national efforts are genuine and in accordance with certain minimum standards. In this sense an initiative like the proposed multilateral treaty also builds on the legacy of international criminal tribunals, as noted by Justice Hassan Jallow, Prosecutor of the Mechanism for International Criminal Tribunals (MICT) and the ICTR. He noted that such a multilateral treaty, duly implemented, would "form an essential building block for a sustainable and truly global system of international criminal justice, ensuring that the legacy of the ICTR and ICTY and the hybrid tribunals extends far beyond what has been achieved by these ad hoc tribunals."[26]

There is one more development that we would like to briefly note in the context of ICTs and domestic institutional change. It was pointed out above that the apparent tensions between the AU and the ICC is real, but perhaps a bit overblown, especially if we look at the AU-ICC relationship beyond the rhetoric and also take into account developments at the national level, for instance the 2016 referral by Gabon to the ICC of a situation; a development that clearly postdates the perceived poor relationship between the AU and the ICC. One event that did occur in the midst of the growing tension between the AU and the ICC was the adoption of the Protocol on Amendments to the Protocol on the Statute of the African Court of Justice and Human Rights, commonly known as the Malabo Protocol, in July 2014.[27] The aim of the Malabo Protocol is to vest the African Court on Human and Peoples' Rights with international criminal jurisdiction. It does not create a new court, but extends the jurisdiction of the regional Human Rights court to be able to try individuals (and corporations) for the atrocity crimes (war crimes, crimes against humanity, and genocide) as well

---

26 Remarks by Justice Hassan Jallow at the event organized by Argentina, Belgium, the Netherlands and Slovenia during the Fourteenth Session of the Assembly of States Parties of the International Criminal Court (ICC), held in The Hague from 18 to 26 November 2015 (available at www.unmict.org/en/news/prosecutor-jallow-delivers-keynote-speech-assembly-states-parties-icc).

27 Adopted at an AU meeting in Malabo, Equatorial Guinea. Text available at www.au.int/en/content/protocol-amendments-protocol-statute-african-court-justice-and-human-rights.

a number of other international and transnational crimes,[28] including the crime of aggression, terrorism, the crime of unconstitutional change of government, corruption, and money laundering.

The Malabo Protocol is sometimes presented as Africa's answer to the ICC, meaning, Africa's alternative to, or substitute for, the ICC.[29] This is, textually at least, not correct. There is no mention of the ICC in the Malabo Protocol. Contextually, there is no doubt that many of the states that were at the forefront of the drive to draft and adopt the Malabo Protocol were also some of the most ardent critics of the ICC. Notable in this regard is Kenya, which was one of the first states to sign the Malabo Protocol.[30] Kenya went even one step further and also committed to financial support[31] for the criminal chamber and the inevitable expansion of staff, most notably, of course, the registry and an Office of the Prosecutor.

The Malabo Protocol, like the Rome Statute of the ICC, is based on the principle of complementarity. Article 46H (2) of the Protocol thus provides:

'The Court shall determine that a case is inadmissible where:

---

28 The list of crimes, to be found in Articles 28A – 28N, go beyond the substantive jurisdiction of any other international criminal tribunal. For a comprehensive commentary on the crimes and other aspects of the Malabo Protocol, see G. Werle and M. Vormbaum (eds) *The African Criminal Court – A commentary on the Malabo Protocol*, Den Haag 2017.

29 For further background, see C. Bhoke Murungu, 'Towards a Criminal Chamber in the African Court of Justice and Human Rights', *Journal of International Criminal Justice* 9 / 2011, 1067–1088; A. Abass, 'The proposed criminal jurisdiction for the African Court: Some problematic aspects' *Netherlands International Law Review* 60 / 2013, 27–50.

30 The context and timeline here is important: In 2013, Kenya, an ICC situation state, acted in terms of the Rome Statute and requested the UN Security Council to support its request for the deferment of the proceedings against President Kenyatta and Deputy-President Ruto. The Security Council refused the request. It was not only Kenya that was deeply disappointed. The AU also expressed its disappointment, thus setting in train more urgent movement towards a regional African criminal jurisdiction. See Decision on the Progress Report of the Commission on the Implementation of the Decisions on the International Criminal Court, Assembly/AU/Dec.493 (XXII) paras 6 and 13.

31 'Malabo Protocol – Legal and institutional implications of the merged and expanded African Court' Amnesty International (2016) 11 (available at www.amnesty.org).

a) The case is being investigated or prosecuted by a State which has jurisdiction over it, unless the State is unwilling or unable to carry out the investigation or prosecution;

b) The case has been investigated by a State which has jurisdiction over it and the State has decided not to prosecute the person concerned, unless the decision resulted from the unwillingness or inability of the State to prosecute;

c) The person concerned has already been tried for conduct which is the subject of the complaint;

d) The case is not of sufficient gravity to justify further action by the Court.'

Article 46H (3) then proceeds to list relevant factors that would determine whether a state is unwilling to investigate or prosecute in a particular case:

a) The proceedings were or are being undertaken or the national decision was made for the purpose of shielding the person concerned from criminal responsibility for crimes within the jurisdiction of the Court;

b) There has been an unjustified delay in the proceedings which in the circumstances is inconsistent with an intent to bring the person concerned to justice;

c) The proceedings were not or are not being conducted independently or impartially, and they were or are being conducted in a manner which, in the circumstances, is inconsistent with an intent to bring the person concerned to justice.'

Article 46H of the Malabo Protocol largely corresponds with Article 17 of the Rome Statute of the ICC, but there are important textual differences. The most remarkable difference is that the Malabo Protocol does not contain the equivalent of Article 17(3) of the Rome Statute, which provides for the factors relevant to determine a state's inability to investigate or prosecute a particular case. The Malabo Protocol is silent on this important aspect of the complementarity and admissibility framework that one finds in the Rome Statute. Nevertheless, it is clear that the overall design of the Malabo Protocol clearly intends the criminal jurisdiction of the African Court to be a court of last resort, with the emphasis on national and sub-regional criminal prosecutions.

Perhaps the most controversial aspect of the Malabo Protocol, and something that clearly sets it apart from the Rome Statute, is the inclusion of an immunity clause, thus providing that 'No charges shall be commenced or continued before the Court against any serving AU Head of State or Government, or anybody acting or entitled to act in such capacity, or other senior state officials based on their functions, during their tenure of office.'[32]

---

32 Art 46A *bis* Malabo Protocol. For a comment, see Dire Tladi 'The immunity provision in the AU Amendment Protocol' 13 *Journal of International Criminal Justice* (2015) 3–17.

The AU decisions and posturing, resulting in a legal framework for an African criminal jurisdiction, against the backdrop of on-going African cases before the ICC, amidst proposals for a more radical form of complementarity and better multilateral cooperation in criminal matters to put the emphasis back on domestic prosecutions of atrocities, may yet lead to a very confusing and ultimately counterproductive proliferation of legal obligations and institutions. There is also a risk that the cacophony of political noise surrounding all these debates may mask, or worse, deter, real institutional change in line with the central rationale of international criminal justice: an end to impunity.

When looking at the states of former Yugoslavia, we can observe two main differences compared to the African countries examined in this publication. First, the criminal cases regarding the states of former Yugoslavia were exclusively subject to the ad hoc International Criminal Tribunal for the former Yugoslavia (with two additional relevant cases in front of the International Court for Justice), while the International Criminal Court played no role. Hence the fact that all former Yugoslav states are signatories and have ratified the Rome Statute is not meaningful, or at least significantly less meaningful than for the African countries observed. As an additional consequence of this, the former Yugoslav countries had no need to use their acceptance of the Rome Statute for political calculations, as we observed it in the African cases, be it by withdrawing from the treaty or by obstructing the activity of the international court by other (legal) means.[33] On the other hand, the fact that the cases regarding the former Yugoslav states were under the jurisdiction of an ad hoc crime tribunal established by the UN-Security Council created a situation in which these states, frankly speaking, could not withdraw and were not even asked whether they agree or not to the jurisdiction of the Tribunal – it was an accomplished fact. Nevertheless, the states of former Yugoslavia did also have ways to obstruct the work of the ICTY, only that this occurred at a very high cost, mainly by hindering their own EU-integration process or by terminating substantial financial development aid. It was these high costs – which the states of former Yugoslavia at one point were not ready to pay anymore – that eventually led to the second difference we can observe when comparing the former Yugoslav and the African

---

33 As in the case when South Africa did not want to arrest the Sudanese president Omar Al Bashir on occasion of his visit to South Africa during the 2015 AU Summit. In the cases of the former Yugoslav states we also cannot observe any initiative for united action against the international court, as the African Union at one moment attempted to take.

countries examined in this publication: In the successor states of Yugoslavia, the impact of international courts – namely the ICTY – on domestic change was certainly more tangible and concrete, especially when it comes to the introduction of completely new institutions, be it special courts or laws. A great part of these domestic changes that have been identified in this publication can, as a matter of fact, only be defined as an indirect, rather than a direct impact of the Tribunal. However, indirect impact in this case does not mean that it also could and would have happened independently of the Tribunal and its work. On the contrary – what at first sight and formally speaking has to be defined as only a secondary, indirect impact of the Tribunal, was in fact a role without which the total impact would have very likely not occurred at all, or for sure not in the way it did. And it is this indirectness – through EU conditionality and the so-called Europeanization on the one hand, and the Completion Strategy of the Tribunal on the other – behind which the explanations for the most important influence of the Tribunal in the former Yugoslav states are to be found.

Out of these two factors, EU-conditionality was the one which was in place earlier.[34] At first, the Tribunal was established as a UN-institution and hence did not have any formal ties with the EU. This changed as soon as the former Yugoslav countries under ICTY jurisdiction were about to formally start their EU integration process, during which they had to – like other aspirant EU members from Central and Eastern European countries – comply with the so-called Copenhagen criteria, which were set out in 1993. These criteria, apart from envisioning functioning democratic institutions, a functioning market economy, the capacity to implement EU legal principles, and the protection of human and minority rights, had also proved to be crucial for the reconciliation and therefore for the overbridging of historical disputes among neighbouring states in Central and Eastern Europe. Based on this good practice, the EU therefore decided in 1999, when launching the first step of the EU integration process for the Western Balkan countries (the Stabilisation and Association Process), to

---

34 For EU-conditionality and the process of Europeanization see A. Elbasani (Ed.), *European Integration and Transformation in the Western Balkans – Europeanization or Business as Usual?*, London 2013; F. Bieber (ed), *EU conditionality in the Western Balkans*, London, 2013; with a focus on the judiciary: K. Bachmann, T. Sparrow-Botero, P. Lambertz, *When Justice Meet Politics – Independence and Autonomy of Ad Hoc International Criminal Tribunals*, Frankfurt/M. 2013; C. Dallara, *Democracy and Judicial Reforms in South-East Europe – Between the EU and the Legacies of the Past*, Cham/Heidelberg/New York/Dordrecht/London 2014; M. Kmezić, *EU Rule of Law Promotion – Judiciary Reform in the Western Balkans*, London 2017.

extend the criteria for the EU integration of the Western Balkan states by additional political conditions (the so-called "Copenhagen Plus criteria") consisting
of the full cooperation with the ICTY, the refugee return and the regional cooperation and reconciliation.[35] Following this decision, the EU started to link its
biannual evaluation of the integration process of the Western Balkan states with
the assessment of the ICTY-Chief Prosecutor about the cooperation of these
countries with the Tribunal. And since these states had a high economic and
political interest to progress in their integration process, the assessment of the
Chief Prosecutor of the ICTY started to play an important role for these states
and societies, especially in Croatia and Serbia, and to indirectly impact domestic
change. The motivations of the ICTY and the EU were however not the same
in this arrangement. While the ICTY primarily had no ambition in spreading
political messages, or in helping the EU integration or the reconciliation process,
but was rather pragmatically interested in focusing on the trials, the intention
of the EU by applying the conditionality was rather value driven. By setting up
conditions, Brussels hoped that the new political elites in the given societies,
mainly in Croatia and Serbia, would reshape the national goals by leaving the
former politics of enmity behind and concentrating on achieving peace, stability,
and prosperity.[36]

Eventually, the policy of conditionality based on the cooperation with the
ICTY brought results, not only in arresting the fugitive defendants, but also in
introducing institutional changes, including new laws and new institutions in
charge of leading, monitoring, and implementing this cooperation. However,
not only were these particular reforms not directly required by the ICTY, but
their introduction paradoxically also made it possible to legally justify lim-
iting cooperation with the Tribunal and hindering its work by legal means. As
shown in the example of the newly created National Council for Cooperation
with the ICTY in Serbia, this institution, officially established to improve and
enforce Serbia's cooperation with the Tribunal, often disabled the cooperation
with the ICTY rather than enabling it. This happened when the Council found
a legal way to not hand over transcripts from meetings of the Supreme Defence
Council claiming that they were state secrets of national interest, although these
documents would have been of high importance for both BiH against Serbia in

---

35 J. Batt, J. Obradović-Worchnik (ed), Conditionality and EU Integration in the Western
    Balkans, European Union Institute for Security Studies, Chaillot Paper Nr. 116, http://
    www.iss.europa.eu/uploads/media/cp116.pdf, 9.
36 Batt, Obradović-Worchnik, *Conditionality*, p. 9.

the case in front of the ICJ as well as for the Prosecution against Milošević in his case in front of the ICTY to prove Serbia's involvement in the genocide of Srebrenica. In a similar manner, the Croatian government refused to hand over artillery logbooks, upon which the Prosecution of the Tribunal had based its case against the Croatian general Gotovina. Therefore, these new institutions, while indirectly impacted by the ICTY, were in fact at the same time indirectly legally obstructing the ICTY and its purpose, and also the wider idea and aim of the EU to trigger a shift of values in the given societies. This shows that institutional changes and reforms, even if introduced, were often only formally adopted in order to show good will and to move on with the EU integration process, or in order to please donors, while there was less interest in a fruitful cooperation with the ICTY and a geniune attempt to disclose crucial information, face the past and work on reconciliation. So, once a further step in the integration process had been reached, the cooperation would usually slow down for some time, until the deadline for the next step would approach. In the case of Croatia, as very well pointed out in Vjeran Pavlaković's chapter, the readiness for additional judiciary reforms related to the procession of war crimes has even diminished after Croatia's accession to the EU.

The question which remains is, however, whether it was in the first place politically realistic to expect that the Tribunal and the EU could create conditions in which the states under their jurisdiction (or in the process of EU integration respectively) would wholeheartedly act and try war criminals as the Tribunal did, and would help the Tribunal to fully establish the truth about the past as a base for reconciliation in the region as the EU had projected. While it would certainly be desirable that state institutions and political elites participate in the uncovering of crimes committed in their state, as well as uncovering the (criminal) role and responsibility the state has played, it does not come as a surprise that in reality states, when in front of an international criminal court, usually behave as any other defendant who is trying to defend him/herself by all means. Confronted with the complexity of domestic and foreign policies, and with the dynamics that arise from it, political elites – independently of whether they played a crucial political role during the time when the crimes were committed or not – tend to be cautious when dealing with the past, especially when the past still is, like in the states of former Yugoslavia, disputed and – since no lustration took place – still strongly linked with the political power, but also to the question of national identity. That is one of the reasons why both in Serbia and in Croatia it was the opponents of the Milošević and the Tuđman regime, respectively, who, once in power after the regime change in 2000 in both countries, did not opt to disclose evidence that would have helped the Prosecution make the case against

Gotovina et. al and against Milošević in front of the ICTY, as well as it would have helped BiH against Serbia in the case in front of the ICJ. And not only did the governments not disclose this information, but they even formed legal teams and allocated significant funds from the state budget to legally protect information that would have helped to uncover the role their states had played during the war.[37]

Such behaviour of states is considered pragmatic in the world of *realpolitik*, while advocates of transitional justice believe that it is an immoral act, since the political elites are de facto averting the full disclosure of the truth about the crime in which their state participated. And certainly the moral aspect is an important point to be made and it would be more than desirable that more attention is paid to it. However, it is rather unlikely that in international politics a state would, without being forced to, admit that it is guilty and disclose all possible evidence in support of its guilt. On the contrary, states have at their disposal a number of legal instruments accepted in the framework of international law, which help them to legally evade a complete disclosure of facts about the role of the state in potential crimes[38], and hence legally limit the space for the reconstruction of the truth. Consequently, it seems less realistic that states and political elites, which are pragmatically doing everything to evade the disclosure of facts about certain crimes the state was involved in, could at the same time be credible in calling for a moral responsibility for the crimes committed and the disclosure of all facts. Which of course does not mean at all that it is not necessary to go on insisting on it, but only that states – when it comes to their own involvement in crimes – tend to comply with pragmatic principles, being at the same time to some extent even covered by international law in doing so, and that hence conditionality as applied in the case of the EU, and by using the ICTY, had from the beginning limited potential for creating long-lasting (value) changes.

In conclusion, while some institutional reforms coming indirectly from the ICTY were triggered by the EU policy of conditionality, this policy did have

---

37 As an illustration, the legal team of the government of Serbia (until 2003 of the Federal Republic of Yugoslavia, between 2003 and 2006 the State Union of Serbia and Montenegro) was made of lawyers and legal experts who were doubtless opponents of Milošević, being before and after 2000 politically active against him and internationally well-known lawyers working in the field of Human Rights protection.

38 There are numerous examples in cases in front of the ICTY and the ICJ showing that also leading western democracies (among others USA) claimed that certain information about assumed involvements of these states in conflicts are to be kept undisclosed due to being state secrets of national interest.

certain limitations and so did the institutional changes evolving from it.[39] On the one hand, these reforms often consisted of only a formal adoption of new laws and institutions for opportunistic reasons in order to please the EU, the Chief Prosecutor or external donors. Consequently, in the long run they were not serving the purpose they were established for. And on the other hand, the policy of conditionality envisaged a model of institutional reforms based on values, which did not seem feasible to be implemented and internalized in the given societies and states in the given time frame.

When it comes to the second channel of influence of the ICTY on institutional change – the process, which followed the announcement of the Completion Strategy – the means were less political and hence the impact more sustainable. Here as well there is rather an indirect and to some extent even unintentional impact to be observed, which, however, would not have occurred without the action of the Tribunal, namely the announcement of the Completion Strategy in 2002. The Strategy's main objective was to complete all trials in the first instance by 2008, and to start transferring cases to domestic courts in the former Yugoslav countries. And since until 2002 the domestic judiciaries in the region had shown varying degrees of intent to process war crime cases[40], and at that point none of them, for different reasons, was determined on it, the Completion Strategy triggered a process which eventually led to substantial institutional reforms throughout the region in order to enable local courts to carry out cases according to international standards. This included reforms reaching from completely new institutions and courts, to the amendment of existing laws and the drafting of new laws. The impact, however, was not the same in all countries. While in BiH the announcement of the Completion Strategy led to the establishment of a War Crimes Chamber based on the initiative of the international administration in BiH, in Serbia and Croatia it had a smaller but nevertheless significant impact in regard to improving the capacities and competences of existing institutions. On the other hand, given that the transfer of cases required quite standardized legislation and clearly defined criteria, the impact on laws throughout the region was comparable so that the notions of war crimes, crimes against humanity, command responsibility, witness protection, and sexual violence have been adjusted to the standards used by the ICTY in all former Yugoslav countries.

---

39 The greatest impact of the EU policy of conditionality, the arrest and extradition of fugitive defendants, remains outside the sphere of institutional reforms.

40 United Nations – International Criminal Tribunal for the Former Yugoslavia, Completion Strategy, http://www.icty.org/sid/10016

However, when taking a deeper look, all these reforms cannot be exclusively attributed to the ICTY. The Tribunal did trigger them by announcing the transfer of cases, but eventually it was on the local actors to comply with the criteria set out, and as shown in this publication, not only did they have different motivations, but none of the local actors seemed to have been driven by the aim of openly and with no strings attached confronting war crimes in domestic trials. In BiH it would have certainly been difficult for the local elites to find a consensus on sensitive issues such as the conditions for war crimes trials in front of domestic courts, and hence the OHR did to some extent simply impose these new institutions and reforms. Croatia at that time went through an important stage of its EU integration and that was an additional, if not the most crucial, motivation and reason to introduce judiciary reforms, among which were also these required for war crimes cases. Therefore, there was most probably also some opportunistic behaviour rather than a genuine need to address war crimes. Finally, in Serbia the reforms turned out to be part of a wider battle against organized crime. Eventually, the US government through USAID, linked its financial support for the establishment of a special court for organized crime with the creation of a war crimes section within this court and therefore it was more the result of opportunism and an attempt to please the donor than the need to create institutional conditions for processing war crimes.

When it comes to the domestic changes triggered by international criminal courts in Kosovo, the situation is different for a number of reasons. First, until 2008, Kosovo was exclusively led by a UN-administration, which was rather randomly than systematically introducing a number of new institutions. After 2008, when Kosovo became independent, the local actors continued to be supported by an EU-mission, which had similar features as the previous UN-mission and continued adjusting the judiciary of Kosovo to international criminal law standards and conventions related to human and minority rights. The second reason for a rather low impact of the ICTY is that the Completion Strategy and the process of finalizing the mission of the Tribunal took place when there were no further defendants from Kosovo and hence there was less pressure to prepare the local courts for the transfer of cases. A third reason for a less intense impact of the ICTY is, as Vjollca Krasniqi points out in the chapter dealing with Kosovo in this volume, that there was resistance towards these kinds of reforms, both within the UNMIK until 2008, and within the local political elite once Kosovo became independent. The reasons for this are again different than those observed in Croatia, BiH or Serbia, and go back to the commonly accepted understanding that the struggle for independence was just in itself and therefore can be neither illegal nor immoral. This also explains why the reaction in Kosovo to the 2016 "Kosovo Relocated Specialist Judicial Institution", a special criminal tribunal set up for potential trials related to crimes committed in Kosovo, was very reserved. While this court is by law not an international court but a genuine court of Kosovo, it was conceived, established and financed by the EU, located in The Hague and staffed by international judges only. Consequently, there is no path that would lead to a direct impact of the ICTY in Kosovo either. It cannot, however, be said that the numerous judiciary reforms in Kosovo carried out alone by the local actors or jointly by them and the international missions were not impacted by the ICTY, given the expertise that already existed in the region once the Completions Strategy was introduced. The same can be said for the special criminal court for Kosovo, which had no direct link to the ICTY, but was conceived and is now run by lawyers and experts who are endorsing the standards set by the ICTY.

Concluding, it can be said that international courts, in particular the ICTY, certainly did trigger a number of changes and judiciary reforms. In the successor states of Yugoslavia, this process was, however, enforced not only by the usage of different political instruments based on conditionality, but it was also driven by different political motivations in the given states and societies. Hence the impact was closely, if not exclusively, linked to political factors and a political will rather than on legal or other reasons. This should certainly not come as a surprise and it only confirms the initial hypothesis of this publication that international criminal courts are actors and subjects of international relations who deal with crimes arising from political conflicts and are consequently as such more exposed to political criticism and pressure, but at the same time also leave more imprints on states and their political and judiciary systems than ordinary courts do.

However, the findings in this volume are far from corroborating the theoretical assumptions in the introduction and provide a multitude of suprising conclusions, which show a variance of influences and different mechanisms, which are at work behind influences triggering domestic change in countries under ICC jurisdiction. The impact of EU conditionality bolstered the influence of the ICTY more than any other factor in Serbia, Croatia, and BiH, but it totally failed with regard to Kosovo. The Completion Strategy, the next important factor, had some significance in Croatia and BiH, but not much in Serbia (to which only one ICTY accused was transferred) and none in Kosovo. But a similar kind of domestic change, as took place in Serbia and Croatia, could also be observed in Rwanda, where no external influence comparable to EU conditionality was at play. In Rwanda, it was the Completion Strategy and its promise to transfer cases back to Rwanda and pressure from foreign countries that had apprehended genocide suspects, but refused to extradite them without legal reform in Rwanda, was paramount. However, the Rwandan case also shows the limits of domestic change under external influence: Rwanda created a two-tier system, under which extradited genocide fugitives were treated differently (and better) than suspects who had been apprehended by the Rwandan judiciary. One might therefore argue that Rwanda's readiness for reform was not so much driven by Human Rights and rule of law considerations, but by the wish to have the country's institutions (especially the judiciary and the penitentiary) recognized as full-fledged partners of the outside world and to bolster the state's internal sovereignty and its monopoly on violence.

This volume also comes with some other surprising findings. The cases of BiH and Kosovo contradict the assumption according to which domestic change is more likely and likely to be deeper and far-reaching in cases where the international community has more leverage and a direct grip on the domestic institutions. This hypothesis is confirmed in BiH, where the international community created and partly ran judicial institutions and domestic change in line with ICTY requirements took place (although much more on the state level than on the entity level); it is disconfirmed with regard to Kosovo, which remained immune against EU conditionality and ICTY pressure despite the leverage the UN administration had over the country. But whereas in Serbia, Croatia and BiH, the UN, the ICTY and the EU mostly spoke with one voice, the interests and preferences of the UN administration and the UN tribunal were often contradictory and allowed the Kosovo judiciary to defy ICTY decisions.

On this list, Sudan is certainly the most intriguing and astonoshing case. Despite the total absence of any regional factor, which could be compared to EU compliance, without anything similar to the ICTY's and the ICTR's Completion Strategy, some limited domestic change, which survived even the conflict with the ICC, took place in this war-tormented, desintegrating country. Some of these changes constituted lip service, paid in the attempt to prove the inadmissibility of the UNSC-referral of the Darfur cases (although Sudan never formally lodged any inadmissibility challenge) and to delegitimize the ICC's intervention in the eyes of the Sudanese public and the international community. This was far from successful, making the abolition of the newly created institutions and legal reforms more likely. However, some of them proved sustainable. More research is needed to explain this, but for the moment, it seems that this phenomen can best be explained as a case of transnational norm proliferation. As has been described in Latin America, sometimes authoritarian governments pay lip service to Human Rights in order to satisfy expectations from other countries during international negotiations. But this lip service, which often comes in the form of declarations or laws those governments never intend to implement, is then taken over by civic actors on the ground, who use it for strategic (and often transnational) litigation. If the judiciary enjoys at least some leeway and autonomy (or prosecutors and judges lack clear guidance from the government in these cases), there is a chance for some of these novelties to become legally binding and practically applicable.

This did not happen in Kenya and Libya. In post-Gaddafi Libya, there were hardly any functioning state institutions, which could have implemented declarations and/or legal novelties from abroad. As we have seen, the entire institutional landscape of the country had to be built from scratch after the revolution, including a quite sustainable constitutional basis. As the case of Sudan shows, this is in itself not an argument against the view according to which even UNSC-referrals may lead to sustainable (though limited) domestic change, even in countries with authoritarian governments. The more puzzling is the case of Kenya, a country with a vibrant civil society and a responsible government, which completely and successfully defied the ICC in a way which very much resembles the strategy followed by Kosovo. One might argue that the ICC so far lacks all the instruments, which the ICTY had at its disposal to further compliance: there is no Completion Strategy, neither is there a strong regional organization like the EU bolstering its influence. In Libya and Sudan, even the UNSC abdicated as an actor of potential change. Transnational norm proliferation did not work either, despite favourable conditions on the ground.

Our volume also shows some need for further research. As the case of Russia and Ukraine shows, our initial assumption about the intrinsic inability of self-referrals to trigger domestic change is only partly correct. Self-referrals may not lead to domestic reform in the countries, whose government lodged them, but they may well lead to adaptation in countries, which are collaterally affected by an ICC intervention, when the ICC's personal jurisdiction extends to citizens of a state other than the self-referring one, or when its territorial jurisdiction extends to territory, which is claimed or occupied by a third party. All in all, the analyses in this publication show a very diverse picture of how and under which circumstandes ICTs can trigger domestic change in countries affected by their jurisdiction. It shows a rather somber outlook for the ICC, a court of last resort, deprived of the ICTY's most effective tools to achieve compliance (EU conditionality and completion), which is highly controversial in many of the states it has intervened in and lacks the unambiguous support by its founders and the UN, which would be needed in order to achieve the results the ICTY achieved in Serbia and Croatia. It is no wonder the ICC is also less ambitious. As the case of Libya has shown, domestic change is not a priority for the judges. Out of necessity (and out of the obvious), the ICC has made a virtue…

Bibliography

Abass, A., 'The proposed criminal jurisdiction for the African Court: Some problematic aspects' *Netherlands International Law Review* (2013) 27–50.

Abdelsalam Babiker, M., 'The Prosecution of International Crimes under Sudan's Criminal and Military Laws', in: Lutz Oette (ed): Criminal law reform and transitional justice: human rights perspectives for Sudan, Burlington 2011.

Adwok Nyaba, P., *South Sudan: The State We Aspire To*, Cape Town 2013.

African Union Peace and Security Council, *Report of the Chairperson of the Commission on the situation in Libya* (presented at the 500. meeting of the Council in April 2015 in Addis Ababa, PSC/PR/3(D)), available at: http://www.peaceau.org/uploads/auc.rpt.libya.psc500.27.04.2015.pdf

Aidoo, A., 'Africa and the International Criminal Court: Moving the narrative forward', Humanity United 8 April 2015, available at https://humanityunited.org/africa-and-the-international-criminal-court-moving-the-narrative-forward/.

Akande, D., 'The Effect of Security Council Resolutions and Domestic Proceedings on State Obligations to Cooperate with the ICC', *Journal of International Criminal Justice*, Vol. 10, Issue 2, May 2012, available also at: http://papers.ssrn.com/sol3/papers.cfm?abstract_id=2038217

Akech, M., *Institutional Reform in the New Constitution of Kenya*, New York 2010.

Akhavan, Payam, 'Beyond Impunity: Can International Criminal Justice Prevent Future Atrocities?' *American Journal of International Law* 95(1) (2001): 7–31.

Ambani, J. O., 'Navigating past the "Dualist Doctrine": The case for progressive jurisprudence on the application of international human rights norms in Kenya', in: M. Killander (ed) *International Law and Domestic Human Rights Litigation in Africa*, Pretoria 2010, 25–30.

Amnesty International, 'Libya: Detention abuses staining the new Libya', available at: http://www.amnesty.org.uk/resources/libya-detention-abuses-staining-new-libya#.Vd8j6cqli1E

Amnesty International, 'Libya: new report shows that abductions by armed groups is rampant', available at:

Amnesty International, *Libya: The battle for Libya: Killings, disappearances and torture*, available at: https://www.amnesty.org/en/documents/MDE19/025/2011/en/

Arendt, H., *Eichmann in Jerusalem: A Report on the Banality of Evil*, London 1994 [1963].

Asaala, E. and Dicker, N., 'Transitional justice in Kenya and the UN Special Rapporteur on Truth and Justice: Where to from here?' *African Human Rights Law Journal* 13 / 2013, 324–355.

Bachmann, K., 'The loathed tribunal. Public opinion in Serbia toward the ICTY' in: K. Bachmann, D. Heidrich (eds), *The Legacy of Crimes and Crises. Transitional Justice, Domestic Change and the Role of the International Community*, Frankfurt/M 2016, 113–134.

Bachmann, K., Fatić, A., *The UN International Criminal Tribunals. Transition without Justice?* London, New York 2015.

Bachmann, K., Sparrow-Botero, T. and Lambertz, P., *When Justice Meets Politics. Independence and Autonomy of Ad Hoc International Criminal Tribunals*, Peter Lang 2013.

Baldwin, D. A., *Neorealizm and neoliberalizm. The contemporary debate*, Columbia University Press, 1993.

Ball, H., *Prosecuting War Crimes and Genocide: The twentieth century experience*, Kansas 1999.

Banning, T., The 'Bonn Powers' of the High Representative in Bosnia and Herzegovina: Tracing a Legal Figment, *Goettingen Journal of International Law* 6 (2014) 2, 259–302, pp. 289–301. (http://www.gojil.eu/issues/62/62_article_banning.pdf)

Barria, L. A., Roper, S. D., 'Judicial capacity building in BiH: Understanding legal reform beyond Completion Strategy of the ICTY', *Human Rights Review*, vol. 9, 2007, pp. 317–330.

Barria, L. and Roper, S., *How effective are the International Criminal Tribunals? An analysis of the ICTY and the ICTR*, available at: http://www.library.eiu.edu/ersvdocs/3800.pdf

Bassiouni, M. C., 'Mixed Models of International Criminal Justice', in: M. Cherif Bassiouni (ed.), *International Criminal Law*, vol. 3, International Enforcement, Leiden 2008, 577–618.

Batt, J., Obradović-Wochnik, J. (ed.), 'War crimes, conditionality and EU integration in the Western Balkans', European Union Institute for Security Studies, Chaillot Paper Nr. 116, http://www.iss.europa.eu/uploads/media/cp116.pdf

Bendor, J., Glazer, A. and Hammond, T., 'Theories of Delegation', *Annual Review of Political Science*. Vol. 4 (2001), 235–269.

Bieber, F.l (ed.), *EU conditionality in the Western Balkans*, London 2013.

Biserko, S., 'Zoran Đinđić i Haški Tribunal', in: L. Perović (ed), *Zoran Đinđić: Etika Odgovornosti*, Belgrade 2006, 226–7, available at:, http://helsinki.org.rs/doc/Svedocanstva25.pdf.

M. Bohlander, 'Last Exit BiH – Transferring War Crimes Prosecution from the International Tribunal to Domestic Courts', in: *Criminal Law Forum* 14 (1), 2003, 59–99.

Boraine, A., *A Life in Transition*, Cape Town 2008.

Borger, J., *The Butcher's Trail: How the Search for Balkan War Criminals Became the World's Most Successful Manhunt*, New York 2016.

Bougarel, X., Helms, E. and Duijzings, G. (eds), The new Bosnian Bosnian mosaic: Identities, memories and moral claims in a post-war society. Abingdon, New York 2007.

Brockman-Hawe, B. E., *Questioning the UN's Immunity in the Dutch Courts: Unresolved Issues in the Mothers of Srebrenica Litigation, Washington University Gobal Study Law Review 10, 727* (2011), available at: http://openscholarship.wustl.edu/law_globalstudies/vol10/iss4/3

Brunk, D., 'Dissecting Darfur: Anatomy of a genocide debate', *International Relations*, vol 22, No 1, 25–44.

Burke-White, W. B., 'The Domestic Influence of International Criminal Tribunals. The International Criminal Tribunal for the Former Yugoslavia and the Creation of the State Court of BiH', *Columbia Journal of Transnational Law* 46 (2006), 279–350.

Bywaters, F., 'Hybrid Courts – A Broken Promise? International Judges and Prosecutors of the War Crimes Chamber of BiH', 1–90, in: Democracy and Human Rights in South-East Europe: Selected master theses for the academic year 2011–2012, Sarajevo 2012.

Campbell, H., *Global NATO and the Catastrophic Failure in Libya*, New York 2013.

Caplan, R., *International Governance of War-Torn Territories: Rule and Reconstruction*, Oxford 2005, 209–210.

Caspersen, N., *Contested Nationalism – Serb Elite Rivalry in Croatia and BiH in the 1990s*. New York/Oxford 2010.

Chandler, D., *Faking Democracy after Dayton*, Chicago 2000.

Chatman, J. A.; Polzer, J. T.; Barsade, S. G.; Neale, M. A., 'Being Different Yet Feeling Similar: The Influence of Demographic Composition and

Organizational Culture on Work Processes and Outcomes', *Administrative Science Quarterly*, vol. 43, No. 4. (Dec., 1998), 749–780.

Chehtman, A., 'Developing BiH's Capacity to Process War Crimes Cases. Critical Notes on a "Success Story"', *Journal of International Criminal Justice no 9 iss. 3* (2011), 547–570.

Chrétien, J. P., *les médias du* génocide, Paris 1995.

Clark, H., *Civil Resistance in Kosovo*, London 2000.

Clark, J. N., 'Collective Guilt, Collective Responsibility and the Serbs', *East European Politics and Societies* (2008) 22, no. 3, 668–692.

Cohen, S., *States of Denial: Knowing about Atrocities and Suffering*, Cambridge 2001.

Cole P. and McQuinn, B. (eds), *The Libyan Revolution and its Aftermath*. Oxford (kindle edition) 2015.

Cole, P. and McQuinn, B., 'The Fall of Tripoli part 1' in: Cole, P. and McQuinn, B. (eds), *The Libyan Revolution and its Aftermath*. Oxford: (kindle edition) 2015.

Cole, P. and McQuinn, B., 'The Fall of Tripoli part 2' in: Cole, P. and McQuinn, B. (eds), *The Libyan Revolution and its Aftermath*. Oxford: (kindle edition) 2015.

Commission of Inquiry into the Post-Election Violence (CIPEV) *Final Report* (15 October 2008) 472–475, available at: http://www.dialoguekenya.org/index.php/reports/commission-reports.html.

Dagn, T., 'Sudan, The Crises in Darfur and the Status of the North-South Peace Agreement', Congressional Research Service Report for Congress, May 28, 2010 available at, http://fpc.state.gov/documents/organization/142785.pdf

Dallara, C., *Democracy and Judicial Reforms in South-East Europe – Between the EU and the Legacies of the Past*, Cham/Heidelberg/New York/Dordrecht/London 2014.

De Vasconcelos, A., 'Preface', in: J. Batt, J. Obradović-Wochnik (eds):, *War Crimes, Conditionality and EU Integration in the Western Balkans*. Paris 2009, 1–23.

de Waal, A., 'Darfur, The court and Khartoum; The politics of State Non-Co-Operation', in: N. Waddell and P. Clark (eds), *Courting Conflict? Justice, Peace and the ICC in Africa*, London: 2008, 29, available at: http://www.lse.ac.uk/internationalDevelopment/research/crisisStates/download/others/ICC%20in%20Africa.pdf

Del Ponte, C. (with Chuck Sudetić), *Madame Prosecutor. Confrontations with Humanity's worst criinals and the culture of impunity*, New York 2008.

Delpla, I.; Bougarel, X.; Fournel, J.-L. (eds.), *Investigating Srebrenica: Institutions, Facts, Responsibilities*, New York, Oxford 2012.

Deng, F. M., 'Customary Law in the Cross Fire of Sudan's War of Identities', available at: http://southsudanhumanitarianproject.com/wp-content/uploads/sites/21/formidable/Deng-2010-Customary-Law-in-the-Cross-Fire-of-Sudan-%E2%80%99-s-War-of-Identities2.pdf.

DeNicola, C., 'Criminal Procedure Reform in BiH: Between Organic Minimalism and Extrinsic Maximalism', Express0 2010, available at: https://works.bepress.com/christopher_denicola/1/

Des Forges, A., *Leave none to tell the story*, New York, 1999.

Dimitrijević, V., *O pravu i nepravu*. Belgrade 2011.

Dimitrova, B., 'Bosniak or Muslim? Dilemma of one Nation with two Names', *Southeast European Politics*, Vol. II, No. 2, October 2001, 94–108.

Dizdić, D, *Bosnian Independence Day Divides Ethnic Communities*, Balkaninsight, available at http://www.balkaninsight.com/en/article/Bosnian-independence-day-still-divides-ethnic-groups.

Douglas, L., *The Memory of Judgment: Making Law and History in the Trials of Holocaust*, New Haven et al. 2001.

Dowden, R., *Africa: Altered States, Ordinary Miracles*, New York, Philadelphia 2010.

Dubljević, M. (ed.), *Procesuiranje ratnih zlocina – Jamstvo procesa suočavanja s prošlošću u Hrvatskoj*, Zagreb 2014, also available at: https://www.documenta.hr/assets/files/publikacije/procesuiranje-ratnih-zlocina-FINAL.pdf

du Plessis, M., *African guide to international criminal justice*, Pretoria, 2008.

du Plessis, M.; Maluwa, T. and O'Reilly, A., 'Africa and the International Criminal Court' Chatham House Occasional Paper, London, 2013/01, 2 (available at www.chathamhouse.org).

Duijzings, G., 'Commemorating Srebrenica: histories of violence and the politics of memory in Eastern BiH', in: Bougarel, X., Helms, E. and Duijzings, G. (eds), The new Bosnian Bosnian mosaic: Identities, memories and moral claims in a post-war society. Abingdon, New York 2007, 141–166.

El Jizooli, K., 'Sudan: the Wrong Confrontation between the Government and the ICC' (a paper prepared for a regional workshop "For the Peace in Darfur), (11–12 May 2007).

El-Gizouli, K., 'The Erroneous Confrontation: The Dialectics of Law, Politics and the Prosecution of War Crimes in Darfur' in: S. M. Hassan and C.

E.Ray (eds), *Darfur and the Crises of Governance in Sudan; A critical Reader*, Ithaka 2009.

Elbasani, A. (ed.), *European Integration and Transformation in the Western Balkans – Europeanization or Business as Usual?*, London 2013.

Elias-Bursac, E., *Translating Evidence and Interpreting Testimony at a War Crimes Tribunal: Working in a Tug-of-War*, London 2015.

Ellis, M. S., 'Bringing Justice to an Embattled Region - Creating and Implementing the 'Rules of the Road' for BiH', *Berkeley Journal of International Law*, 5-6(1999), 1–25.

Engelbrekt, K.; Wagnsson, C.; Mohlin, M. (eds), *The NATO Intervention in Libya*. New York, London 2015.

European Union Election Observation Mission, *Final Report on Kenya, General Elections 27 December 2007* (3 April 2008), 36, available at: http://www.eods. eu/library/FR%20KENYA%2003.04.2008_en.pdf.

Futamura, M. and Gow, J., 'The strategic purpose of the ICTY and international peace and security', in: James Gow, Rachel Kerr and Zoran Pajić (eds.), *Prosecuting War Crimes: Lessons and Legacies of the International Criminal Tribunal for the Former Yugoslavia*, London and New York 2014.

Gagnon, V. P., *The myth of ethnic war. Serbia and Croatia in the 1990s*, Ithaka and London 2006.

Gahima, G., *Transitional Justice in Rwanda. Accountability for atrocity*, London 2013.

Gallannt, K. S., 'Securing the presence of defendants before the International Tribunal for the Former Yugoslavia: Breaking with extradition', *Criminal Law Forum*, (1994) Vol. 5, No. 2, 557–588.

Gardetto, J. C., *Report to the Council of Europe: The protection of witnesses as a cornerstone for justice and reconciliation in the Balkans*, 23–4, available at: http://assembly.coe.int/CommitteeDocs/2010/20100622_ ProtectionWitnesses_E.pdf.

Glaurdić, J., *The Hour of Europe: Western Powers and the Breakup of Yugoslavia*, New Haven 2011.

Goldstein, I., *Croatia: A History*, Montreal 1999.

Gordy, E., *Guilt, Responsibility, and Denial: The Past at Stake in Post-Miloševic Serbia*. Philadelphia 2013.

Gregulska, J., *Memory Work in Srebrenica: Serb Women Tell their Stories*. Budapest, (CEU, Master Thesis).

Guichaoua, A., *De la guerre au génocide. Des politiques criminelles au Rwanda*, Paris, 2010.

Hansen, K. F., 'Political and Economic Effects of Qaddafi's Death on Chad', *Notes de l'IFRI*, December 2013, available at: www.ifri.org/sites/default/files/atoms/files/noteifriocpkfhansen.pdf

Hartmann, F., 'The ICTY and EU conditionality', in: J. Batt and J. Obradović-Wochnik (eds), 'War crimes, conditionality and EU integration in the Western Balkans', *Challiot Paper* No. 116, (Paris: EU Institute for Security Studies), 72–76.

Hayden, R, '"Genocide Denial" Laws as Secular Heresy: A Critical Analysis with Reference to BiH', Slavic Review, Vol. 67, No. 2 (Summer, 2008), 384–407.

Hayden, R., 'Genocide Denial Laws as Secular Heresy: A Critical Analysis with Reference to BiH', *Slavic Review* Vol. 67, No 2 (2008), 384–407.

Heller, K. J., 'Radical Complementarity', *Journal of International Criminal Justice* 14 (2016) 637–665.

Helmes, E., *Victimhood and Innocence: Gender, Nation, and Women's Activism in Postwar BiH*, Madison 2014.

Holbrooke, R., *To End a War*', New York 1998.

http://scholarlycommons.law.northwestern.edu/njihr/vol8/iss3/3

http://www.amnesty.org.uk/press-releases/libya-new-report-shows-abductions-armed-groups-rampant

Human Rights Watch, 'South Sudan's New War: Abuses by Government and Opposition Forces', HRC report, August 2014 available at: https://www.hrw.org/report/2014/08/07/south-sudans-new-war/abuses-government-and-opposition-forces

Human Rights Watch, *Ending the Era of Injustice; Advancing Prosecutions for Serious Crimes Committed in South Sudan*, December 2014, available at: https://www.hrw.org/report/2014/12/10/ending-era-injustice/advancing-prosecutions-serious-crimes-committed-south-sudans

Human Rights Watch, *Justice at Risk: War Crimes Trials in Croatia, BiH, and Serbia and Montenegro*, HRW report vol. 16, No. 7(D), 21–22, available at: https://www.hrw.org/reports/2004/icty1004/icty1004.pdf.

Human Rights Watch, *Still Waiting Bringing Justice for War Crimes, Crimes against Humanity, and Genocide in BiH's Cantonal and District Courts.* Human Rights Watch, 2008.

Human Rights Watch, *Turning Pebbles: Evading Accountability for Post-Election Violence in Kenya* (2011) 3–4, available at

Human Watch Rights, 'BiH: Looking For Justice – The War Crimes Chamber in BiH',

Humanitarian Law Center, *Ten Years of War Crimes Prosecutions in Serbia: Contours of Justice: Analysis of the Prosecution of War Crimes in Serbia 2004–2013*, Belgrade 2014.

Ingimundarson, V., 'The Last Colony in Europe': The New Empire, Democratization and Nation-Building' in: V. Ingimundarson, K.

Internal Displacement Monitoring Centre (IDMC), *Speedy reforms needed to deal with past injustices and prevent future displacement* (10 June 2010), available at: http://www.internal- displacement.org/countries/Kenya.

International Crises Group, 'Sudan: Justice, Peace and the ICC', Africa Report N.152-17 July 2009, http://www.crisisgroup.org/~/media/Files/africa/ horn-of africa/sudan/Sudan%20Justice%20Peace%20and%20the%20ICC. ashx

Ivanišević, B., Uprkos okolnostima – Krivični postupci za ratne zločine u Srbiji, International Center for Transitional Justice, New York 2007.

Izveštaj o tranzicionoj pravdi u Srbiji, Crnoj Gori i na Kosovu 1999 – 2005, Belgrade: Fond za humanitarno pravo, 2006, p. 31, http://www.hlc-rdc.org/ images/stories/publikacije/03-tranzicija-srpski.pdf.

Jacobs, D., 'A narrative of Justice and the (Re) Writing of History: Lessons Learned from World War II French Trials in: K. J. Heller and G. Simpson (eds.), *The Hidden Histories of War Crimes Trials*, Oxford: Oxford University Press 2013, 122–136.

Jeroen K. van Ginneken and Wiegers, M., 'Various causes of the 1994 genocide in Rwanda with emphasis on the role of population pressure', available at http://paa2005.princeton.edu/papers/51066.

Johnson, H. F., *Waging Peace in Sudan: The Inside Story of the Negotiations That Ended Africa's Longest Civil War*, Eastbourne 2011.

Josipović, I., 'Implementation of the International Criminal Law in the National Legal System and the Liability for War Crimes,' in: Ivo Josipović (ed.), *Responsibility for War Crimes: Croatian Perspective – Selected Issues*, Zagreb 2005, 185–234.

Josipović, I., *Ratni zločini: priručnik za praćenje suđenja*, Osijek 2007.

Kabagema, I., *Ruanda unter deutscher Kolonialherrschaft 1899–1916*, Frankfurt am Main 1993.

Kamatali, J. M., *From the ICTR to ICC: learning from the ICTR experience in bringing justice to Rwandans*, available at: http://www.nesl.edu/userfiles/file/ nejicl/vol12/kamatali.pdf

Kapralski, J., 'The Jedwabne Village Green? The Memory and Counter-Memory of the Crime', *History & Memory*, vol. 18, no. 1, 179–194.

Kemp, G., 'International and transnational criminal procedure' in: Du Toit et al, Commentary on the Criminal Procedure Act (Revision Service 57) Appendix B1, App B66 at B59, Cape Town 2016.

Kemp, G., 'The implementation of the Rome Statute in Africa', in: G. Werle, L. Fernandez and M. Vormbaum (eds), *Africa and the International Criminal Court*, The Hague 2014, pp. 61–77.

Keppler, E., 'Managing Setbacks for the International Criminal Court in Africa', *Journal of African Law* 2011, 1–14.

Kersten, M., 'Justice after the war: The International Criminal Court and post-Gaddafi Libya' in: K. Fisher and R. Stewart (eds), *Transitional Justice and the Arab Spring*. London, New York 2014, 172–183.

Khan, M. I., 'Historical Record and the legacy of the International Criminal Tribunal for the former Yugoslavia' in: J. Gow, R. Kerr and Z. Pajić (eds.), *Prosecuting War Crimes: Lessons and Legacies of the International Criminal Tribunal for the Former Yugoslavia*, London and New York, Routledge 2014, 88–102.

Kmezić, M., *EU Rule of Law Promotion – Judiciary Reform in the Western Balkans*, London 2017.

Koshkina, C., Maidan. Njekasskazannaja Istorija, Kiev 2015. (Кошкина, С., *Майдан. Нерассказанная история*, Киев 2015.)

Krasniqi, V., 'Kosovo: Topography of the Construction of the Nation', in: Pål Kolstø (ed.) *Strategies of Symbolic Nation-Building in South Eastern Europe*, London 2014, 139–165.

Lacey, N., 'Criminal Justice' in: Robert E. Goodin, P. Petit and T. Pogge (eds.), *A Companion to Contemporary Political Philosophy*, Oxford, Wiley-Blackwell 2012, 511–520.

Lamont, C. K., *International Criminal Justice and the Politics of Compliance*. Farnham and Burlington, 2010.

Lamont, C., *International Criminal Justice and the Politics of Compliance*, Farnham 2010.

Lapid, Y., 'The third debate. On the prospects of International Theory in a post-positivist era.' *International Studies Quarterly* 1989, vol. 33, 235–254.

Larson, G.; Biar, P.; Ajak, P. B. and Pritchett, L., 'South Sudan's Capability Trap: Building a State with Disruptive Innovation,' UNU-WIDER Working Paper No. 2013/120, October 2013, available at www.wider.unu.edu/publications/working-papers/2013/en_GB/wp2013-120/

Leonardo, C.; Moro, L. N.; Santschi, N.; Isser, D. H., 'Local Justice in Southern Sudan', Washington, D. C.: United States Institute of Peace and Rift Valley

Institute 2010, available at: http://www.usip.org/sites/default/files/PW66%20 -%20Local%20Justice%20in%20Southern%20Sudan.pdf

Leydesdorf, S., *Surviving the Bosnian Genocide: The Women of Srebrenica Speak*, Bloomington 2011.

Loftsdóttir, I. Erlingsdóttir (eds), *Topographies of Globalization: Politics, Culture, Language*, Reykjavik 2004, 67–91.

Lumumb, L. G. and Franceschi, L., *The Constitution of Kenya, 2010 – An Introductory Commentary*, Nairobi 2014.

Lunch, G., Zgonec-Rožej, M., *The ICC Intervention in Kenya*, London, Chatham House, available at

Lyubashenko, I., 'Euromaidan: From the students' protest to mass uprising', in: K. Bachmann, I. Lyubashenko (eds.), *The Maidan Uprising, Separatism and Foreign Intervention. Ukraine's complex transition*, Frankfurt/M. 2014, 61–86.

Magaš, B. and Žanić, I. (eds.), *Rat u Hrvatskoj i Bosni i Hercegovini, 1991–1995*, Zagreb 1999.

Martin-Ortega, O., 'Beyond The Hague: Prosecuting War Crimes in Bosnia and Herzegovina' in: J. Gow, R. Kerr and Z. Pajić (eds.), *Prosecuting War Crimes: Lessons and Legacies of the International Criminal Tribunal for the Former Yugoslavia*, London and New York, Routledge 2014, 116–132.

Martin-Ortega, O.,'Prosecuting war crimes at home: lessons from the War Crimes Chamber in the State Court of BiH', *International Criminal Law Review* vol. 12, 2012, 589–628.

Materu, S. F., 'A strained relationship: reflections on the African Union's stand towards the International Criminal Court from the Kenya experience' in: G. Werle, L. Fernandez & M. Vormbaum, *Africa and the International Criminal Court*, The Hague, Asser Press/Springer, 211–226.

Materu, S. F., *The Post-Election Violence in Kenya*, The Hague 2015.

Meernik, J., 'Justice and Peace? How the International Criminal Tribunal Affects Societal Peace in BiH,' *Journal of Peace Research* 42(3) (2005): 271–289.

Mekki Medani, A., *Crimes Against International Humanitarian Law in Sudan (1989–2000)*, Dar El Mostaqbal El Arabi 2001.

Melvern, L., *Conspiracy to Murder: The Rwandan Genocide*, London, 2006.

Mertus, J., 'Shouting from the bottom of the well: the impact of international trials for wartime rape on women's agency', *International Feminist Journal of Politics* vol. 6. No.1, 2004, 110–128.

Mihajlović Trbovc J. and Petrović, V., 'Impact of the ICTY on Democratisation in Yugoslav Successor States,' in, S. P. Ramet, C. M. Hassenstab, and O. Listhaug (eds), Building Democracy in the Yugoslav Successor States. Accomplishments, Setbacks, and Challenges since 1990. Cambridge 2017, 135–161.

Mihajlović Trbovc, J., Public Narratives of the Past in the Framework of Transitional Justice Processes: The Case of BiH, PhD Thesis, University of Ljubljana 2014.

Miller, P., 'Contested Memories: The Bosnian Genocide in Serb and Muslim Minds' *Journal of Genocide Research* vol. 8 iss. 3 (Sept. 2006), 311–324.

Moghalu, K., *Rwanda's Genocide. The Politics of Global Justice*, New York, 2005.

Moravcsik, A., 'A New Statecraft? Supranational Entrepreneurs and International Cooperation', *International Organization* 53 (2), 1999, 267–306.

Moravcsik, A., 'The Origins of Human Rights Regimes: Democratic Delegation in Postwar Europe', *International Organization*, Vol. 54, No. 2 (Spring, 2000), 217–252.

Mueller, J. (ed), *Memory and Power in Post-War Europe: Studies in the Presence of the Past*, Cambridge et al. 2002.

Mugesera, A., *The Persecution of Rwandan Tutsi before the 1990–1994 Genocide.* Kigali 2014.

Mujuzi, J. D., 'steps taken in Rwanda's efforts to qualify for the referral of accused from the ICTR', in: *Journal of International Criminal Justice* 8 (2010), 237–248.

Murithi, T., 'The African Union and the International Criminal Court: An embattled relationship?' Institute for Justice and Reconciliation, Policy Brief, March 2013, available at http://www.ijr.org.za/publications/pdfs/IJR%20 Policy%20Brief%20No%208%20Tim%20Miruthi.pdf.

Murungu, C. B., 'Towards a Criminal Chamber in the African Court of Justice and Human Rights' *Journal of International Criminal Justice* (2011), 1067–1088.

Nalepa, M., *Skeletons in the Closet. Transitional Justice in Post-Communist Europe*, Cambridge 2010, 42–44.

Nazaro, S. G., 'Istine i zablude o zaštiti svedoka', *Pravda u tranziciji* No. 1 (2005), available at: http://www.tuzilastvorz.org.rs/html_trz/(CASOPIS)/ SRP/SRP01/49.pdf.

Nettelfied, L. J., *Courting Democracy in BiH: The Hague Tribunal's Impact in Postwar State.* Cambridge University Press 2010.

Nettelfield, L. J. and Wagner, S. (eds), *Srebrenica in the Aftermath of Genocide*, New York 2014.

Nielsen, A., 'Surmounting the Myopic Focus on Genocide: The Case of the War in BiH', *Journal of Southeast European and Black Sea Studies*, vol. 13, No. 1, 2013, 110–112.

Nora, P., Realms of Memory, Rethinking the French Past, Vol. 1 - Conflicts and Divisions, New York 1996.

Nouwen, S. M. H. and Werner, W. G., 'Doing Justice to the Political: The International Criminal Court in Uganda and Sudan', *The European Journal of International Law* Vol.21 (2010) available at: http://www.ejil.org/pdfs/21/4/2120.pdf

Novoselec, P., 'Substantive International Criminal Law in the Amendments of the Croatian Criminal Code of 15 July 2004', in Josipović, I. (ed), *Responsibility for War Crimes*, pp. 255–264.

Ntaganda, E., 'Le TPIR a la *croisée des chemins; bilans mitigé et défis de coopération avec le Rwanda'* in: Anastase Shyaka (ed) *la Résolution des Conflits en Afrique des Grands Lacs. Revue critique des Mécanismes Interantionaux.* Butare 2004, 149–158.

Nuhanović, H., *Under The UN Flag; The International Community and the Srebrenica Genocide.* Sarajevo 2007.

Obeid, K. M., *Darfur - The Absent Truth*, Khartoum 2005.

Obradovic - Wochnik, J., *Ethnic Conflict and War Crimes in the Balkans: the Narratives of Denial in Post-Conflict Serbia*, London: IB Tauris 2013.

Orentlicher, D. F., *That Somebody Guilty Be Punished: The Impact of the ICTY in BiH*. New York: Open Society Institute 2010.

Orentlicher, D. F., 'Shrinking the Space for Denial: The Impact of the ICTY in Serbia.' Belgrade 2008: Center for Transitional Processes, available at: http://www.opensocietyfoundations.org/sites/default/files/serbia_20080501.pdf.

OSCE Misja u Srbij i Crnoj Gori, *Ratni zločini pred domaćim sudovima: Praćenje suđenja za ratne zločine i podrška domaćim sudovima za njihovo sprovođenje*, Beograd, 2003, available at: http://www.osce.org/sr/serbia/13495?download=true.

OSCE, Combating Impunity for Conflict-Related Sexual Violence in BiH: Progress and Challenges (2004–2014), http://www.osce.org/bih/171906.

OSCE: 'Witness Protection and Support in BiH Domestic War Crimes Trials: Obstacles and recommendations a year a er adoption of the National Strategy for War Crimes Processing', January 2010, available at http://www.oscebih.org/documents/osce_bih_doc_2010122314375593eng.pdf

Ostojić, M., *Between Justice and Stability: The Politics of War Crimes Prosecutions in Post-Milošević Serbia*, Farnham and Burlington 2014.

Owiye Asaala, E., 'Prosecuting crimes related to the 2007 post-election violence in Kenyan courts: issues and challenges', in: H. J. van der Merwe and G. Kemp, *International Criminal Justice in Africa*, Nairobi 2016, 27–46.

Owiye Asaala, E., 'The International Criminal Court factor on transitional justice in Kenya' in: K. Ambos & O. Maunganidze (eds), *Power and Prosecution*, Göttingen 2012, 119–144.

Pavlaković, V., "Croatia, the International Criminal Tribunal for the former Yugoslavia, and General Gotovina as a Political Symbol," *Europe-Asia Studies*, Vol. 62, No. 10 (2010), 1707–1740.

Pejić, J., 'The Yugoslav Truth and Reconciliation Commission: A Shaky Start', *Fordham International Law Journal* 25, no. 1 (2001), 1–22.

Peskin, V., *International Justice in Rwanda and the Balkans. Virtual Trials and the Struggle for State Cooperation*, Cambridge 2008.

Petrović, V., 'A Crack in the Wall of Denial: The Scorpions Video in and out of the Courtroom', in: D. Žarkov and M. Glasius, *Narratives of Justice In and Out of the Courtroom: Former Yugoslavia and Beyond*, Cham 2014, 89–110.

Pimentel, D., 'Rule of Law Reform Without Cultural Imperialism? Reinforcing Customary Justice Through Collateral Review in Southern Sudan', *Hague Journal on the Rule of Law*, 2/1/2010, 1–28.

Pollack, G. E., 'Intentions of Burial: Mourning, Politics, and Memorials following the Massacre at Srebrenica', *Death Studies*, 27 (2003), 125–42.

Pollack, G. E., 'Burial at Srebrenica: Linking Place and Trauma', *Social Science and Medicine*, 56 (2003), 793–801.

Pollack, G. E., 'Returning to a Safe Area? The Importance of Burial for Return to Srebrenica', *Journal of Refugee Studies*, 16/2 (2003), 186–201.

Popović, D. and Janković, M. D., *Implementation of Transitional Law in Serbia*, Belgrade, 2005, available at: http://www.hunsor.se/dosszie/translaws_in_serbia.pdf.

Prashad, V.,: *Arab Spring, Libyan Winter*. Okaland, Baltimore, Edinburgh 2012.

Ramet, S. P., Clewing, K., and Lukić, R. (eds.), *Croatia since Independence: War, Politics, Society, Foreign Relations*, Munich 2008.

Risse, T.; Sikkink, K. and Ropp, S. C. (eds), *The Power of Human Rights. International Norms and Domestic Change*, New York 1999.

Rohde, D., *A Safe Area: Srebrenica, Europe's Worst Massacre since the Second World War*, London 1997.

Ronen, Y., 'The Impact of the on Atrocity-Related Prosecutions in the Courts of BiH', *Pennsylvania State Journal of Legal and International Affairs*, April 2014 (113), Vol.3, Issue 1, 112–160, available at:: http://elibrary.law.psu.edu/jlia/vol3/iss1/4/

Rumiya, J., *Le Rwanda sous le régime du mandat belge (1916–1931)*, Paris 1992.

Schwendiman, D., 'Prosecuting Atrocity Crimes In National Courts: Looking Back On 2009 in BiH', Northwestern Journal of International Human Rights 8/2010, 269–300.

Schwendiman, D., Ellis, M. S., *The Legacy of the ICTY: National and International Efforts in Capacity Building. In Assessing the Legacy of the ICTY*, Leiden-Boston 2011.

Shany, Y., 'Two Sides of the Same Coin? Judging Milošević and Serbia before the ICTY and ICJ', in T. W. Waters (ed), *The Milošević Trial: An Autopsy*, Oxford and New York, 2013, 451–454.

Shany, Y., 'How Can International Criminal Courts Have a Greater Impact upon National Criminal Proceedings? Lessons from the First Two Decades of International Criminal Justice in Operation', Israel Law Review 46 / 3 / Nov. 2013, 431–453.

Shapovalova, N., 'The Role of Crimea in Ukraine – Russia relations' in: K. Bachmann, I. Lyubashenko (eds.), *The Maidan Uprising, Separatism and Foreign Intervention. Ukraine's complex transition*, Frankfurt/M. 2014, 227–266.

Shyaka, A., 'Justice and Reconciliation in Post-Genocide Rwanda. Assessing the Impact of the International Criminal Tribunal for Rwanda', in: *The Review of International Affairs* (Belgrade), vol LIX, no. 1127–1131, April/September 2008, 15–25.

Sikkink, K., *The Justice Cascade. How Human Rights Prosecutions are changing world politics*. London, New York 2011.

Simić, O., 'Remembering, Visiting and Placing the Dead: Law, Authority and Genocide in Srebrenica', *Law Text Culture*, 13(1), 2009, available at:http://ro.uow.edu.au/ltc/vol13/iss1/13.

Sjekavica, M., 'Procesuiranje zločina počinjena tijekom VRA Oluja I nakon nje', in: M. Dubljević,(ed.), *Procesuiranje ratnih zlocina – Jamstvo procesa suočavanja s prošlošću u Hrvatskoj*, Zagreb 2014, 209–212.

Skocpol, T., *Protecting Soldiers and Mothers: The Politics of Social Policy in the United States*, Cambridge 1992.

Sparks, A., *Tomorrow is Another Country: The inside story of South Africa's negotiated revolution*, Chicago 1995.

Stahn, C., 'Admissibility challenges before the ICC from quasi-primacy to qualified deference?' in C. Stahn (ed) *The Law and Practice of the International Criminal Court*, Oxford 2015, 228–259.

Stahn, C. (ed), *The Law and Practice of the International Criminal Court*, Oxford 2015.

Steinberg, R. S. (ed): *Assessing the Legacy of the ICTY*, Leiden Boston 2011.

Stojanović, M. and Čalić Jelić, M. (eds), *Monitoring War Crime Trials Report for 2013*, Zagreb 2014.

Stojanović, M., and Sjekavica, M. (eds.), *Monitoring War Crime Trials: A Report for 2011*, Osijek 2012.

Stojanović, M., Čalić Jelić, M., and Sjekavica, M. (eds.), *Ensuring the Right to "Effective Remedy" for War Crime Victims: Monitoring War Crime Trials Report for 2012*, Zagreb 2013.

Strizek, H., *Geschenkte Kolonien. Ruanda und Burundi unter deutscher Herrschaft*. Berlin 2006.

Subašić, H. and Curak, N., 'History, the ICTY's Record and the Bosnian Serb Culture of Denial', in: J. Gow et al. (eds), *Prosecuting War Crimes: Lessons and Legacies of the International Criminal Tribunal for the Former Yugoslavia*, New York 2014; 133–151.

Subotić, J., 'Europe is a State of Mind: Identity and Europeanization in the Balkans', *International Studies Quarterly*, vol. 55 (2011), 309–330.

Subotić, J., *Hijacked Justice: Dealing with the Past in the Balkans*, Ithaca and London 2009.

Suljagic, E., *Postcards from the Grave*. Saqi 2005.

Swart, B., Zahar, A., Sluiter, G., (eds), *The legacy of the International Criminal Tribunal for the former Yugoslavia*, Oxford, New York 2011.

Swart, M., and Krisch, K., 'Irreconcilable differences?', *African Journal of International Criminal Justice*, Issue 0 2014, available at http://www.elevenjournals.com/tijdschrift/AJ/2014/0/AJ_2352-068X_2014_001_000_003/fullscreen.

Szewczyk, B. M. J., 'The EU in BiH: powers, decisions and legitimacy', EUISS Occasional Paper, available at: http://www.iss.europa.eu/uploads/media/OccasionalPaper83.pdf.

Tanner, M., *Croatia: A Nation Forged in War*, 3rd ed., New Haven 2010.

The Human Rights Center and the International Human Rights Law Clinic, University of Berkeley, and the Centre for Human Rights, University of Sarajevo, 'Justice, Accountability and Social Reconstruction: An Interview Study of Bosnian Judges and Prosecutors', *Berkley Journal of International*

Law, vol. 18, issue 1, 2000, 102–164, available at: http://scholarship.law. berkeley.edu/cgi/viewcontent.cgi?article=1184&context=bjil

Thoms, O. N. T., Ron, J., and Paris, R., 'State-Level Effects of Transitional Justice: What do we Know?' *The International Journal of Transitional Justice*, vol. 4, 2010, 329–354.

Tladi, D., 'The duty on South Africa to arrest and surrender President Al Bashir under South African and international law' *Journal of International Criminal Justice* 13 (2015) 1027–1047.

Tønnessen, L., 'From impunity to Prosecution? Sexual Violence in Sudan beyond Darfur', NOREF Report, February 2012, available at: http://www. peacebuilding.no/Regions/Africa/Sudan-and-South-Sudan/Publications/ From-impunity-to-prosecution-Sexual-violence-in-Sudan-beyond-Darfur

Tranziciona pravda u postjugoslovenskim zemljama: Izveštaj za 2009. godinu, Beograd, Zagreb (Fond za humanitarno pravo, BIRN, Documenta), 13, available at: http://www.hlc-rdc.org/?p=13826.

Udumbana, N. J. (ed), 'Who blinks first? The International Criminal Court, the Arican Union and the Problematic of International Criminal Justice', in T. Maluwa (ed), *Law, Politics and Rights: Essays in Memory of Kader Asmal*, Leiden, Boston 2013, 92–118.

UNDP, 'Capacity Needs Assessment for enhancing provision of victim/witness support during the pre-investigative stage of criminal proceedings in BiH', 2013, available at: http://www.ba.undp.org/content/dam/Bosnia_and_ herzegovina/docs/Research&Publications/Crises%20Prevention%20and%20 Recovery/Capacity%20needs%20assessment%20for%20enhancing%20 provision%20of%20victim-witness%20support/Izvjestaj%20ENG%20-%20 WEB.pdf

Vanderwalle, D, 'Libya's uncertain revolution', in: P. Cole, and B. McQuinn (eds), The Libyan Revolution and its aftermath, Oxford, New York: Oxford University Press (kindle edition) 2015.

Vansina, J., *Évolution du royaume Rwanda des origines à 1900*, Bruxelles 1962, 32–65.

Várady, T., 'Ambiguous Choices in the Trials of Milošević's Serbia', in T. W. Waters (ed), *The Milošević Trial: An Autopsy*, Oxford and New York 2013, 459–467.

S. Vasiljević, *Development of a Victim and Witness Support System. Croatian Experience: good practices and lessons learned*, UNDP 2014, available at: http://www.eurasia.undp.org/content/dam/rbec/docs/UNDP-CROATIA%20-%20Witness%20and%20Victim.pdf

Ventura, M., 'Escape from Johannesburg – Sudanese President Al Bashir visits South Africa, and the implicit removal of head of state immunity by the UN Security Council in light of Al-Jedda', *Journal of International Criminal Justice* 13 (2015), 995–1025.

Verdery, K., *The Political Lives of Dead Bodies: Reburial and Postsocialist Change*, New York 1999.

Vijgen, I., *Tussen mandaat en kolonie. Rwanda, Burundi en het Belgisch bestuur in opdracht van de Volkenbond (1916–1932)*, Leuven 2005.

Wagner, E. *To Know Where He Lies: DNA Technology and the Search for the Srebrenica Missing*, Oakland 2008.

Waterman, R. and Meier, K., 'Principal-Agent Models: An Expansion?' *Journal of Public Administration Research and Theory*. 8,2,1998, 173–202.

Wehrey, F., 'NATO's Intervention' in: Cole P. and McQuinn, B. (eds), *The Libyan Revolution and its Aftermath*. Oxford (kindle edition) 2015.

Wendt, A., 'On constitution and causation in International Relations', *Review of International Studies* (1998), 24, 101–118.

Werle, G. and Jessberger, F., *Principles of International Criminal Law* Oxford (3ed) 2014.

Werle, G., and Vormbaum, M. (eds), *The African Criminal Court – A commentary on the Malabo Protocol*, Den Haag 2017.

Williams, S., 'ICTY Referrals to National Jurisdictions:. A Fair Trial or a Fair Price?', *Criminal Law Forum* Vol.2006/17 (4), 177–222.

Wilson, A., *Ukraine Crisis. What It Means for the West*, Yale 2014.

Young, J., *The fate of Sudan: The Origins and Consequences of A Flawed Peace Process*, London 2012.

Young, John, *The fate of Sudan: The Origins and Consequences of A Flawed Peace Process*, London 2012.

Zawati, H. M., 'The Challenge of Prosecuting Conflict-related Gender-Bases Crimes under Libyan Transitional Justice', *The Journal of International Law and International Relations* 10 (2014), 45–91 available at: http://www.jilir. org/docs/issues/volume_10/10_5_ZAWATI_FINAL.pdf

Zertal, I., *Israel's Holocaust and the Politics of Nationhood*, Cambridge et al. 2005.

Magaš, B. and Žanić, I. (eds.), *Rat u Hrvatskoj i Bosni i Hercegovini, 1991–1995*, Zagreb 1999.

List of Names

Studies in Political Transition

Edited by Klaus Bachmann

www.peterlang.com